THE ESSENCE OF
DATABASES

THE ESSENCE OF COMPUTING SERIES

Published titles
The Essence of Program Design
The Essence of Discrete Mathematics
The Essence of Logic
The Essence of Programming Using C++

Forthcoming titles
The Essence of Artificial Intelligence
The Essence of Human–Computer Interaction
The Essence of Compilers
The Essence of Z
The Essence of Systems Analysis and Design

THE ESSENCE OF

DATABASES

F.D. Rolland

An imprint of **Pearson Education**

Harlow, England · London · New York · Reading, Massachusetts · San Francisco · Toronto · Don Mills, Ontario · Sydney
Tokyo · Singapore · Hong Kong · Seoul · Taipei · Cape Town · Madrid · Mexico City · Amsterdam · Munich · Paris · Milan

Pearson Education Limited
Edinburgh Gate,
Harlow,
Essex, CM20 2JE
England

and Associated Companies throughout the world

Visit us on the World Wide Web at:
http://www.pearsoneduc.com

Typeset in 10/12 pt Times
by Photoprint, Torquay

Printed and bound in Great Britain by
TJ International Ltd., Padstow, Cornwall

Library of Congress Cataloging-in-Publication Data

Rolland, F. D.
   The essence of databases / F.D. Rolland.
     p. cm. – (The essence of computing series)
   Includes bibliographical references and index.
   ISBN 0–13–727827–6
   1. Database management. I. Title. II. Series.
QA76.9.D3R654 1998
005.74–dc21   97–2835
                                    CIP

British Library Cataloguing in Publication Data

A catalogue record for this book is available from
the British Library

ISBN 0-13-727827-6

---

9 8 7 6 5 4
04 03 02 01 00

Contents

Foreword

As the consulting editor for the Essence of Computing Series it is my role to encourage the production of well-focused, high-quality textbooks at prices which students can afford. Since most computing courses are modular in structure, we aim to produce books which will cover the essential material for a typical module.

I want to maintain a consistent style for the series so that whenever you pick up an Essence book you know what to expect. For example, each book contains important features such as end-of-chapter summaries and exercises and a glossary of terms, if appropriate. Of course, the quality of the series depends crucially on the skills of its authors and all the books are written by lecturers who have honed their material in the classroom. Each book in the series takes a pragmatic approach and emphasises practical examples and case studies.

Our aim is that each book will become essential reading material for students attending core modules in computing. However, we expect students to want to go beyond the Essence books and so all books contain guidance on further reading and related work.

I would expect a module on databases to be an essential part of the curriculum for all students of computing and also associated courses such as information technology and business information systems. This book provides an introduction to databases suitable for all such courses. Starting from the basic concepts, it covers data modelling, relational databases in some detail, then other database models, including object-oriented databases, implementation issues and an introduction to distributed databases. After reading this book you should have a basic understanding of all the major issues in databases and be well prepared for more advanced study.

RAY WELLAND
Department of Computing Science
University of Glasgow
(e-mail: ray@dcs.gla.ac.uk)

Preface

Database systems is an important subject on many undergraduate courses. It frequently appears as a compulsory subject for students following courses in areas such as computer science, information systems, software engineering and information technology. It is also commonly offered as an optional subject for courses in related areas such as business studies and public administration. The subject itself has greatly expanded in the last 10 years. Within specialist computing degrees, it tends to be offered at two levels: 'introductory' and 'advanced'.

This book is targeted primarily at students following courses in database systems at the introductory level. No prior knowledge of the subject area is assumed, though a basic level of computer literacy is expected of the reader. The book should serve as a course text for lecturers delivering database units at the first or second level of a typical bachelor's degree or higher diploma. It can also serve as a refresher text for students on more advanced courses.

I have tried to make the text as informal as possible without sacrificing technical precision. I have also attempted to keep it as concise as possible whilst, hopefully, achieving a comprehensive coverage of the main areas. While the main audience for this book is the university student population, it is anticipated that anyone who wishes to become acquainted with the study and use of databases will find this a useful and informative read.

Acknowledgements

I should like to thank everyone at Prentice Hall, especially Jackie Harbor and Derek Moseley, for their highly professional and enthusiastic support of this project. I should also like to thank the mainly anonymous set of reviewers who gave my original drafts such a thorough inspection and who made numerous helpful comments. My wife Linda, as always, has provided a constant supply of encouragement and confidence. Certain friends of mine seem determined to provide a financial imperative. They know who they are. I must also acknowledge the role played by the students at MMU who have been the unwitting testers of so much of the material in this book. Without them, none of this would have been possible.

CHAPTER 1
The basics

In this chapter, we shall define the basic concepts that underpin the technology of database systems. We shall define what a database system is, explain why it is so important and outline the main types of database system.

At the end of this chapter, the reader should be able to:

1. Explain the benefits of a database system.
2. List the main components of a database system and describe their respective functions.
3. Explain the concept of data independence and how it is achieved.
4. Differentiate between the main types of database system.

1.1 What is a database system?

A database system is any computer-based information system where the data that supports that system may be shared. By 'shared', we mean that the data can be used by a wide variety of applications and is not arranged in such a way that it can only support one particular application.

1.2 Database systems and file processing systems

Computers store data in files. A file is a collection of records on a common theme. For instance, we can have a stock file consisting of stock records, a customer file consisting of customer records and so on. Each record consists of data that is subdivided into fields. For instance, we could have a book file consisting of book records, with each book record having fields for ISBN number, title and author. In a traditional file processing system, specific sets of files are created and manipulated by specific applications. A database system is different. With a database system, files are not tied to and maintainned by specific applications. Instead, they are integrated in such a way that the data within them may be shared by an indeterminate set of applications.

Why are database systems so important? In order to answer this question, we have to look at the alternative.

It is a relatively straightforward task to create an application with its own dedicated set of files. Suppose, for instance, a manufacturing firm wished to computerize its stock control system. In order to do this, it would need to create an application for the Production Department that used a stock file consisting of stock records which included, amongst other things, the following fields:

StockNo Description Level Re_Order_Level Unit_Cost

Suppose the Sales Department at the same time implemented an order processing system. This system would maintain an invoice file containing minimally the following fields:

Customer_Name Address Invoice_No ItemNo Description Amount Item_ Cost Order_Cost Credit_Limit

There could also be an application running in the Finance Department for a credit control system that used a customer file with the following fields:

CustomerName Invoice_No Order_Cost Payment_Received Credit_Limit

We would now have three separate files with a considerable amount of 'redundant' data. Redundancy is the term used to describe the situation when the same data is stored in more than one file. This redundancy is dangerous for a number of reasons:

1. Ambiguity. In the case above, there are examples of what could be the same thing being referred to by a different name according to the file in which it occurs. For instance, is 'StockNo' in the stock file referring to the same data as 'ItemNo' in the invoice file? It is imperative for the efficient running of an enterprise that such ambiguities are resolved.
2. Inconsistency. When applications have their own versions of what is essentially the same data, we have an unlimited potential for inconsistency. If, for instance, the price of an item of stock were to change it would not be sufficient just to change it within the stock control system. We would also have to change it within the order processing system and within any other systems that used a version of this piece of data. We call this 'update propagation'.

    Apart from data value inconsistencies, we can have data representation inconsistencies. If 'ItemNo' and 'StockNo' refer to the same thing, then it is imperative that they are represented in the same way. It would be undesirable for one application to treat this data as a fixed length number while another treats it as, for instance, a variable length string of numeric characters.
3. Wasted effort. Creating records with data to support a particular application when much of that data already exists is a considerable waste of time, effort and money.

In the traditional file processing environment where separate applications create and maintain their own files, the potential for ambiguity, inconsistency and wasted effort is infinite. Moreover, in the example above, we have three separate applications that should be working together in an integrated manner, but instead are potentially working against each other by maintaining different versions of what should be the same data. We can avoid these problems by associating all of the data together within a database system.

Ideally, all of the data that supports a varied set of applications is stored just once within a single 'database'. The different applications can then access those parts of the database that they require (Figure 1.1). Redundancy is eliminated and the applications become truly integrated. In practice, as we shall see later within this text, complete elimination of redundancy is frequently not achievable. In such situations, the important feature of a database system is that it provides control over data redundancy and delivers the means by which applications can work together in an integrated manner.

Every major organization has turned to using database systems for the storage and organization of their data. It is not just major organizations that benefit from the database approach. With the simplicity and power of modern

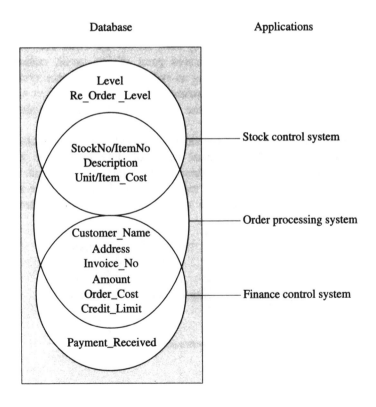

Figure 1.1 Sharing data amongst applications.

desktop packages, even very small enterprises benefit from the use of a database system to organize their data resource.

1.3 Components of a database system

A fundamental characteristic that distinguishes a database system from a traditional file processing system is that a database system allows many different uses to be made of the same data. The use of the data is not tied to or controlled by any single application. Instead, it is shared amongst different applications. This is achieved by removing the responsibility for creating and maintaining the stored data away from the individual applications and passing this to an underlying layer of software known as a 'database management system' (DBMS). The DBMS acts as a controlling layer between the users of applications and the data itself (Figure 1.2).

The data itself will probably still be stored in a number of files. For instance, in our example enterprise, we would probably have files of stock, orders, customers and invoices. The important thing is that different applications can access different parts of what is now a common set of files. For instance, the stock control system would probably only access the stock file, whereas the order processing system would access parts of the stock, customers and invoices files whilst also maintaining an orders file. The finance system would access parts of the invoices and customers files. Each application will require what is effectively a subset of the entire set of data controlled by the system.

The subset of the database required by a particular application is often referred to as a 'view'. Individual items of data may have a different appearance according to the view through which they are accessed. What may be a decimal number in one view might be treated as an integer in another. Different names may be ascribed to the same data. Thus, 'ItemNo' and

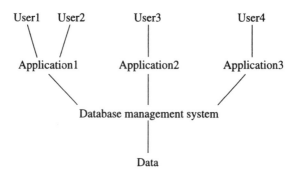

Figure 1.2 An integrated database system.

'StockNo' may indeed be referring to the same piece of data. A DBMS must be capable of supporting multiple views of the same dataset.

Implied in the concept of an integrated set of applications is the idea not only that data may be shared amongst different applications, but also that the same data may be used by different applications at the same time. This is known as 'concurrency'. A database system should provide facilities that enable and control concurrent access to the same data. Concurrency must be controlled otherwise data can easily be corrupted by, for instance, one application updating a piece of data whilst it is still being used by another.

As well as concurrency, a database system should provide facilities for ensuring the security and integrity of the database. Computer users must be able to protect their data against unwarranted intrusion, and be able to restore it in the case of some sort of system breakdown. Centralized data security is a significant feature of a database system. One of the great advantages of a database system is that it also provides the means by which centralized data integrity may be provided. For instance, having established that a 'StockNo' must be a six-digit integer, then all applications can be required by the DBMS to use it in that manner. Modern systems provide for quite complex integrity control as we shall see later in the text.

Thus, a DBMS provides facilities for:

1. The sharing and integration of data between different applications.
2. The ability to support multiple views of the same data.
3. Controlled concurrent access to data.
4. Ensuring the security and integrity of data.

In its totality, a database system has the following components:

1. Users. The people who make use of the data.
2. Applications. Programs used by the users who require data from the system.
3. The DBMS. Software that controls all access to the data, providing the facilities of a database system as described above.
4. The data. The raw data held in computer files.
5. The host system. The computer system on which the files are held. Access to the raw data is performed by the host system. The role of the DBMS is to issue requests to use the host system file storage facilities in order to service the different applications. Thus, the DBMS sits as an extra layer of software on top of the host system software.

A database system is best viewed as a series of layers. We illustrate the above by expanding and simplifying Figure 1.2 into Figure 1.3.

At the bottom level we have the data stored in a set of physical files. This is the physical storage of the database. At the top level we have the applications with their own individual views of the same physical data. Each view of the database represents a 'logical' rearrangement of the underlying physical data.

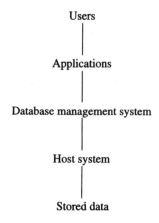

Figure 1.3 The layering of a database system.

In order to provide an interface between the physical storage of the database and its multiple logical versions as represented by the set of supported views, the DBMS must itself be internally layered.

1.4 DBMS layering

Central to any database system is what is known as the 'conceptual level'. This is a logical description of all the data within the system. The conceptual level must have the following characteristics:

1. It is a logical data description. It is independent from any considerations of how the data is actually stored.
2. It is complete. It contains a description of the entire data content of the database system.

The conceptual level of a database consists of all of the 'database objects' available to users and their applications. A database object is any logical item within the database. It may, for example, be a file, a record structure, a field, a set of fields and so on. There exist many different types of database, as explained in section 1.5 below. The type of the database will determine the range of database object types that are made available to its users. A database system will maintain a data dictionary which stores, amongst other things, the list of database objects that currently exist within it. For every database 'object' in a system, there will exist one and only one entry for it within the data dictionary.

In order to build a data dictionary, a database system must be given a complete description of all of the logical database objects that it is required to store. This description is known as the 'conceptual schema'.

The conceptual level of a database system as described in its conceptual schema and recorded in its data dictionary is the lowest form of representation available to a database user. The database users are completely and deliberately shielded from considerations of how the data is actually stored at the physical level.

We have established that a DBMS must be capable of supporting multiple views of the same data. A view is essentially a mapping between the representation of the data within the database (at the conceptual level) and the representation of the same data as it is required by a given application or set of applications. Different views may be mapped from the same set of database objects. The mapping of a view to a set of database objects is known as its 'definition'. All view definitions are kept in the data dictionary and become database objects in their own right. By storing view definitions in the data dictionary, it becomes possible for the same view to be used by many applications. The entire set of view definitions comprise what is known as the 'external' layer of the database. This is the layer that represents the interface between the database and its users. If the conceptual schema of the database is modified, then all view definitions affected by the modification will need to be rewritten in order that the view will appear, to its users, not to have changed, even though it may now be based on a completely different part of the logical database. In this way applications can be shielded from database modifications at the logical level. We call this 'logical data independence'.

Logical data independence is the shielding of users and applications from changes to the logical representation of the database. There is another form of data independence known as 'physical data independence'. This is the shielding of users and applications from changes in the physical storage of the database.

The physical storage of a large database will be frequently updated and altered, partly to improve performance and partly to reflect changes in the 'real' world. At the lowest level, the DBMS must map the conceptual schema representation of the database to its physical representation. This mapping is known as the 'internal layer' of a database system. It represents the interface between a DBMS and the actual computer system on which it runs. When the actual physical storage of a database is altered, then the DBMS must, at the internal level, have its conceptual schema remapped to a new physical representation. The conceptual schema must itself remain constant. In this way, applications may continue to proceed as if nothing had changed.

The DBMS thus comprises three layers: a set of mappings from the conceptual level to the user views, the conceptual level itself and a mapping from the conceptual level to the physical storage. These three layers are referred to as the external layer, the conceptual layer and the internal layer respectively (Figure 1.4).

Database layering is a long-established concept, being originally proposed as a standard by ANSI/SPARC (1978). In reality this neat layering is seldom

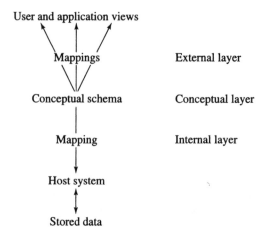

Figure 1.4 Layering of a database management system.

precisely achieved in practice. In particular, for performance reasons alone, the separation of the DBMS from the underlying host system facilities is frequently adapted, with the DBMS itself taking on many of the host system operations concerned with file management. In some systems, the host system is completely bypassed, with the DBMS directly accessing and organizing the 'raw' data stored on disk.

1.5 Types of database

The need for a 'database approach' to the organization of data in a large enterprise has long been appreciated. Over the years, a number of models have been adopted for implementing database systems. Here we will briefly review the four most commonly used approaches to the design of database management systems: hierarchic, network, relational and object-oriented. Each one will receive further consideration in the main part of the text. It is true that the first two of these approaches (hierarchic and network) are increasingly of historical rather than technical interest. However, there still exist many large databases in active use that are based on the principles of these approaches and they are of interest for this reason alone. In recent years, the majority of newly developed systems incorporate major aspects of the relational approach. Relational databases will therefore receive most attention in the text. However, relational databases do have significant shortcomings, many of which are tackled by object-oriented systems. There are still, at the time of writing, very few object-oriented database systems in live commercial use. This is likely to change rapidly in the near future, and the majority of research interest is in the object-oriented area.

1.5.1 Hierarchic databases

In 1968, IBM introduced its customers to its information management system (IMS). This was an early attempt to achieve at least some of the aims of the database approach to file management and is one of the earliest examples of a database management system. In IMS, a database is conceptually represented as a hierarchy. Records are organized into sets which are connected to each other by 'ownership' links.

Take a simple order processing system where customers place orders against items of stock. Each order may be for a collection of items. The same item may appear on a number of different orders. To model this in a hierarchic schema, we show a customer record 'owning' a set of orders, with each order record 'owning' a set of stock records and so on. Any record type may only appear at one position in the hierarchy, meaning that if we say that an order may own a set of stock records, then a stock record cannot own a set of orders. This way, the data is physically organized along strict hierarchical grounds (Figure 1.5).

Hierarchic databases are well suited to those information systems that can be based naturally on the hierarchical model, and there are a number of high performance large scale systems in use that have been built with IMS. However, most systems cannot be implemented in a simple manner in IMS without a dangerously wasteful level of duplication of data. In Figure 1.5, we

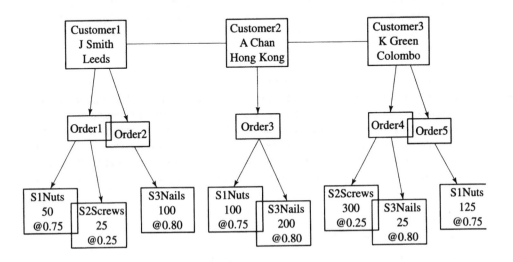

Figure 1.5 A hierarchic database.

have the same stock information replicated across a number of orders. Moreover, we have no information regarding items for which there are no orders. Thus, we have both duplication and loss of data. This can be overcome in IMS by creating another database for stock alone and then setting up a series of elaborate links between the stock and customers databases. In reality, the hierarchic view of the world is far too inflexible for the majority of database applications.

1.5.2 Network databases

In the 1970s, the Conference On Data Systems Languages (CODASYL) set up a Database Task Group specifically to produce a set of guidelines for realizing the database approach to file management. What they produced was a report (CODASYL, 1975) which was essentially a modification of the hierarchic model. (The hierarchic model was never precisely defined prior to its first implementation.) This new model has become known as the CODASYL or 'network' model.

In the network model, we have two basic constructs: records and links. A link is a set of physical pointers that establish an 'ownership' between one set of records and another. Thus we can say that a customer 'owns' a set of orders and that an order 'owns' a set of stock items, as in the hierarchic model. However, we are not constrained solely to ownership in one direction only, and a set of records may participate in any number of 'ownership' links.

In our sample database, rather than an order owning a set of stock items, we would say that an order owned a set of quantities, each of which in itself is owned by a given stock item. Thus a stock item also owns a set of quantities. Each quantity is associated with a given order and item by means of the ownership links in which it participates. This can be represented diagrammatically by means of pointers linking a record from one file to a set of records that it owns in another (Figure 1.6).

With the network approach, careful data analysis removes redundancies and the files within a system become truly integrated. However, this integration is achieved at the cost of complexity. Network databases are characterized by large numbers of sets of records, each containing a small amount of information and a large number of pointers to other sets of records. Writing the most straightforward of queries can involve an intricate navigation of the database from one record set to another. Examples in Chapter 6 will make this apparent.

1.5.3 Relational databases

Relational databases were originally proposed in the 1970s by Dr E.F. Codd (1970). His 'relational' model for database systems was markedly different to

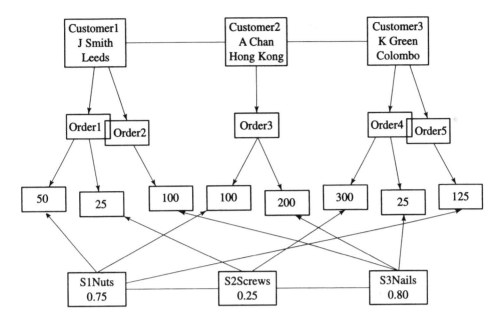

Figure 1.6 A network database.

the previously described models and by the 1980s it had become generally accepted as the most coherent and usable model for DBMS development.

In the relational approach, data is conceptually represented in two-dimensional tables consisting of rows and columns. Strictly speaking, the tables are called 'relations', the rows 'tuples' and the columns 'attributes'. The tuples are roughly equivalent to what is usually understood to be the records in a file, with the attributes indicating the meanings of the values in each tuple. Thus our sample database would be presented as in Table 1.1.

We have four relations which we shall call CUSTOMERS, ORDERS, STOCK and ORDERLINES. The CUSTOMERS relation has three attributes (CUSTNO, CUST-NAME and CITY) and three tuples. The STOCK relation also has three attributes and three tuples. The ORDERS relation consists of two attributes and five tuples, indicating that there currently exist five orders in this database. The ORDER-LINES table has three attributes, but eight tuples, one for each time an item of stock appears on an order.

A relational database uses attribute values to associate data from different tables rather than the explicit pointers used to link record sets together in the network approach. In our example database, we can deduce that ORDERS tuples with a CUSTNO of C1 relate to orders placed by the customer C1 in the CUSTOMERS relation. The items pertaining to a particular order are deduced by looking up its ORDERNO value in the ORDERLINES table and checking which

Table 1.1 A Relational Database

CUSTOMERS

CUSTNO	CUSTNAME	CITY
C1	J Smith	Leeds
C2	A Chan	Hong Kong
C3	K Green	Colombo

ORDERS

ORDERNO	CUSTNO
O1	C1
O2	C2
O3	C3
O4	C4
O5	C5

STOCK

STOCKNO	SNAME	SPRICE
S1	Nuts	0.75
S2	Screws	0.25
S3	Nails	0.80

ORDERLINES

ORDERNO	STOCKNO	AMOUNT
O1	S1	50
O1	S2	25
O2	S3	100
O3	S1	100
O3	S3	200
O4	S2	300
O4	S3	25
O5	S1	125

STOCKNO values it is matched against. For instance, ORDERNO O1 is matched against items S1 and S2, meaning that order O1 is for items S1 (Nuts) and S2 (Screws). The function of the ORDERLINES relation is to establish a 'relationship' between ORDERS and STOCK. In a relational database, relationships may be established between any two attributes that have compatible data values. An attribute in one relation that consists solely of numeric values can be related to any attribute in any other relation that also consists solely of numbers. In this way, logical links between relations are very easy to establish.

Relational systems provide a development environment that is significantly easier to use than that provided by the previous approaches. The data structures are simple to build and easy to understand and the writing of programs to manipulate them relatively straightforward. For these reasons, in recent years, the vast majority of producers of new DBMSs base their offerings to a greater or lesser extent on the relational model. However, there are shortcomings with the relational model that are partly addressed by the object-oriented approach to database management.

1.5.4 Object-oriented databases

One of the major criticisms of the so-called 'classic' approaches to the implementation of DBMSs as described above is that they are all based on the idea of a passive set of data. There is nothing in them that allows for the modelling of how data actually behaves. Moreover, they are very limited in terms of semantics: there is very little that can be represented in terms of what the data actually means.

Object-oriented database technology represents an attempt to redress such shortcomings. An object-oriented database schema consists of a collection of 'classes'. A class is a collection of objects that are structured and behave in the same manner as all other objects in the same class. The visible structure of an object is defined by its class 'properties'. For instance, a customer would have properties such as number, name, address, status and so on. The behaviour of an object is determined by its class 'methods'. A method is, loosely, an operation that may be applied to an object. It represents what we would wish an object to be able to do. For instance, a customer might raise an order, pay an invoice and so on. We would have methods for each of these activities.

In our sample database, we would almost certainly have object classes to represent customers, orders and stock items respectively. We might not necessarily have 'OrderLine' as an object class in itself. It could simply be part of an Order object. If we had a method for Customers such as 'Raise_an_ Order', it would inevitably involve interaction with Stock and Order objects. The important thing about an object-oriented database is that a user would not necessarily have to know this. The user would simply access a Customer object and make use of the 'Raise_an_Order' method. The fact that this is affecting other objects in the database may or may not be hidden from the user.

What can also be hidden from the user are all sorts of semantic rules governing the use of an object. For instance, 'Raise_an_Order' may in itself call methods for checking the creditworthiness of a customer or checking whether certain kinds of item may not be sold to certain types of customer.

It is possible to do this in a more traditional type of database by means of writing applications that present an interface to the database user that do things 'in the background' to the other parts of the database. The important difference with an object-oriented database is that such activities can become part of the definition of a database object and thus part of the database, rather than being separately encoded in applications. By using objects and methods, we can store and share not just the structure of a database object, but also its behaviour.

At the time of writing, only a small percentage of live database systems are object-oriented. Despite ongoing attempts at standardization, the definition of the term 'object oriented database' suffers in comparison with the very precise definition of the relational model. This has led to a large diversity in the way that object-oriented databases are implemented. These two factors naturally tend to deter prospective purchasers of such systems who are familiar with the well-understood relational model and relative uniformity of relational products. However, a number of leading relational products are now being extended to encompass some of the advantages of object-oriented technology and the object-oriented field is by far the greatest single area of database research.

Summary

- A database system provides the means by which access to a set of data may be shared and integrated amongst a set of applications.
- The main components of a database system are the users, the applications, the database management system, the host system and the data.
- Physical data independence is the immunity of applications to changes in the underlying storage. Logical data independence is the immunity of applications to changes in the logical database representation.
- A database management system should be arranged into layers whereby there exists a single 'logical' layer which supports the various application views of the data and which has a one-to-one mapping to the stored data. Access to the stored data may or may not be via the host operating system.
- The major approaches to the implementation of database management systems are hierarchic, network, relational and object-oriented.

Exercises

1   Study the following scenario:

The EverCare County General Hospital makes extensive use of computers to monitor and calculate the costs of patient care. The computer system maintains a number of master files, each with the following details:

Patient File: Patient Id, Patient Name, Home Address, Ward, Date of Admission, Date of Release, Conditions Diagnosed, Consultant, Treatments Received (each with a date, a Drug Id, DrugName, Amount and the name of the Nurse administering the treatment)

Ward File: Ward Sister, Names of Assigned Nurses, Names of Patients

Doctor File: Consultant Id, Consultant Name, Names of Patients

Nurse File: Nurse Id, NurseName, Ward, Treatments Administered (each with a Date, Drug Id, DrugName, Dosage and name of the patient receiving the treatment)

Drug File: Drug Id, DrugName, Recommended Dosage

(a)   What does the term 'redundant data' mean in the context of database systems?

(b)   Identify the redundancies that exist within these files. What problems might arise from these redundancies?

(c)   Suggest a reorganization of these files so that redundancy can be eliminated.
2   What are the differences between a database system and a file processing system? Make reference to the facilities that a database management system should provide.
3   What is data independence? Explain how this is provided by layering a database management system. Why is it so important?
4   What are the main differences in the basic data models supported by hierarchic, network, relational and object-oriented systems?

Further reading

Date (1995) Chapters 1 and 2
Delobel *et al.* (1995) Chapter 1
Elmasri and Navathe (1994) Chapters 1 and 2
Korth and Silberschatz (1991) Chapter 1
Kroenke (1995) Chapters 1 and 2

References

ANSI/SPARC (1978) 'DBMS Framework: Report on the Study of Data Base Management Systems', *Information Systems*, Vol. 3
CODASYL (1975) 'Data Base Task Group Report 1971', Association for Computing Machinery
Codd, E.F. (1970) 'A Relational Model of Data for Large Shared Databanks', *Communications of the ACM*, 13, June

CHAPTER 2
Database design

Database design is fundamental to the study of databases. In this chapter, we present the concepts that underpin 'semantic modelling'. Semantic modelling is the process by which we attempt to model 'meaning' in a database. We also present methodologies that are used for designing databases that each support a greater or lesser range of semantic modelling concepts.

By the end of the chapter, the reader should be able to:

1. Explain what a conceptual model is.
2. Describe the main stages in designing a database.
3. Define the basic semantic modelling concepts of assertion, convertibility, relatability, object relativity, generalization, specialization and grouping.
4. Outline the main features of entity/relationship modelling, functional data modelling and semantic object modelling.
5. Apply entity/relationship modelling to the modelling of a simple database.

2.1 The design process

In the previous chapter, examples of different types of database system were given. For any system, we must first identify its data requirements and then organize it into the types of data object that can be represented by the type of database management system that we are using. For instance, with a relational database, we need to organize the data into relational tables. A network database will require the data to be organized into record sets and connecting ownership links. Having identified our set of database objects, we can produce our conceptual schema for the database.

With a trivial system, it is possible to determine a conceptual schema directly from an analysis of the system requirements. However, with larger systems, a preceding stage design is required. This is known as the 'conceptual design'. A conceptual design attempts to present a logical model of a database at a higher level than a conceptual schema. Such a model is known as the 'conceptual model' of the database. Conceptual models are derived using some form of methodology for 'semantic modelling'. Semantic modelling is concerned with the creation of models that represent the meaning of data. There are various semantic modelling methodologies for the design of databases. They share the same general aims:

1. They can be used to model many different types of database system.
2. They are capable of capturing and representing more of the semantic requirements of a database than those allowed by the 'classic' database models.
3. They can be used as a convenient form of communicating database requirements.

Aim 1 above allows for a certain amount of DBMS independence. With a well-defined conceptual model, it becomes possible for a database user to choose between the various types of system available for implementing a database and even to change the system if it is found to be unsuitable. In reality, most of the methodologies tend to be particularly well suited to a given type of system, so DBMS independence is often more apparent than real.

The second aim is a particularly important feature. The classic approaches to implementing a DBMS are very constrained in terms of their semantic power. That is, they tell you very little about the real meaning of the data and its requirements. Conceptual models attempt to communicate a lot more in terms of semantics than that which is allowed by the various implementation approaches. The next section will define the basic forms of semantic information that a good methodology should be able to capture.

For the final aim, the design of large databases is typically a team effort and ideally should involve the end users of a system as well as the technical specialists charged with its implementation. A large database will also have a life beyond its initial implementation. It is therefore important that its design is well documented and understandable. For these reasons, a large proportion of methodologies make heavy use of diagrams and simple forms of notation. In this chapter we shall look at three methods of database design, all of which have a well-established approach to diagrammatic forms of representation.

The process of designing a large database can therefore be broken down into two basic stages:

1. Capture the database users' requirements and represent these in the form of a conceptual model.
2. Convert the conceptual model to a conceptual schema that can be implemented on a given DBMS.

A conceptual schema is sometimes misleadingly referred to as the 'physical design' of a database. As explained in the previous chapter, a true conceptual schema describes the lowest level of database representation made available to a database user and should not have to concern itself with physical details of how the database is actually stored. However, because it represents the lowest available form of database representation, it is sometimes treated as if it represented the actual physical storage. Many texts refer to the first stage as the 'conceptual design stage' and the second stage as the 'physical design stage'. The real physical design stage is where a Database Administrator, behind the scenes, will configure and tune a database system so that certain logical structures (e.g. relations in a relational database) are stored in a particular physical manner.

In this chapter, the examples used will be at the point where the user's requirements have been captured and the conceptual model must be built. The process of capturing a user's requirements comes under the related discipline of systems analysis and design which is outside the scope of this text. Converting a conceptual model to a conceptual schema design is particular to the type of system used and will be examined in the relevant later chapters.

2.2 Semantic modelling concepts

When designing a database, we aim at the construction of a representation of some part of the real world which has a meaning for its users. Semantics is the discipline of dealing with the relationships between 'words' and the real world items that words refer to. Database semantics are concerned with the relationship between a given set of data and the real world items that this dataset represents. The semantics of a natural language are complex, informal and frequently ambiguous. Database semantics are formalized and have a deliberately restricted complexity in order that they can be clearly understood.

We shall briefly examine a series of database semantic concepts.

2.2.1 Assertions

A database consists of a series of assertions. An assertion is a 'fact' that is true according to the semantics of the given system. Anything that contradicts the given semantics cannot be asserted and thus cannot be stored by the database.

For instance, suppose we defined a type of object in a database that we called a 'body' and we said that a 'body' may have properties such as 'head', 'trunk', 'hands', 'arms' and 'feet' and that we may give a range of descriptions to each of these properties. Thus, we can store assertions such as 'My body has big hands', 'My body has small feet' and so on. If we attempted to make an assertion such as 'My body has a large wheelbarrow' we would be contradicting the type definition for 'body' as there is no reference to 'wheelbarrow' as being a property of 'body'. This assertion would be rejected. Clearly, the semantics have done part of their job in rejecting an assertion that could not be true in the real world.

However, semantics should also be sufficient to represent all the truth that a database user might want to capture. We could not represent an assertion such as 'My body has 10 fingers' despite its truth in the real world because our type definition does not include the property 'finger'. This, however, is only important if the database user wanted to store information about fingers. There is no point in adding semantics about fingers if the database user has no interest in them. The aim of database semantics is not to provide a framework by which all valid assertions about the real world assertions may be recorded. Besides not being feasible, the effort involved would be out of all proportion to any benefit derived. Instead, database semantics aim to provide an abstract model that captures those parts of the real world that are of interest to the database user.

2.2.2 Convertibility

Every assertion in a database consists of a subject about which the assertion is made and a predicate which is applied to that subject. Suppose we formalized our type definition for 'body' thus:

type body = head, trunk, hands, arms, feet

This gives us a format for making assertions about bodies such as:

Abdul: large head, small trunk, 2 hands, long arms, 1 foot

In this assertion, 'Abdul' is the subject and the things we say about the properties of his body are the predicate. Together, they yield a piece of information. Suppose we had an assertion about another subject who happened to be called Abdul:

Abdul: large head, small trunk, 2 hands, long arms, 1 foot

Note that this assertion is identical to the previous one. We have no way of knowing whether this is a different subject with the same name and property values or whether this is the same subject as before who has been erroneously introduced a second time.

The convertibility rule states that a given subject and a given predicate are tied together in a one-to-one relationship. No two subjects may share the same predicate. Thus all assertions are unique. If our database semantics allow for the possibility of non-unique assertions, then we must extend them to avoid this. The classic, but not the only, way in which this is done is to introduce some sort of identifying property for all subjects in a database. Thus, in our bodies database we might introduce a property 'Body_Number', with no two subjects having the same Body_Number. Thus the assertions:

Abdul: Body_Number 1, large head, small trunk, long arms, 2 hands, 1 foot
Abdul: Body_Number 2, large head, small trunk, long arms, 2 hands, 1 foot

would satisfy the convertibility rule as they are both unique. The possible confusion regarding whether the given properties refer to the same body is removed by means of the Body_Number.

Convertibility also applies to data type definitions. If we declare two data types with exactly the same properties, then they must be the same data type. For instance, if we had a data type 'Monkey' which also had the properties 'Body_Number, head, trunk, arms, hands, feet', then we would have to regard the type Monkey as the same as the type Body as there is nothing to differentiate them.

2.2.3 Relatability

The relatability concept is applied when we have different types of object in a database. Suppose we had a database in a travel agent's office which stored details of bookings and holidays according to the following type definitions:

> type Booking = Customer, Holiday, Payments_Received
> type Holiday = HolidayRefNo, Resort, Cost, Departure_Date

We have here a semantic link between our two types of object, the link being that 'Holiday' is a property of 'Booking'. We say that the values that we give to a Holiday in instances of the Booking type are related to instances of the type Holiday. The relatability rule states that each value we use to establish such a relationship must be related to one and only one instance in the related type. In other words, in this example, a Booking instance may refer to only one Holiday.

2.2.4 Object relativity

In the examples above, we have some simple type definitions of the form:

> typename = property list

Such simple definitions provide us with a means of making assertions. A classic problem with many forms of semantic modelling is that of forcing everything in the model to be either a 'type' or a 'property'. However, in the real world, things are much more complex than this. In our example above, 'Holiday' exists both as a property of 'Booking' and as a type in its own right. The object relativity principle states that 'type' and 'property' are just different interpretations of the same object.

There are a number of semantic modelling abstractions that allow us to support the principle of object relativity, as follows.

Generalization and specialization
Generalization is the process by which we take a series of object types and associate them together in a generalized type. Take the following types:

type secretary = employee_number, department, start_date, typing_speed
type programmer = employee_number, department, start_date, grade

We might deduce that there are certain properties (employee_number, department, start_date) that are common to all employees in a firm. If this were the case, we could make explicit the fact that secretaries and programmers were both the same type of object by introducing a 'supertype' employee:

type employee = employee_number, department, start_date

Secretary and Programmer would then become subtypes:

type secretary = IS-A-employee, typing_speed
type programmer = IS-A-employee, grade

IS-A makes explicit that secretary and programmer objects are also employee objects. Thus, a given instance of a secretary may at some points be regarded as an employee and at other times as a secretary who also happens to be an employee. This allows us to define general semantics that we would wish to apply to all employees and particular semantics to particular types of employee.

Specialization is the inverse of generalization. We may have started from a generalized type 'employee' and then specialized into particular types of employee. Having performed our generalization, we may introduce a new specialization, for example:

type house_staff = IS-A-employee, house_staff_role

Aggregation

Aggregation is the process by which we take a series of otherwise independent types and associate them together in an aggregated type, for example:

type engine = engine no, factory, date_of_manufacture, engine_type
type body = style, no_of_doors, batch_no, factory
type wheelset = batch_no, source, wheel_type
type suspension_system = product_no, factory
type car = engine, body, wheels, suspension_system

The type 'car' consists of objects that are in no way related to each other but which may be put together to make another type of object. This association may be represented by making an explicit IS-PART-OF extension to our definitions, for example:

type engine = engine_no, factory, date_of_manufacture, engine_type, IS-PART-OF car

Grouping

Grouping is represented by a TYPE-OF association between two objects. When we say engine IS-PART-OF car, we assign an engine to a particular car. A given set of engines will have the same basic given design. This can be represented by a TYPE-OF association. TYPE-OF associations take a set of objects and associate them with one particular object of a related type. We could create a type that records different sorts of engine design, for example:

type engine_type = capacity, no_of_cylinders, camshaft_type

and then explicitly associate all engines together that share the same design characteristics:

type engine = engine_no, factory, date_of_manufacture, TYPE-OF-engine_type, IS-PART-OF-car

This represents the idea that we can have many instances of the same object, with each of these instances in some way being unique. Thus we have a many-to-one mapping between a type and a related type.

This is quite different to the IS-A type of relationship. When we establish an IS-A relationship between one type and another, we map instances of this relationship in a strictly one-to-one manner, for example each secretary maps to exactly one employee and that mapping is unique. No two secretaries may map to the same employee.

2.3 Database modelling

In this section, we shall briefly examine some major forms of conceptual modelling. We shall apply each type of model to the same basic scenario as follows:

The Rock Solid Banking Corporation stores details of its accounts with the following information for each account: Customer Details (Reference_Number, Name, Address, Status), Account_Number, Balance. Accounts may be of two types: deposit and current. Customers may have any number of accounts. Account numbers uniquely identify an account. An account may be shared by more than one customer. Each customer has a unique reference number. Each account is handled at a distinct branch of the bank. Branch details include Branch Name, Address and Manager. No two branches have the same name.

2.3.1 The entity/relationship model

Entity/relationship modelling is an approach to semantic modelling originally defined by Chen (1976) and very much refined since. It is not without its deficiencies, but it has the benefit of being relatively simple and highly applicable to business-type scenarios such as the one above. It is probably, in

BANK	CUSTOMER	ACCOUNT

Figure 2.1 Entities.

its variations, the most widely used form of database modelling. For convenience, we shall use the common abbreviation E/R modelling.

An E/R model of a database has three fundamental components:

1.   Entities: These are items in the real world that are capable of a unique existence. In the above scenario, accounts, customers and branches would be examples of entities. An entity is represented in an E/R diagram by means of a box labelled with the name of the entity. (Figure 2.1).

2.   Attributes: These are the things that describe an entity. They are represented by labelled ovals attached to an entity. A simple attribute would be the name of a customer, the manager of a branch, the balance of an account (Figure 2.2). Attributes may be multi-valued. For instance, if a customer could have two addresses. we would have shown this by drawing a double oval around Address.

A very important attribute is the key attribute. A key attribute is that part of an entity which gives it a unique identity. In our scenario above, the key attributes are Reference_Number for CUSTOMER, Account_No for ACCOUNT and Branch_Name for BRANCH. We underline key attributes as shown in Figure. 2.2. Key attributes need not be simple attributes. There can be occasions when a number of simple attributes need to be combined to form a composite key. Suppose for instance we had a database of people's names consisting of forename, surname and date of birth. If we had semantics that stated that two people may have the same forename or the same surname or the same date of birth but no two people can have the same values recorded for all three, then we could have a composite key consisting of all three attributes.

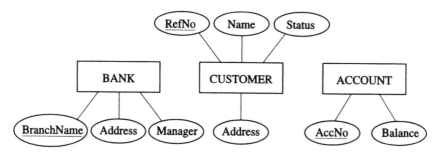

Figure 2.2 Entities with attributes.

Figure 2.3 A 1–M cardinality.

3. Relationships: A relationship represents the interaction between entities. It is diagrammatically represented by means of a diamond connecting the entities participating in the relationship. A relationship has a 'degree' indicating the number of entities participating in the relationship and each interaction has a cardinality. In our scenario above we have an interaction between accounts and customers and another one between accounts and branches. As each of these interactions involves two entities, they have a degree of two. We have said that an account is handled by one branch. Assuming that a branch may have any number of accounts, we have a many-to-one (M–1) cardinality between accounts and branches (Figure 2.3).

As an account may be shared by a number of customers and a customer may have many accounts, we have a many-to-many (M–N) cardinality for this relationship. One-to-one cardinalities are possible. For instance, we might need to treat MANAGER as a separate entity. If a manager can only manage one branch, then we would have a one-to-one relationship between MANAGER and BRANCH.

Our scenario above could be represented by the E/R diagram shown in Figure 2.4.

Relationships may in themselves become entities. Take the relationship between ACCOUNT and CUSTOMER. Suppose for shared accounts we

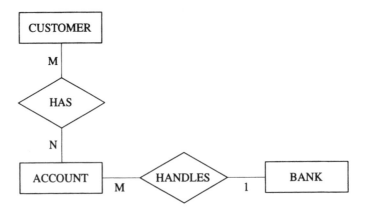

Figure 2.4 An entity/relationship data model.

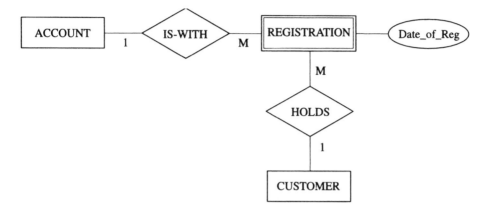

Figure 2.5 A weak entity.

wished to record the date each time a given customer was allocated to a given account. This means that the relationship itself now has an attribute ('Date of Registration'). We must now represent the relationship as an Entity in its own right (Figure 2.5). Note how the M–N cardinality has been replaced by two 1-M cardinalities indicating that ACCOUNT may have many registrations, one for each customer, and that CUSTOMER may have many registrations, each one for a unique account. Note also how we have drawn a double box around Registration. This is because it is a special type of entity known as a 'Weak Entity'.

A weak entity is one that is not capable of an independent existence. Instead it can only exist in terms of the relationships in which it participates. A Registration cannot exist in itself; it requires an account and a customer. With weak entities we can use the participating entities to generate its unique identity. In this case we can identify a Registration by the combination of AccountNo and RefNo. A weak entity may itself have attributes.

One of the problems of E/R modelling is that it is not always obvious on initial analysis whether an item should be represented as an entity or an attribute. For instance, suppose we wished to represent the set of employees working at a branch. We might show this as in Figure 2.6.

The problem with this is that it does not capture the idea that managers are themselves employees and that they are in charge of the employees at a branch. We can show this in Figure 2.7 by use of a recursive relationship.

The attribute 'Manager' is now replaced by a relationship 'Managed_by' linking a branch to a particular employee. 'Supervise' is a recursive relationship, indicating that all employees are supervised by one particular employee. However, this does not capture the fact that the manager of a set of employees must also be the manager of their particular branch. Extensions to

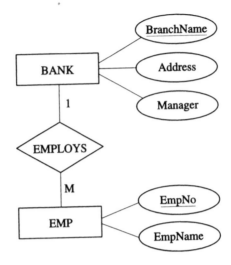

Figure 2.6 Introducing a new entity.

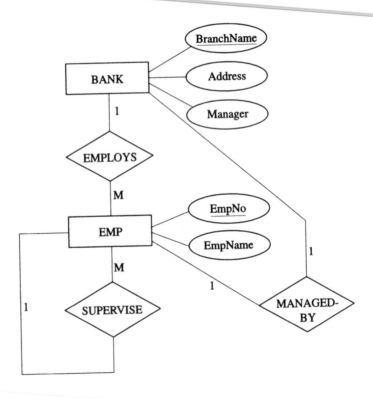

Figure 2.7 A recursive relationship.

E/R modelling (collectively known as 'extended E/R') make this easier to represent.

The most important extension to E/R modelling is the notion of subtyping and its refinements. In our first diagram we failed to show that accounts may be of two types (deposit or current). It is possible to do this using the method shown in Figure 2.8

In Figure 2.9 we show MANAGER as a subtype of EMPLOYEE who supervises other employees. We can also show that one (and one only) of the

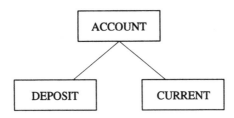

Figure 2.8 Subtyping in an E/R diagram.

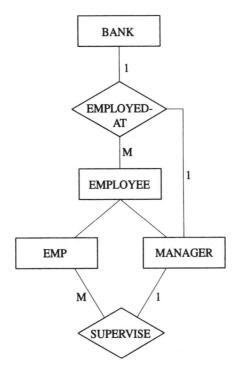

Figure 2.9 Further subtyping with a ternary relationship.

employees at a given branch may be a manager by making the 'employed at' relationship a three-way ('ternary') between one manager, one branch and a set of employees.

Extensions to subtyping allow generalization and specialization to be incorporated into E/R diagrams. We already have an implicit amount of specialization. MANAGER IS-A type of EMPLOYEE. DEPOSIT and CURRENT are both IS-A types of ACCOUNT.

We can create generalized types from within subtypes. For instance, suppose we identified amongst our employees various roles such as clerk, secretary, programmer, system designer. We might generalize the first two into a type 'clerical' and the other two into a type 'technical' and state that nobody can be both. We would represent this as in Figure 2.10.

Note how we have now started using subset notation to indicate a subtype/ supertype relationship. The subset symbol between MANAGER and

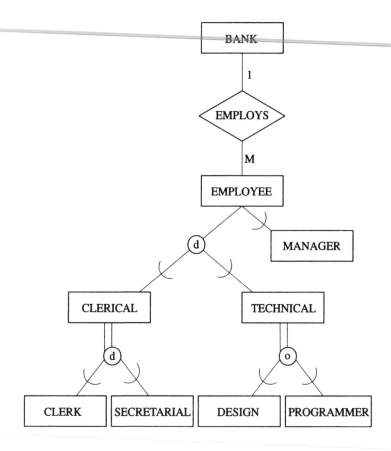

Figure 2.10 Specialization in an E/R diagram.

EMPLOYEE indicates that MANAGER is a subtype of EMPLOYEE. TECHNICAL and CLERICAL are also both subtypes of EMPLOYEE. The use of the 'd' indicates the notion of disjoint sets, meaning that no employee may be a member of the clerical and technical particular subtypes; 'o' indicates that an employee may belong to either or both of two subtypes, and thus a technical worker may be both a programmer and a designer.

Note that there is no subset symbol above the disjoint symbol that separates clerical from technical workers. This means that this particular specialization is separate from the specialization into the manager subtype. The manager subtyping is thus distinct from the clerical/technical subtyping. Thus, the same set of employees may be classified as managers/non-managers as well as being classified as technical/clerical.

We have double lines connecting CLERICAL and TECHNICAL to their subtypes. This indicates a 'must be' mapping; that is, all clerical workers must be either clerks or secretaries, all technicians must be programmers and/or designers. We do not have a double line below EMPLOYEE, indicating that there may be employees who do not belong to any of the specializations indicated.

In Figure 2.11, we create a new type from existing types. Here we combine the types 'manager' and 'clerical' into a new type 'clerical manager' which shares the attributes of both a clerical worker and a manager.

Aggregation is achieved in E/R modelling by taking a single entity such as a car and, in this case, drawing a series of one-to-one relationships with the items of which it is composed. In Figure 2.12, we show that a car has one body, one engine, one wheel system, and one suspension system, showing that these are all PART-OF an engine. The many-to-one mappings on the other side of the diagram show that, for instance, a number of engines may have the same design. This represents a TYPE-OF relationship. All cars whose engine is related to the same engine design can be said to have the same TYPE-OF engine.

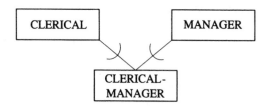

Figure 2.11 Creating a subtype from existing subtypes.

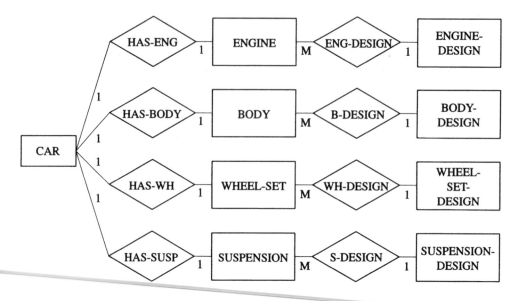

Figure 2.12 Aggregation and groupings in an E/R diagram.

2.3.2 Functional data modelling

The functional data model was first presented by Shipman (1981). It is based on the notion that the relationships amongst data in a database can be represented using the notation of a mathematical function.

A mathematical function is an entity that, given certain argument values, will yield a result. With a functional data model (FDM), we model the database as a series of functions which are applied to entities to return information. Thus, an FDM has two basic modelling primitives: a function and an entity. An entity may be 'primitive' or 'abstract'. Primitive entities are items such as text strings and numbers. Abstract entities are types that correspond to real world items. FDM diagrams can be drawn which bear a superficial similarity to E/R diagrams, except that the relationship between one entity and another is represented as a function (Figure 2.13).

Note how we have represented what might be regarded as the attributes of an entity in an E/R database as functions of an entity. Some functions may be multi-valued. For instance, the HOLDS function applied to BRANCH yields a set of accounts, rendering it a multi-valued function.

FDM data modelling languages exist to describe a functional database. They take the form of a series of function declarations with the given results. Starting from our main entities, we would say:

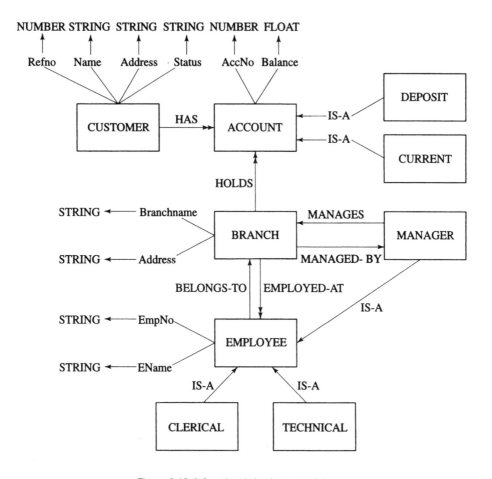

Figure 2.13 A functional database model.

```
CUSTOMER( ) - - > >  ENTITY
ACCOUNT ( ) - - > >  ENTITY
BRANCH ( ) - - > >  ENTITY
EMPLOYEE ( ) - - > >  ENTITY
```

These declarations indicate that each function in itself yields an entity set. To yield properties of an entity, we apply a function to that entity, for example:

```
NAME(CUSTOMER) - - >  String
ACCNO(ACCOUNT) - - >  Number
```

Relationships between entities are indicated by applying a function to an entity which in itself yields an entity, for example:

HAS(CUSTOMER) - - > > ACCOUNT
BELONGS_TO(EMPLOYEE) - - > BRANCH

The first of these yields the accounts held by a customer. The second yields the branch where EMPLOYEE is located. One problem with FDMs is the one-way nature of the declarations. If we wished to yield the set of customers for an account or the set of employees for a branch we could connect them to the above declarations thus:

CUSTOMER(ACCOUNT) - - > > INVERSE OF HAS(CUSTOMER)
EMPLOYED_AT(BRANCH)   - - > >   INVERSE   OF   BELONGS_
TO(EMPLOYEE)

Multi-argumented functions can take the place of weak entities. For instance, to derive the date of the registration of an account with a particular customer, we can declare:

REGISTRATION_DATE(ACCOUNT,CUSTOMER) - - > String

Specializations are indicated by an IS-A function:

IS-A-EMPLOYEE(TECHNICIAN) - - > EMPLOYEE
IS-A-TECHNICIAN(PROGRAMMER) - - > TECHNICIAN

This means that functions can be passed from a supertype to a subtype, for example:

EMPNAME(TECHNICIAN) - - > EMPNAME(IS-A-EMPLOYEE
(TECHNICIAN))

This means that the name of a technician is yielded by applying the name function to the entity Employee that represents the technician.

Aggregated types are easily defined in a functional database. Each function simply yields an entity, for example:

ENGINE(CAR) - - > ENGINE
BODY(CAR) - - > BODY
WHEELS(CAR) - - > > WHEELS

A grouping semantic such as the example given in section 2.2.4 would be represented as an inverse function, that is:

TYPES_OF_CAR(CAR) - - > > PRODUCED_CAR
TYPE_OF_CAR(PRODUCED_CAR) - - > INVERSE OF TYPES_OF_
CAR(CAR)

We can define constraints to ensure the integrity of a database. The fact that an employee can only manage employees in his or her own branch can be asserted thus:

DEFINE CONSTRAINT MANAGES_BRANCH(BRANCH) - - >
BELONGS_TO(MANAGER(BRANCH)) = BRANCH

This means that when we apply the BELONGS_TO function the manager of a
particular branch, we get back the branch that he or she manages.

2.3.3 Semantic objects

Semantic object modelling was first presented by Kroenke (1988) and is based
on concepts originally published by Hammer and Macleod (1981) and Codd
(1979). With semantic object modelling, we represent a database as a series of
semantic objects. A semantic object is similar in some ways to an entity in E/R
modelling in that it represents an identifiable item in a database. Like an entity,
it is characterized by a series of attributes. However, unlike E/R modelling,
when two or more objects interact, we represent this as an attribute of the two
objects. In this way, semantic objects are in themselves complete descriptions
of everything that is of interest to the user of that object.

In Figure 2.14 we have drawn semantic object diagrams to represent the
CUSTOMER, BANK, and ACCOUNTS objects. In BRANCH, we have a
series of simple attributes: BranchName, Address and Manager. Note how we
have given each one a cardinality of 1,1. This determines the minimum and
maximum occurrences of an attribute within an object; 1,1 means that branch
must have at least one and at most one BranchName. BranchName also has ID
indicated next to it, showing that this is used as an identifier for the object. ID
is underlined in this instance, showing that it must have a unique value. In
semantic object diagrams, the identifying attribute need not necessarily be
unique. We also have an object type attribute 'Account' indicated by the
rectangle with a cardinality 0,N. This means that there are associated with a
branch at least zero and possibly many accounts. Attributes that can take on
more than one value are called multi-valued.

In the object CUSTOMER we have a group attribute 'Address'. Here a line
is drawn around the group showing those attributes that contribute to the
address. Each attribute within the group must have a cardinality as well as a

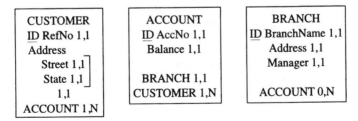

Figure 2.14 Semantic objects.

cardinality for the group as a whole. If a customer could have more than one address, we would give the group as a whole a cardinality of 1,N. Again we have an object attribute 'Account'. We have given this a cardinality of 1,N, indicating that a customer must have at least one account and possibly many.

With ACCOUNT, we have simple attributes 'AccNo' and 'Balance'. We have an object attribute 'Customer'. This has a 1,N cardinality, indicating that an account is associated with at least one and possibly many CUSTOMER objects.

With semantic objects, whenever an object attribute appears in one object, that object must appear as an attribute in the other object, completing the relationship. Thus, because ACCOUNT appears as an attribute of CUSTOMER and BRANCH, then CUSTOMER and BRANCH must appear as attributes of ACCOUNT.

As we noted in the section on E/R modelling, when two objects such as CUSTOMER and ACCOUNT are associated together, we may wish to record values pertinent to that association. In Figure 2.15, we have an association object ('Registration') which has an attribute to record the date when a particular customer became connected to a particular account. CUSTOMER and ACCOUNT now have REGISTRATION as an object type attribute. The cardinalities indicate that accounts and customers may have many registrations, but each registration pertains to precisely one customer and one account.

Semantic object diagrams can also encompass subclassing allowing for specialization and generalization. In Figure 2.16 we have slightly altered the diagram for BRANCH to include employee objects and a manager object. We have introduced objects for employees and managers and used special notation to indicate a subtype relationship between EMPLOYEE and MANAGER.

In this instance, instead of a cardinality, we have placed 0,ST next to the manager attribute in EMPLOYEE. This indicates that MANAGER is a subtype of EMPLOYEE. The '0' indicates that an employee need not be a manager. In

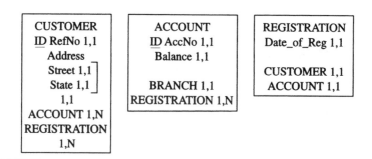

Figure 2.15 Introducing an association object.

```
 ┌─────────────────┐  ┌─────────────────┐  ┌─────────────────┐
 │     BRANCH      │  │      EMP        │  │    MANAGER      │
 │ ID BranchName 1,1│  │ ID EmpNo 1,1    │  │    EMP P        │
 │   Address 1,1   │  │  Insur_No 1,1   │  │   Grade 1,1     │
 │                 │  │    Name 1,1     │  │                 │
 │  ACCOUNT 0,N    │  │                 │  │   BRANCH 1,1    │
 │    EMP 1,N      │  │   BRANCH 1,1    │  └─────────────────┘
 │  MANAGER 1,1    │  │  MANAGER 0,ST   │
 └─────────────────┘  └─────────────────┘
```

Figure 2.16 Subtyping with semantic objects.

```
        ┌─────────────────────┐
        │         EMP         │
        │   ID EmpNo 1,1      │
        │    Insur_No 1,1     │
        │                     │
        │ TECHNICAL 0,ST ⎤    │
        │ CLERICAL 0,ST  ⎦0,1,1│
        └─────────────────────┘
```

Figure 2.17 Disjoint subtypes with semantic objects.

MANAGER, we place 'P' next to the employee attribute, indicating that the employee object is the 'Parent' of MANAGER, that is all the characteristics of an employee also apply to a manager. Note how we have introduced connections between BRANCH and EMP and BRANCH and MANAGER showing that a branch may have many employees but just one manager.

In Figure 2.17, we show disjoint subtyping by placing a grouping around a collection of subtypes and giving this grouping a three-way cardinality 0,1,1. This means that an employee need not be a programmer or a technician, but if employees are, they must be at least one of these and at most one.

Aggregated objects are quite easy to represent. We simply create an object with a series of 1,1 cardinalities with other objects (Figure 2.18).

In Figure 2.19, we model a TYPE-OF grouping showing that a given object (ENGINE) must be associated with a given ENGINE_TYPE. ENGINE_TYPE can be associated with a number of engines, indicating that a large number of engines may share the same basic characteristics.

Summary

- Database design is the process by which the requirements of a database are modelled prior to implementation.

```
┌─────────────────────────────┐
│             CAR             │
│                             │
│          ID CAR_No          │
│      Date_of_Manufacture    │
│          ENGINE 1,1         │
│           BODY 1,1          │
│         WHEELSET 1,1        │
│        SUSPENSION 1,1       │
└─────────────────────────────┘
```

Figure 2.18 An aggregated object.

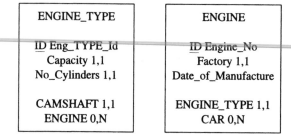

Figure 2.19 A grouped object.

- The conceptual model of a database is a logical data model independent of any particular form of implementation.
- There are various approaches to conceptual modelling, all of which incorporate certain aspects of semantic data modelling.
- Semantic data modelling proposes concepts such as assertions, convertibility, relatability and object relativity to enable useful and accurate conceptual models to be built.
- Generalization, specialization, aggregation and grouping are important aspects of object relativity that a conceptual model should attempt to represent.
- The entity/relationship model enables conceptual models to be built using entities and the relationships between them. It represents these using diagrams.
- Functional data modelling uses both diagrams and notation to represent a database as a series of mathematical functions.
- Semantic object modelling uses diagrams to represent a database as a series of interacting semantic objects.

- Each of the above approaches to conceptual modelling can represent most of the important semantic modelling concepts with varying degrees of ease.

Exercises

Here is a restatement of the scenario at the EverCare County General Hospital as set out in Chapter 1, except using narrative rather than file descriptions:

At the EverCare County General Hospital, patients are admitted and given a unique Patient Id. We record their name, home address and date of admission. They are assigned to a ward and to a consultant. They may then be diagnosed a set of conditions. Whilst in our care, they will receive a set of treatments. Each treatment will have a date and details of the nurse administering the treatment, the drug being administered and the dosage. Drugs have a unique Drug Id, a name and a recommended dosage (which may not be the same as the dosage given in individual treatments). Nurses have a Nurse Id and a name and are assigned to a ward. Each ward has a Sister (who is a nurse). Consultants have a Doctor Id and a name.

1 Represent the above scenario as
    (a) a set of entities and relationships;
    (b) a set of semantic objects.
2 A refinement is required of the above scenario. Consultants are either physicians or surgeons. Wards are either medical (meaning that all patients within them are assigned to physicians) or surgical (meaning that all patients within them are assigned to surgeons). Extend your answers to 1(a) and 1(b) using subsets and/or subtypes where necessary.

Further reading

Date (1995) Chapter 12
Delobel *et al.* (1995) Chapters 4, 5 and 6
Elmasri and Navathe (1994) Chapters 3 and 21
Hawryszkiewycz (1991) Chapters 6, 7 and 8
Hughes (1991) Chapter 1
Korth and Silberschatz (1991) Chapter 1
Kroenke (1995) Chapters 3 and 4
Paton *et al.* 1996 Chapter 4
Ryan and Smith (1995) Chapters 3 and 4
Ter Bekke (1992) Chapters 3, 4, 5, 8 and 9

References

Codd, E.F. (1979) 'Extending the Relational Model to Capture More Meaning', *Transactions on Database Systems*, 4, December

Chen, P. (1976) 'The Entity-Relationship Model: Toward a unified view of data', *ACM Transactions on Database Systems*, 1, March

Hammer, M. and Macleod, D. (1981) 'Database Description with SDM: A Semantic Database Model', *Transactions on Database Systems*, 6, September

Kroenke, D.M. (1988) *Database Processing*, 3rd edn, Prentice Hall International

Shipman, D.W. (1981) The Functional Data Model and the Language DAPLEX', *Transactions on Database Systems*, 6, March

CHAPTER 3

Relational databases 1 – Basic concepts

Relational database technology dominates the current database market. It provides a remarkably simple means of representing and manipulating data. It also has a thorough theoretical grounding. In this chapter, we will outline the main aspects of the relational model with simple definitions and examples.

By the end of this chapter, the reader should be able to:

1. Describe the major characteristics of a relational database.
2. Explain the major components of relational theory, namely relational data structures, relational data manipulation and relational data integrity.
3. Understand the meaning of the terms 'minimally relational', 'relationally complete' and 'fully relational'.

There are three main components of relational theory: data structures, data manipulation and data integrity. We will examine each of these in turn.

3.1 Relational data structures

In a relational database, all data is stored in simple two-dimensional tables known as relations. In Table 3.1 we have an example of a relation that stores data regarding a number of employees in a firm.

All tables in a relational database take this form. As stated above, tables are strictly referred to as relations, though we shall use the two terms inter-changeably. Broadly speaking, a relation equates approximately (though not necessarily precisely) to an entity in an entity/relationship diagram. We

Table 3.1 A relation

```
EMP
|--------------------------------------------|
| EMPNO   | EMPNAME   | DEPTNAME  | GRADE |
|---------|-----------|-----------|-------|
| 1       | F Jones   | SALES     | 6     |
| 2       | P Smith   | ACCOUNTS  | 6     |
| 3       | K Chan    | SALES     | 4     |
| 6       | J Peters  | SALES     | 5     |
| 9       | S Abdul   | ACCOUNTS  | 3     |
|--------------------------------------------|
```

construct a relation to represent each item of interest in a database. All items that have the same characteristics are stored in the same relation. The characteristics of an item are represented by the column headings (EMPNO, EMPNAME, DEPTNAME, GRADE) at the head of the table. The occurrences of this particular item (EMP) are represented by the rows of data underneath the column headings. The meaning of each row is quite easy to interpret: for example, the first row represents an EMP with an EMPNO of 1, an EMPNAME P Jones, a DEPTNAME of SALES and a GRADE of 6. This table has a number of features that all tables must have in a relational database.

3.1.1 Headings and bodies

1. The heading. All relations must have a heading. The heading consists of the name of the relation (EMP) and the names of the columns that comprise the relation. The columns of a relation are strictly referred to as attributes. The number of attributes determines the 'degree' of the relation. This particular relation is a four-degree relation. In relational theory, there is no limit to the number of attributes that a relation may be assigned, though in practice most relational DBMS products will usually place an upper limit on this.
2. The body. The rows of a relation comprise its body. Strictly speaking, these are referred to as tuples. A tuple is an ordered list of values. The meaning of each value is determined by its position in the tuple. Thus, in the first tuple the first value (1) represents the EMPNO, the second value (P Jones) represents the EMPNAME and so on. The number of tuples in a relation determines its cardinality. Thus, we have a relation with a cardinality of five.

One important feature of a tuple set in a relation is that it is a true set in the mathematical sense. A set is an unordered collection of distinct items. The set of tuples above is displayed in EMPNO sequence. This sequencing is of no consequence in itself. There is no inferred information such as EMPNO 1 is 'greater than' EMPNO 6. Tuples in a relation may be stored and displayed in any

Table 3.2 Adding a tuple

EMP

EMPNO	EMPNAME	DEPTNAME	GRADE
1	F Jones	SALES	6
2	P Smith	ACCOUNTS	6
3	K Chan	SALES	4
6	J Peters	SALES	5
9	S Abdul	ACCOUNTS	3
5	J Lewis	RESEARCH	5

sequence. In most relational systems, tuples are simply stored and displayed in the order in which they are added to the table. Adding a new EMP with an EMPNO of 5 would result in the relation now looking like Table 3.2.

3.1.2 Domains

For each attribute, there is clearly some sort of restriction upon the data that can be assigned. Under EMPNO, we have simple integers, EMPNAME is clearly a string of characters, and so on. The range of values that can be assigned to an attribute is known as its domain. At one level, a domain is conceptually very similar to a data type in programming. As with a data type, a domain not only defines the set of values that can be assigned to an attribute, but also determines the range of allowable operations on each value, for example adding or subtracting a number, splitting and concatenating strings and so on. At a higher level, domains have a semantic connotation. For instance, one could have a domain 'kilogram' to represent weight values and another domain 'money' for representing money values. Both domains would be built over a range of decimal numbers, but values from one domain could not be said to be compatible with values from another. This higher level of domain support is not usually found with most relational products.

When defining an attribute, we must give it a name and a domain. From thereon, every value given to an attribute must conform to its domain. Domains may be very general, for example 'all positive integers within 00000 to 99999', 'all strings of not more that 20 characters', or they may be very specific, for example 'one of SALES, ACCOUNTS, RESEARCH'. Most relational products provide general domains in the form of basic data types. There are very few that provide the facility for database users to define their own domains except in a very rudimentary fashion.

One very important feature of all relational domains is that they must be simple, meaning that they consist of single values only. For each tuple in EMP, we can assign one and one only EMPNO, EMPNAME, DEPTNAME and GRADE. We cannot have multi-valued domains. If we discover an entity with an attribute that is multi-valued, then we must create additional relations to cater for this.

For instance, suppose we wished to record the skills pertaining to each employee in a database, and that an employee could have a number of skills. The representation shown in Table 3.3 would be disallowed.

We have a domain SKILLS which is 'non-atomic'. By this we mean that it is capable of having values that are not simple 'atoms'. An atom is something that cannot be divided. In a relational database, all domains must be atomic. With this problem, we would have to reorganize our database into two tables, leaving the EMP table as before and introducing a SKILLS table as in Table 3.4.

Table 3.3 Disallowed non-atomic domain

EMP

EMPNO	EMPNAME	DEPTNAME	GRADE	SKILLS
1	F Jones	SALES	6	{German}
2	P Smith	ACCOUNTS	6	{Typing, Shorthand, French}
3	K Chan	SALES	4	{German, French}
6	J Peters	SALES	5	{French, Typing}
9	S Abdul	ACCOUNTS	3	{French, German, COBOL}
5	J Lewis	RESEARCH	5	{Piano}

We now represent SKILL as atomic, with each row on the SKILLs table the possession of one skill by one employee. If an employee has three skills, then this is represented by three tuples in the SKILLs table.

3.1.3 Null values

Suppose we wished to add an employee to our database who was not assigned to any particular department, and that the semantics of the database allowed for this. We would therefore add a new tuple as in Table 3.5.

In this case, we say that the tuple for the EMP with EMPNO 10 has the value NULL for DEPTNAME. NULL is a special value meaning 'not equal to anything', including itself. We cannot say that two employees with a null DEPTNAME have an equal value for this attribute. We can say that all the other Employees have a DEPTNAME that is not null (note: 'not null', not ' < > null').

When defining an attribute, we must not only state its domain, but also state whether or not its domain includes the value NULL. If not, then all tuples in the

Table 3.4 An acceptable relation with atomic values

SKILL

EMPNO	SKILL
1	German
2	Typing
2	Shorthand
2	French
3	German
3	French
6	French
6	Typing
9	French
9	German
9	COBOL
5	Piano

Table 3.5 Adding a tuple with a null value

EMP

EMPNO	EMPNAME	DEPTNAME	GRADE
1	F Jones	SALES	6
2	P Smith	ACCOUNTS	6
3	K Chan	SALES	4
6	J Peters	SALES	5
9	S Abdul	ACCOUNTS	3
5	J Lewis	RESEARCH	5
10	J Major		1

given relation must have a value for that attribute. Clearly, those attributes that give a unique identity to a tuple should never be allowed to take a null value, such as EMPNO in the EMP relation. We shall discuss this further in the section on entity integrity (3.2.2). Other attributes may or may not take null values depending on the semantic requirements of the database.

3.1.4 Base relations and views

The examples given so far are of a particular type of relation, known as a 'base relation'. A base relation is the lowest level of data representation available to the relational database user. All data in a relational database is ultimately stored in a set of base relations. However, data may also be retrieved and manipulated through 'views'. A view is a logical relation which takes its data either directly or indirectly from the base relations.

A view may be a simple subset of a base relation. Table 3.6 shows a view SALES which is a subset of the EMP relation.

In this view, we have created a relation consisting of all EMPs with a DEPTNAME of SALES. Clearly, we have a certain amount of redundancy here. We do not really need to show the fact that they all have the same DEPTNAME. Views may also be based on subsets of attributes (Table 3.7).

Views may combine data from more than one table as well as being subsets. Table 3.8 gives a view combining the EMPNAME attribute from EMP with just those tuples in SKILL of employees who can speak German.

Table 3.6 A simple view

EMP

EMPNO	EMPNAME	DEPTNAME	GRADE
1	F Jones	SALES	6
3	K Chan	SALES	4
6	J Peters	SALES	5

Table 3.7 A more refined view

```
SALES_1
| --------------------------------|
| EMPNO    | EMPNAME    | GRADE  |
| -------- ----------- ----------|
| 1        | F Jones    | 6      |
| 2        | K Chan     | 4      |
| 6        | J Peters   | 5      |
| --------------------------------|
```

We could then create a view as in Table 3.9 where we combine the data from SALES_1 with the data from GERMAN_SPEAKERS to show all employees in SALES who speak German.

To a certain extent, views can be treated as base tables in a relational database in that they may be used for retrieving data and, within certain constraints, for inserting, deleting and updating data. These constraints will be considered in a later section. When defining a view, the domains are determined by the base tables that hold the data for the view, including any rules regarding null values for a given attribute. The definition of a view is a specification of the views and/or base tables which contribute to that view. When a base table is removed from a relational database, then all views that are derived from that table, whether wholly or partially, directly or indirectly, will logically cease to exist.

Table 3.8 A view from two base tables

```
GERMAN_SPEAKERS
| --------------------|
| EMPNO    | EMPNAME  |
| -------- -----------|
| 1        | F Jones  |
| 3        | K Chan   |
| 9        | S Abdul  |
| --------------------|
```

Table 3.9 A view derived from 2 views

```
GERMAN_SALES_SPEAKERS
| --------------------|
| EMPNO    | EMPNAME  |
| -------- -----------|
| 1        | F Jones  |
| 3        | K Chan   |
| --------------------|
```

3.2 Relational data integrity

3.2.1 Keys

Data integrity in a relational database is based on the concept of keys. There are three types of key in a relational database: candidate keys, primary keys and foreign keys.

A candidate key is an attribute or set of attributes that can be used to identify uniquely each tuple in a relation. For instance, EMPNO is clearly a candidate key for the table EMP. Each row in EMP has a different EMPNO value. Sometimes attributes may be combined to identify tuples. In the SKILLs table, EMPNO values are not unique to any row; neither are the values under SKILL. However, if no employee can have the same skill twice, then each row will have a unique value for the combination of EMPNO and SKILL. This is what we call a composite candidate key.

A primary key is a special form of candidate key. It may be possible to have more than one candidate key for a relation. For instance, we could introduce an attribute TAX_NUMBER to our EMP table for the purposes of attaching an employee to a unique tax reference number elsewhere. If TAX_NUMBER was unique to each employee, then we would have two candidate keys. In this situation, where we have alternate candidate keys, we must nominate one of them to be the primary key. Nominating an attribute or set of attributes as the primary key has particular implications for that attribute set (see below). A table may have any number of candidate keys, but must have one, and only one, primary key. When there is only one candidate key in a table, then it is by default the primary key

A foreign key is an attribute (or set of attributes) that exists in more than one table and which is the primary key for one of those tables. EMPNO exists in both the SKILLs and the EMP tables. As it is the primary key for EMP, it therefore exists as a foreign key on SKILLs. Foreign keys are very important in relational databases. They are the major means by which data in one table may be related to data in another table. We can relate the rows in EMP to the corresponding rows in SKILLs by means of the EMPNO foreign key in SKILLs. When we do this, we say that we are establishing a relationship between the two tables. In order that relationships are valid, we must apply certain rules to the use of foreign keys (see section 3.2.3 below).

3.2.2 Entity integrity

Entity integrity is concerned with the reality of a database. The definition of an entity is an item which is capable of an independent existence. An entity set is a collection of items which have the same properties. In order that items within the same entity set can have an independent existence, there must be some way of differentiating them. In a relational database, we use base relations to model entity sets. A base relation consists of a set of tuples, all of which have the same attributes. In order that the tuples in a relation belong to a true set of distinct items, and, moreover, such a set is analogous to an entity set, they must each have a distinct identity.

It is for this reason that every base relation in a relational database must have a primary key. Moreover, we must ensure that every row has a distinct value for its primary key otherwise it has no unique identity. We therefore do not allow null values to be assigned to any attribute that forms part of the primary key. Thus, in our EMP table, all rows must have a value for EMPNO. In the SKILLs table where the primary key is composite, every row must have a value for both EMPNO and SKILL. If we allowed a null value for either of these attributes, then we could end up with two rows with, for instance, the same SKILL but no EMPNO. There would be nothing to differentiate such rows. Thus entity integrity requires that every attribute that participates in a primary key is *not* allowed to take a null value.

Entity integrity only applies to the primary key. If a table has alternate candidate keys, then the non-primary candidate keys may take a partial or total null value. However, the database designer may decide to debar null values for such keys and also for non-key attributes, depending on the semantic requirements of the system in question. Such decisions are specific to a particular system. Entity integrity is a theoretic requirement for all relational systems. (We say 'theoretic' as there are many relational database products that allow tables to be built without primary keys.)

To summarize, entity integrity requires that the value NULL may not be assigned to any attribute that forms part of a primary key.

3.2.3 Referential integrity

Referential integrity concerns the use of foreign keys. In our SKILLs table, EMPNO exists as a foreign key for EMP. How do we ensure that only valid EMP references are made in this table? We do this by applying the referential integrity rule.

Referential integrity states that every non-null value that exists in a foreign key attribute must also exist in the relation for which it is the primary key. Thus, we may not have any EMPNO values in SKILLs that do not also exist in EMP. This way, all references from SKILLs to EMP are valid. We can only enter up SKILL values for employees that actually exist.

Referential integrity brings up special problems regarding the updating or deleting of rows in a table. What happens if we change or alter an EMPNO value in EMP, thus invalidating all references to the previous EMPNO? There are three possible strategies:

1.   Restrict. With this strategy, we ban any alterations to a primary key if there are foreign key references to it. Thus, if we wanted to remove

EMPNO 1 from the EMP table, or alter the value of EMPNO 1 from 1 to 7, we would not be allowed to do this. We could only delete or change EMPNO values for those employees who did not have an entry in the SKILLs table.

2. Cascade. In this case, we 'cascade' the effect of the operation on the original row to all rows in all tables that reference it. If we wished to delete the row for EMPNO 1 from EMP, then we would also have to delete all rows with EMPNO 1 from the SKILLs table. If we change any EMPNO value in EMP, then we must change the corresponding EMPNO values in SKILLs.

3. Set to null. In this case, we allow the update or deletion to take place in the original table, but in order to maintain referential integrity, we set all corresponding foreign key values to null. In the example above, this would in fact have the effect of deleting rows from the SKILLs table as EMPNO is part of the primary key for SKILLs. A better example would be if we had another table DEPT as follows:

```
DEPT
| ------------------------------------------- |
| DEPTNAME    | MGR_EMPNO    | BUDGET    |
| ----------- ------------- ------------ -
| SALES       | 3            |  200000   |
| ACCOUNTS    | 2            | 5000000   |
| RESEARCH    | 5            |     100   |
| ------------------------------------------- |
```

In this table, DEPTNAME is the primary key and it now exists as a foreign key in EMP. This means that if we were to change the name of the SALES Department, a 'set to null' strategy would cause all EMP rows with SALES as the DEPTNAME to have a null value entered. This would have no effect on the entity integrity of these rows as DEPTNAME is not part of the primary key.

The reader may note that we have an attribute MGR_EMPNO in DEPT. This is a foreign key into EMP, indicating the EMPNO of the manager of a department. Foreign keys do not have to have the same label across tables. Referential integrity still applies. We have to decide what to do with rows in the DEPT table if updates or deletions are performed on EMPNO values in EMP; for example, if we delete EMPNO 2, do we disallow this because this exists as a value in DEPT ('restrict'), do we remove the corresponding row in DEPT ('cascade') or do we set the value for MGR_EMPNO for ACCOUNTS to null? This has to be defined for every foreign key in a database.

Note that referential integrity works in one direction only. We can update or delete EMPNO values in SKILLs, DEPTNAME values in DEPT or MGR_EMPNO values in DEPT as much as we like so long as they maintain a reference to a primary key value that actually exists. If it is not possible to establish a reference to a primary key value that actually exists, then the relevant foreign key value must be set to null.

To summarize, referential integrity requires that every foreign key value must reference a primary key value that actually exists, otherwise it must be set to null.

3.3 Relational data manipulation

One of the great benefits of relational databases is that data can be retrieved from any set of relational tables using a combination of just eight intuitively simple relational operations. These comprise what is known as the 'relational algebra'. The five basic operations of relational algebra are RESTRICT, PROJECT, TIMES, UNION and MINUS. There are additionally three derived operations: JOIN, INTERSECT and DIVIDE. They are derived in that they can be built from the basic operations. However, it is convenient to treat them as if they were basic operations. The JOIN operation in particular is one of the most commonly used relational operations and merits considerable attention in its own right.

All relational systems use the algebra to return data from tables. However, the algebra is very rarely supported directly by a system. Most systems provide an additional interface, frequently in the form of the SQL language, which is the topic of Chapter 5. SQL is a declarative database language where users can write a statement that 'describes' a given set of data. The task of the SQL interpreter is to break the given SQL statement down into the series of algebraic operations that will build the dataset described by the statement.

One major principle of the relational algebra is that all of its operations work at the relation level alone. The only argument they take is a relation or a set of relations and all that they return is a single relation that satisfies the constraints placed by the operation. The relations provided to the argument must, by definition, exist within the given database, either as base relations or views. The resulting relation is a temporary relation that has been derived by applying an operation to the given relations.

We will now describe the operations that comprise the relational algebra.

3.3.1 The RESTRICT operation

RESTRICT is frequently referred to as the relational SELECT. However, SELECT also exists as a command in SQL and has a far wider meaning in that language. To avoid confusion, we shall use the term RESTRICT when referring to the algebra.

RESTRICT returns tuples from a relation. For instance, the operation:

```
RESTRICT (EMP);
```

will return all of the rows from the EMP table.

RESTRICT may be used with conditions. The operation:

```
RESTRICT (EMP)
DEPTNAME = 'ACCOUNTS';
```

will return:

EMPNO	EMPNAME	DEPTNAME	GRADE
2	P Smith	ACCOUNTS	6
9	S Abdul	ACCOUNTS	3

representing all tuples with the DEPTNAME with the value 'ACCOUNTS'.

Constraints in relational operations may use a combination of conditions using the usual logical operations AND, OR and NOT. For instance, the operation:

```
RESTRICT (EMP)
DEPTNAME = 'ACCOUNTS'
AND GRADE = 6;
```

will return:

EMPNO	EMPNAME	DEPTNAME	GRADE
2	P Smith	ACCOUNTS	6

whereas:

```
RESTRICT (EMP)
DEPTNAME = 'ACCOUNTS'
OR GRADE = 6
```

will return:

EMPNO	EMPNAME	DEPTNAME	GRADE
1	F Jones	SALES	6
2	P Smith	ACCOUNTS	6
9	S Abdul	ACCOUNTS	3

giving the tuples for all employees whose DEPTNAME is 'ACCOUNTS' or whose GRADE is 6.

3.3.2 The PROJECT operation

PROJECT is another operation which can be used on single relations only. Whereas RESTRICT return sets of complete tuples, PROJECT returns tuples with a restricted set of attributes. For instance, the operation:

```
PROJECT EMPNAME(EMP);
```

will return:

```
| ---------- |
| EMPNAME    |
 ----------
| F Jones    |
| P Smith    |
| K Chan     |
| J Peters   |
| S Abdul    |
| J Lewis    |
| J Major    |
| ---------- |
```

representing the set of values under the attribute EMPNAME in EMP. Note how we had to provide as an argument the column over which we wished the PROJECTion to be performed.

We can perform PROJECTs over sets of columns. For instance, the operation:

```
PROJECT EMPNAME,DEPTNAME (EMP);
```

will return

```
| ----------------------- |
| EMPNAME    | DEPTNAME   |
 ----------   -----------
| F Jones    | SALES      |
| P Smith    | ACCOUNTS   |
| K Chan     | SALES      |
| J Peters   | SALES      |
| S Abdul    | ACCOUNTS   |
| J Lewis    | RESEARCH   |
| J Major    |            |
| ----------------------- |
```

When using a relational operation, what is returned is a relation in the strict sense, that is a set of tuples. Sets have no repeating items. Thus, the operation:

```
PROJECT DEPTNAME (EMP);
```

will return:

```
| ------------|
| DEPTNAME    |
 ------------
| SALES       |
| ACCOUNTS    |
| RESEARCH    |
| -----------|
```

representing the set of values stored under this attribute. Although there are seven tuples in the original table, there are only three tuples in the result, representing the three distinct values under this attribute. There is one tuple in the EMP table with a NULL value for DEPTNAME. This is not represented in the PROJECT result as this is a tuple with literally no (distinct) value for this attribute.

Relational operations may be combined. If we wished to find the names of employees in the ACCOUNTS Department, we would specify:

```
PROJECT EMPNAME  (RESTRICT (EMP)
                  DEPTNAME = 'ACCOUNTS');
```

giving:

```
| ---------|
| EMPNAME  |
 ----------
| F Jones  |
| S Abdul  |
| ---------|
```

In this example, we have passed RESTRICT (EMP) DEPTNAME = 'ACCOUNTS' as the argument to the PROJECT operation. The RESTRICT operation returns a temporary relation which can then be used as an argument by the outer PROJECT operation.

3.3.3 The TIMES operation

The TIMES operation is also known as the PRODUCT operation. It returns the Cartesian product of two relations. By this, we mean that it takes two relations and returns a relation where every tuple in one relation is concatenated with every tuple in the other. The operation:

```
EMP TIMES DEPT;
```

will give:

EMPNO	EMPNAME	DEPTNAME	GRADE	DEPTNAME	MGR_EMPNO	BUDGET
1	F Jones	SALES	6	SALES	3	200000
2	P Smith	ACCOUNTS	6	SALES	3	200000
3	K Chan	SALES	4	SALES	3	200000
6	J Peters	SALES	5	SALES	3	200000
9	S Abdul	ACCOUNTS	3	SALES	3	200000
5	J Lewis	RESEARCH	5	SALES	3	200000
10	J Major		1	SALES	3	200000
1	F Jones	SALES	6	ACCOUNTS	2	5000000
2	P Smith	ACCOUNTS	6	ACCOUNTS	2	5000000
3	K Chan	SALES	4	ACCOUNTS	2	5000000
6	J Peters	SALES	5	ACCOUNTS	2	5000000
9	S Abdul	ACCOUNTS	3	ACCOUNTS	2	5000000
5	J Lewis	RESEARCH	5	ACCOUNTS	2	5000000
10	J Major		1	ACCOUNTS	2	5000000
1	F Jones	SALES	6	RESEARCH	5	100
2	P Smith	ACCOUNTS	6	RESEARCH	5	100
3	K Chan	SALES	4	RESEARCH	5	100
6	J Peters	SALES	5	RESEARCH	5	100
9	S Abdul	ACCOUNTS	3	RESEARCH	5	100
5	J Lewis	RESEARCH	5	RESEARCH	5	100
10	J Major		1	RESEARCH	5	100

With this operation, we have concatenated every tuple in the EMP table with every tuple in the DEPT table, resulting in a table with 21 tuples (seven rows in EMP × 3 rows in DEPT). The result of this example is not particularly useful in itself. A more useful result would be one where we concatenate each EMP tuple with just the DEPT tuple relating to the the department to which the employee actually belongs. What we are describing here is a special form of the TIMES operation known as the JOIN.

3.3.4 The JOIN operation

The JOIN operation is a refinement of the TIMES operation where the concatenation of the tuples is based on a given attribute, or set of attributes, from each of the two relations. The values in the given attributes may be compared in order that some sort of constraint may be placed on the result.

The most common form of join is the 'natural join'. This is where two relations have a common attribute and the result only contains rows whose values in this common attribute are the same. For instance, in EMP and DEPT, we have the common attribute DEPTNAME. We can join these:

```
NATURAL JOIN (EMP, DEPT);
```

giving:

EMPNO	EMPNAME	DEPTNAME	GRADE	MGR_EMPNO	BUDGET
1	F Jones	SALES	6	3	200000
2	P Smith	ACCOUNTS	6	2	5000000
3	K Chan	SALES	4	3	200000
6	J Peters	SALES	5	3	200000
9	S Abdul	ACCOUNTS	3	2	5000000
5	J Lewis	RESEARCH	5	5	100

In this result, every EMP tuple has been joined with the DEPT tuple that has the same DEPTNAME value. We now have a genuinely useful result where we are expanding our information on employees with details of the department that each one belongs to.

Note how we did not get a row for the last EMP in the EMP relation in our result. This is because this EMP has a null value under DEPTNAME, meaning that there is no row in the DEPT table that it could join to. This is the standard form of JOIN, known as the 'inner join'. However, there is also another form of JOIN known as the 'outer join'. In this form of the join, any tuple that cannot be joined to a tuple in the corresponding table is displayed with null values in the 'joined' attributes, for example:

```
NATURAL OUTER JOIN (EMP, DEPT);
```

giving:

EMPNO	EMPNAME	DEPTNAME	GRADE	MGR_EMPNO	BUDGET
1	F Jones	SALES	6	3	200000
2	P Smith	ACCOUNTS	6	2	5000000
3	K Chan	SALES	4	3	200000
6	J Peters	SALES	5	3·	200000
9	S Abdul	ACCOUNTS	3	2	5000000
5	J Lewis	RESEARCH	5	5	100
10	J Major		1		

Relations may be JOINed over any two attributes with 'compatible' domains. By 'compatible', we mean that data values from one domain may be meaningfully compared with data values in another. Another JOIN that we could perform is to compare EMPNO values in EMP with MGR_EMPNO values in DEPT. Where the values are equal, this would tell us which employees are managers of their department:

```
JOIN  (EMP, DEPT)
        EMPNO = MGR_EMPNO;
```

giving:

EMPNO	EMPNAME	DEPTNAME	GRADE	MGR_EMPNO	BUDGET
2	P Smith	ACCOUNTS	6	2	5000000
3	K Chan	SALES	4	3	200000
5	J Lewis	RESEARCH	5	5	100

In this example, we perform a join of EMP and DEPT but specify that this join is to be done over EMPNO in EMP matching MGR_EMPNO in DEPT, rather than the natural join over DEPTNAME.

The above examples are joins of two tables. Joins may be nested, enabling multi-table joins to be performed. For instance, suppose we had another table PURCHASES which recorded items of expenditure by individual departments, each item having an ORDER_NO, an AMOUNT and a DEPTNAME indicating the department raising the order:

PURCHASES

ORDER_NO	DEPTNAME	AMOUNT
1	ACCOUNTS	2000
2	SALES	32000
3	RESEARCH	565
4	SALES	2450
6	RESEARCH	245

In this table, ORDER_NO is the primary key and DEPTNAME is a foreign key into DEPT. If we wished to ascertain details of the employees responsible for raising these orders (i.e. the managers), we would have to perform a natural join PURCHASES with DEPT, and then join this with EMP thus:

```
JOIN  (EMP, (NATURAL JOIN DEPT, PURCHASES))
        EMPNO = MGR_EMPNO;
```

This would give us a rather wide table with a lot of columns. We could reduce the number of columns using a PROJECT on this operation thus:

```
PROJECT EMPNAME, ORDERNO, DEPTNAME, AMOUNT, BUDGET
        (JOIN (EMP, (NATURAL JOIN DEPT,PURCHASES))
              EMPNO = MGR_EMPNO);
```

giving:

EMPNAME	ORDER_NO	DEPTNAME	AMOUNT	BUDGET
P Smith	1	ACCOUNTS	2000	5000000
K Chan	2	SALES	32000	200000
J Lewis	3	RESEARCH	565	100
K Chan	4	SALES	2450	200000
J Lewis	6	RESEARCH	245	100

We can further RESTRICT the result to just those managers who have exceeded their budget thus:

```
RESTRICT
        (PROJECT EMPNAME, ORDER_NO, DEPTNAME, AMOUNT, BUDGET
                (JOIN (EMP, (NATURAL JOIN DEPT, PURCHASES))
                      EMPNO = MGR_EMPNO))
    AMOUNT > BUDGET;
```

giving:

EMPNAME	ORDER_NO	DEPTNAME	AMOUNT	BUDGET
J Lewis	3	RESEARCH	565	100
J Lewis	6	RESEARCH	245	100

RESTRICT, PROJECT and JOIN are fundamental relational operators, and in order to be minimally relational, a database system must provide the functionality of these three types of operation.

3.3.5 The UNION operator

The UNION operator is the standard mathematical set operator applied to relations, which in themselves are sets of tuples. In order that two relations may be passed as arguments to the UNION operator, their tuples must be compatible. This means that they must have the same number of attributes and that each attribute must have a domain that is compatible with its equivalent attribute in the other relation. For example, a relation with three attributes cannot be UNIONed with a relation with four attributes. Two relations each with three attributes may be UNIONed as long as the first, second and third attributes in the first relation are respectively compatible with the first, second and third attributes in the second relation. In other words, if the first attribute in the first relation has a domain of simple integers, then the first attribute in the second relation must also have a domain based on simple integers and so on.

The UNION operator returns a set of tuples which are in either or both of two given relations.

With our example database, let us have two views based on employees' skills derived from a JOIN of EMP and SKILLS showing those employees with a language skill:

GERMAN_SPEAKERS

EMPNO	EMPNAME
1	F Jones
3	K Chan
9	S Abdul

FRENCH_SPEAKERS

EMPNO	EMPNAME
2	P Smith
3	K Chan
6	J Peters
9	S Abdul

These tables are clearly compatible. The UNION of these is obtained thus:

GERMAN_SPEAKERS UNION FRENCH_SPEAKERS;

giving:

EMPNO	EMPNAME
1	F Jones
3	K Chan
9	S Abdul
2	P Smith
6	J Peters

Note how we do not get any duplicate tuples in our result. This is because UNION is a true set operator, returning a true set of tuples as the result, a set being an unordered series of distinct items. UNION returns those tuples that are in either or both of two relations. If there are no tuples common to both of the given relations, then the result will contain the total number of tuples belonging to the two relations. For instance, the view representing owners of the typing skill would be:

```
TYPING
| -------- | --------- |
| EMPNO    | EMPNAME   |
| -------- | --------- |
| 2        | P Smith   |
| 6        | J Peters  |
| ----------------- |
```

and the operation:

GERMAN_SPEAKERS UNION TYPING;

would give:

```
| -------- | --------- |
| EMPNO    | EMPNAME   |
| -------- | --------- |
| 1        | F Jones   |
| 3        | K Chan    |
| 9        | S Abdul   |
| 2        | P Smith   |
| 6        | J Peters  |
| ----------------- |
```

which, by coincidence, is the same result as the previous UNION of two different tables. As there are no tuples common to both tables, the result has five tuples (three from the first, two from the second).

The operation:

FRENCH_SPEAKERS UNION TYPING;

would give:

```
| -------- | --------- |
| EMPNO    | EMPNAME   |
| -------- | --------- |
| 2        | P Smith   |
| 3        | K Chan    |
| 6        | J Peters  |
| 9        | S Abdul   |
| ----------------- |
```

which is the same as the view FRENCH_SPEAKERS. This means that TYPING adds no extra tuples to the result, indicating that all employees with the typing skill also happen to speak French.

UNION is a commutative operator, meaning that you get the same result regardless of the order of the arguments given to the operation. FRENCH_SPEAKERS UNION GERMAN_SPEAKERS will yield the same set of tuples as GERMAN_SPEAKERS UNION FRENCH_SPEAKERS.

3.3.6 The MINUS operator

MINUS is another set operator which may be applied to compatible relations. Given two relations, the MINUS operator returns those tuples which are only in the first relation. Those tuples which are also in the second are 'subtracted' from the result.

The operation:

```
GERMAN_SPEAKERS MINUS FRENCH_SPEAKERS;
```

would give:

```
| -------- | --------- |
| EMPNO    | EMPNAME   |
| -------- | --------- |
| 1        | F. Jones  |
| ------------------- |
```

indicating that EMPNO 1 is the only employee who speaks German, but not French.

MINUS is not commutative. The order in which the arguments are given to the operation does make a difference. The operation:

```
FRENCH_SPEAKERS MINUS GERMAN_SPEAKERS;
```

would give:

```
| -------- | --------- |
| EMPNO    | EMPNAME   |
| -------- | --------- |
| 2        | P Smith   |
| 6        | J Peters  |
| ------------------- |
```

indicating those employees who speak French but who cannot speak German.

The operation:

```
FRENCH_SPEAKERS MINUS TYPING;
```

would give:

```
| -------- | --------- |.
| EMPNO    | EMPNAME   |
| -------- | --------- |
| 3        | K Chan    |
| 9        | S Abdul   |
| ----------------- |
```

whereas:

```
TYPING MINUS FRENCH_SKILLS;
```

would return an empty set as there is no one in the TYPING table who does not speak French.

3.3.7 The INTERSECT operator

The INTERSECT operator returns tuples from two compatible relations that exist in both of these relations. The operation:

```
GERMAN_SPEAKERS INTERSECT FRENCH_SPEAKERS;
```

would give:

```
| -------- | --------- |
| EMPNO    | EMPNAME   |
| -------- | --------- |
| 3        | K Chan    |
| 9        | S Abdul   |
| ----------------- |
```

showing those employees who speak both languages. If there are no tuples common to two relations, then the result is an empty set. For instance, GERMAN_SPEAKERS INTERSECT TYPING would give an empty relation, showing that there is no one with both of these skills.

It is possible to build the result of an intersection using UNION and MINUS thus:

```
(GERMAN_SPEAKERS   MINUS(GERMAN_SPEAKERS   MINUS   FRENCH_
SPEAKERS))
UNION
(FRENCH_SPEAKERS   MINUS(FRENCH_SPEAKERS   MINUS   GERMAN_
SPEAKERS));
```

The above removes from GERMAN_SPEAKERS those who do not speak French and UNIONs this with FRENCH_SPEAKERS with non-German speakers removed. It is obviously a lot more convenient to represent INTERSECT as an operation in its own right.

INTERSECT is a commutative operator.

3.3.8 The DIVIDE operator

The DIVIDE operator is another derived operator in that it can be built from the other operations. However, it is a very useful operator that is more conveniently regarded as an operation in its own right.

DIVIDE is concerned with relations with overlapping attribute sets where the attributes of one relation are a subset of the attributes in the other. When we have two such relations, DIVIDE returns all of the tuples in the first relation that can be matched against all of the values in the second (smaller) relation.

For instance, let us take our SKILLs table as before and create a LANGUAGE_SKILL table (Table 3.10). We can DIVIDE SKILL by LANGUAGE_SKILL as they have overlapping sets of attributes (the overlap being the attribute SKILL).

The result of SKILL DIVIDE LANGUAGE_SKILL would be:

```
| -------- |
| EMPNO    |
| -------- |
| 9        |
| -------- |
```

This represents the only EMPNO value in SKILL that is associated in tuples with SKILL values that match all of the SKILL values in the LANGUAGE_SKILL relation. DIVIDE returns the non-overlapping attribute. If we removed the tuple COBOL from the language skills, the result would be:

```
| -------- |
| EMPNO    |
| -------- |
| 3        |
| 9        |
| -------- |
```

As there would now only be two values under SKILL in LANGUAGE_SKILL (French and German), those EMPNO values that were associated in tuples with both of these would be returned.

Table 3.10 Two dividable tables

```
SKILL                                    LANGUAGE SKILL
|-----------------------|                |--------|
| EMPNO   | SKILL       |                | SKILL  |
|-----------------------|                |--------|
| 1       | German      |                | French |
| 2       | Typing      |                | German |
| 2       | Shorthand   |                | COBOL  |
| 2       | French      |                |--------|
| 3       | German      |
| 3       | French      |
| 6       | French      |
| 6       | Typing      |
| 9       | French      |
| 9       | German      |
| 9       | COBOL       |
| 5       | Piano       |
|-----------------------|
```

3.4 Satisfying the relational definition

In section 3.3.4 above, we made reference to the notion that a system must have certain features to be 'minimally' relational. There are certain aspects of the relational model, some of which are essential, the rest of which are desirable. These aspects are classified into three levels: minimal (that which is essential), relationally complete (that which is highly desirable) and fully relational.

To be minimally relational, a system must:

1. At the lowest level available to the user, store all of its data in tables using simple domains.
2. Provide the functionality of the RESTRICT, PROJECT and JOIN operators.

To be relationally complete, a system must:

1. Be minimally relational.
2. Provide the functionality of UNION and MINUS.

To be fully relational, a system must:

1. Be relationally complete.
2. Support entity and referential integrity.
3. Provide for user-defined domains.

An increasing number of products are now fully relational, though there still exist a large number that are not yet even minimally relational even though they claim to be 'relational'.

Summary

- Relational databases are the most commonly used type of database at the present time.
- Data is stored in a relational database in two-dimensional tables using simple domains.
- Integrity of a relational database is maintained by the entity and referential integrity rules.
- Access to data in a relational database is provided by the relational algebra, which consists of a restricted set of operations.
- There are levels of conformance to the relational model which different systems satisfy.

Exercises

Examine the following set of relations:

CUSTOMERS

CUSTNO	CUSTNAME
1	P Jones
2	H Chan
4	S Abdul
6	K Smith
7	N Le Mer

FLIGHTS

FLIGHTNO	DESTINATION	DAY	TIME	COST
FL2X	Paris	Tuesday	1400	78.95
HK101	Hong Kong	Sunday	0900	525.00
JX74	Bahrain	Monday	1300	275.75

RESERVATIONS

CUSTNO	FLIGHTNO
1	FL2X
1	HK101
2	HK101
6	JX74
7	JX74
1	JX74

1   Identify the primary keys and the foreign keys apparent in the above relations.

2 Give examples of data that could be entered into these relations that would make them contradict referential and/or entity integrity.

3 What difficulty might arise if we were to delete one of the flights? What are the alternative strategies that we could employ to counteract this?

4 Specify the operations in the relational algebra necessary to:
   (a) Find the tuple of the customer whose CUSTNO is 4.
   (b) Generate a list of flight destinations
   (c) Find the destination of flight JX74.
   (d) Build a table that shows the CUSTNOs of customers for each flight reservation as well as the flight information.
   (e) Build a table with the columns CUSTNAME, FLIGHTNO, DESTINATION, DAY, TIME relating to each reservation made.
   (f) Find the CUSTNOs for FLIGHTNO HK101.
   (g) Find the CUSTNOs for customers who are on flights HK101 and JX74.
   (h) Find the CUSTNOs for customers who are on flight HK101, but not on JX74.
   (i) Find the names of customers who have made a reservation for all flights.

Further reading

Date (1995) Chapters 3, 4, 5 and 6
Delobel *et al.* (1995) Chapter 2
Elmasri and Navathe (1994) Chapter 6
Gardarin and Valduriez (1989) Chapter 4
Hawryszkiewycz (1991) Chapter 2
Korth and Silberschatz (1991) Chapters 3 and 5
Kroenke (1995) Chapters 5 and 9
Ozkarahan (1990) Chapter 5
Ryan and Smith (1995) Chapter 13

Relational databases 2 – Design

In this chapter, we shall examine how we can take a database designed using entity/relationship modelling and implement it as a relational database. We shall also examine the technique of normalization. This is a specialized form of database design which has its basis in relational database theory. It assists the designer of a relational database in ensuring that a particular set of tables is the most efficient method of representing a given dataset. Normalization may be used as a complete design methodology in its own right. However, it has severe semantic limitations and is not as intuitively straightforward as E/R modelling. It is now widespread practice to use a form of E/R modelling to derive a semantic model of a relational database, transform this into a set of relations using the techniques described in this chapter and then to use normalization to refine the resulting design.

At the end of this chapter, the reader should be able to:

1. Transform an E/R model of a database into a relational database consisting of a set of tables.
2. Use normalization techniques to ensure that a given set of tables is an 'efficient' implementation of a relational database.

We shall examine the meaning of the term 'efficient' in the section on normalization.

4.1 Transforming an E/R model into a relational database

In this section, we shall use the example database in Chapter 2 and implement it as a relational database. We will reproduce some of the diagrams from that chapter. In E/R modelling, entities are characterized by their attributes. In a relational database, relations have attributes. The meaning of the term 'attribute' in relational theory is slightly different to that in E/R modelling. In order to avoid confusion, we shall use the term 'column' in this section when referring to the attributes of a relation.

The transformation of an E/R model into a relational database can be represented as a series of simple steps.

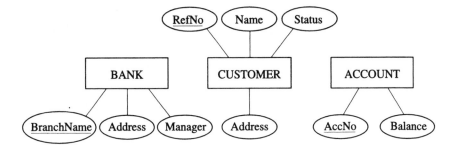

Figure 2.2 Entities with attributes.

Step 1

For each 'strong' entity in the E/R model, create a base relation with a column for each simple attribute of that entity. The key attribute for the entity becomes the primary key of the relation.

In Figure 2.2, we had BANK, CUSTOMER and ACCOUNT as entities. We would therefore create a relation for each of these entities. With BANK, we would have columns for BranchName, Address and Manager, with Branch-Name being the primary key. For ACCOUNT, we would have columns for AccNo and Balance, AccNo being the primary key.

In the case of a composite key, we must have a column for each part of that key, and then define that collection of columns to be the primary of the relation.

Step 2

For each weak entity, create a relation consisting of all the simple attributes of that entity and also include columns for the primary keys of those entities on whose existence it is dependent.

In Figure 2.5, we had the weak entity REGISTRATION with the single simple attribute 'Date_of_Reg'. This entity participates in relationships with CUSTOMER and ACCOUNT. We must include in the relation REGISTRA-TION columns for AccNo indicating the Account and RefNo indicating the customer owning the account registration. Thus each tuple in the relation REGISTRATION will have three columns: AccNo, RefNo and Date_of_Reg. These foreign keys are semantically necessary as, by definition, a weak entity is one that is incapable of an independent existence. It must have an explicit link to those entities on whose existence it depends. In a relational database, such links are established by means of a foreign key relationship. Moreover, with this particular entity, there is no primary key attribute. In this situation, the primary key becomes the composite of the foreign keys for those entities on whose existence it depends. Thus, the key for the REGISTER relation is a composite of AccNo and RefNo.

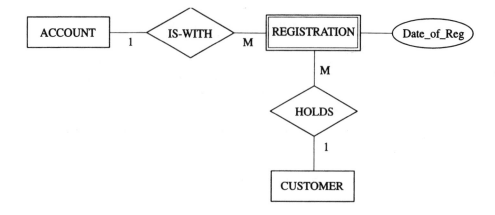

Figure 2.5 A weak entity.

Step 3

When two entities participate in a one-to-many (1–M) relationship, the relation representing the entity with the M (Many) cardinality must have a foreign key column representing this relationship.

There are a number of 1–M relationships in Chapter 2. The relationship between BANK and ACCOUNT in Figure 2.3 is 1–M, meaning that the relation for ACCOUNT must include BranchName as a foreign key.

Figure 2.3 A 1–M cardinality.

Step 4

When two entities participate in a 1–1 relationship, a foreign key column must be included in the relation that represents one of those entities.

In Figure 2.7, there exists a 1–1 relationship ('managed-by') between BANK and EMP, representing that a bank has one employee that is the manager of that bank and that an employee may only manage one bank. We could either place a foreign key EmpNo in the BANK relation to demonstrate this or place a foreign key BranchName in the relation EMP. We would not place the foreign key in both relations as this would give an opportunity for inconsistent data to be recorded. For instance, we could enter in the EMP relation the fact that EMP 'X' manages BANK 'Y' whilst entering in the BANK relation a foreign key reference to EMP 'Z' as the manager of BANK 'Y'. If our foreign key references were all correct, we would have an element of redundancy in the

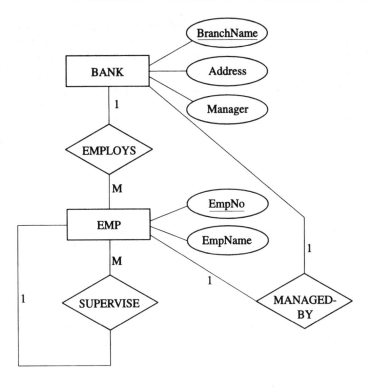

Figure 2.7 A recursive relationship.

database as the same 'fact' (e.g. 'X' manages 'Y') would be recorded in two separate relations.

According to step 3 above, we should be including BranchName as a foreign key in the EMP relation to represent the 1–M relationship 'EMPLOYS' between BANK and EMP. If we also include BranchName as a foreign key in EMP for the purpose of referencing the branch managed by an employee, we would have to call this column by a different name to the column used to reference the branch where an employee works. Thus, we would probably call one of these columns something like 'employed-at' and the other 'managed-by', both referencing the BranchName primary key in BANK. It is perfectly allowable for two different columns to reference the same primary key. We need to separate them out when they have a different underlying semantic such as in this example.

The question to be addressed is which relation would be the 'better' one to have a foreign key column? This is easily answered in this example because for one of the entities, the participation in the relationship is 'total'. An entity is said to have a total participation in a relationship when every member of that set must participate in it. Every bank must have a manager, whereas not all employees are managers. Thus, for BANK, the participation in the managed-by relationship is total, but not for EMP. In this case, it is better to put the foreign key EmpNo in the BANK relation. Every tuple in the BANK relation will now have an EmpNo value indicating its manager. If instead we put a foreign key 'managed-by' in the EMP relation that references BranchName in the BANK relation, there would be a lot of EMP tuples with a null value for this column as most employees are not managers. It is always best to minimize the use of null values in a relational database as they waste space and their meaning may be ambiguous.

Thus, as a guideline, in a 1–1 relationship, the foreign key should be included in the relation that represents the entity that is nearest to a total participation in the relationship.

Sometimes, we may get a 1–1 relationship that is total for both entities. If these entities do not participate in any other relationships, then it may well be worth considering merging them into one relation. One further thing to note is that when a foreign key represents a 1–1 relationship, then duplicate values for that key must be disallowed.

Step 5

When two entities participate in a many-to-many (M–N) relationship, then a relation must be created consisting of foreign keys for the two relations representing the participating entities.

The 'has' relationship in Figure 2.4 is M–N between CUSTOMER and ACCOUNT. In order to represent this, we need to create a relation HAS consisting of the columns RefNo (for CUSTOMER) and AccNo (for AC-COUNT). The primary key for this table would be a composite of these two columns. Each tuple would thus be a pair of values matching the RefNo of a customer paired with an AccNo for an account that the customer owns. A

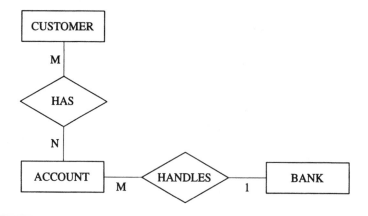

Figure 2.4 An entity/relationship data model.

Table 4.1 A relation representing a M–N relationship

```
HAS_ACCOUNT
- - - - - - - - - - - - - - - - - - - - - - - -
| REFNO       | ACCNO      |
- - - - - - - - - - - - - - - - -
| 12345       | 56930      |
| 12345       | 87306      |
| 12345       | 56789      |
| 39205       | 56789      |
| 98508       | 56789      |
| 92056       | 56789      |
- - - - - - - - - - - - - - - - - - - - - - - -
```

customer owning three accounts will have three tuples in that relation with their RefNo. Likewise an account with four owners will generate four tuples with the AccNo paired with the RefNos of the four customers that own that account. This is shown in Table 4.1. Customer 12345 has three accounts, whereas account 56789 is shared by four customers.

Step 6

Where an entity has a multi-valued attribute, create a relation with a column as a foreign key to the relation that represents the entity and a column for the multi-valued attribute. The primary key is a composite of the two columns. We must do this owing to the atomic nature of data in a relational database.

Suppose we had an attribute Telephone_No for the entity CUSTOMER and that this attribute was multi-valued indicating that a customer may have a series of possible telephone numbers. We could not include this as a column in the CUSTOMER relation. Instead, we would have to create an extra relation (CUSTOMER_TELEPHONE) with the columns Refno (foreign key to Customer) and Telephone_No, the primary key being a composite of these two columns. A tuple would be entered into this table for every telephone number relating to a given customer. In Table 4.2, customer 12345 has three telephone numbers whereas customer 67859 only has one.

If the multi-valued attribute was a composite, then the resulting relation would have a column for each part of the composite attribute.

Table 4.2 Implementing a multivalued attribute

```
CUSTOMER_TELEPHONE
- - - - - - - - - - - - - - - - - - - - - - - -
| REFNO    | TELEPHONE_NO  |
- - - - - - - - - - - - - - -
| 12345    | 687-69449     |
| 12345    | 687-09382     |
| 12345    | 02-578-59483  |
| 67859    | 657-03938     |
- - - - - - - - - - - - - - - - - - - - - - - -
```

Step 7

When more than two entities participate in a relationship, then a relation must be created consisting of foreign keys to those relations representing the entities participating in that relationship.

Suppose that in our sample database we had a relationship 'commends' which was a ternary one between EMP, MANAGER and BRANCH to record the fact that a manager has commended a particular employee and, moreover, any manager can commend any employee at any branch regardless of whether that manager is the manager of the branch or whether the employee belongs to that branch. This relationship has a single attribute 'Date_of_Commendation' (Figure 4.1).

We would have to represent this as a relation COMMENDS consisting of the foreign keys EmpNo (for the employee), EmpNo (for the manager) and BranchName (for the branch). We would also have a column for the date of the commendation. If a manager can only commend an employee once at a given branch, then the three foreign keys would comprise the primary key. If a manager can commend an employee more than once at a branch, the Date_of_ Commendation would have to be included as part of the key. If such a commendation could take place more than once on a given day, then an extra column (commendation number?) would have to be inserted.

This step changes if cardinalities of one exist in the relationship. In Figure 2.9, we have a ternary relationship EMPLOYS between BANK, EMP and MANAGER. In this relationship, only one manager and one bank may participate in each instance of this relationship. We thus have a 1–1 relationship between BANK and MANAGER. In this case, we should apply the rule of step 4 and enter a foreign key into one of these relations. For both entities, the participation is total, meaning that we can enter either the EmpNo of a bank's manager into the BANK relation or the BranchName of the bank managed by

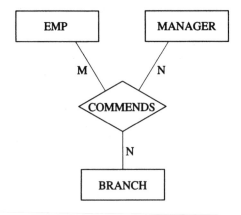

Figure 4.1 An M–N ternary relationship.

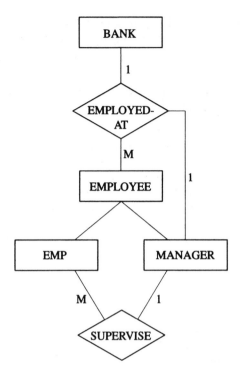

Figure 2.9 Further subtyping with a ternary relationship.

a manager into the MANAGER relation. In either case, the ternary relationship is completed by entering a foreign key column into the EMP relation that references the relevant relation. For example, if we put BranchName as a foreign key into MANAGER to represent this relationship, then we must put the EMPNO of the manager of the branch at which an employee is employed into the EMP relation as a foreign key.

The foregoing discussion assumes that a separate relation has been created for the entity MANAGER which is a subtype of EMP. Whether or not we do this is determined by the next step.

Step 8

Where a subtyping is 'attribute defined', create separate relations for each subtype consisting of those attributes which are peculiar to the given subtype.

In Figure 2.9, we had a subtyping of EMPLOYEE into MANAGER and EMP. If the only difference between the two subtypes was that managers were, for instance, all on a particular grade (a 'condition-defined' subtyping) then it is most sensible to create a single base relation for all employees and then define a view 'Manager' consisting of all employees on the managerial grade and a view 'EMP' consisting of all employees on the non-managerial grade. However, suppose we had the following attributes for the employee entity and its subtypes:

EMPLOYEE: EMPNO, EMPNAME, OFFICE, GRADE
EMP: EMPNO, FUNCTION
MANAGER: EMPNO, PARKING_LOT

It would now be sensible to create a relation EMPLOYEE consisting of those attributes that are common to all employees and then separate relations for EMP and MANAGER consisting of those attributes that are peculiar to their subtypes along with the primary key EMPNO which also acts as a foreign key to the supertype relation. We could implement this as a single relation, but this would result in attributes with a large number of null values (EMP-type tuples with no PARKING_LOT value, MANAGER-type tuples with no FUNCTION value). This would contravene one of the rules of database efficiency as described in the next section.

4.2 Normalization

4.2.1 Database efficiency

Normalization is a process by which we can ensure that the data structures in a relational database are 'efficient'.

A relational database can be described as efficient when it has the following characteristics:

1. Absence of redundancy. A system with redundancy is one where the same data can appear in more than one place. As well as wasting storage space, this gives potential for the data to be inconsistent and ambiguous.

    In Table 4.3 we have a relation that records the presence of students on various courses. There is a lot of redundancy in this relation in that the course data is replicated for every student on a given course. This can give rise to certain anomalies:

    (a) Update anomalies. If we decided to change the name of one of the courses, we would have to propagate that name change to all tuples for students on that course, otherwise our database is inconsistent.

    (b) Insert anomalies. When we enter a student into a database, we must ensure that the course details entered are the same as those for all other students on that course. The current representation provides the opportunity for two students with the same COURSENO to be on different courses with different tutors.

Table 4.3 An inefficient relational database

STUDENTS

SNO	SNAME	COURSENO	COURSENAME	TUTOR
1	J Smith	1264	French Pt 1	J LeClerc
4	S Abdul	1564	Spanish Pt 3	F Rodriguez
7	K Chan	1264	French Pt 1	J LeClerc
11	J Jones	1265	French Pt 2	
13	M Jones	1265	French Pt 2	
16	K Saunders	1264	French Pt 1	J Le Clerc
18	J Ngugih	1265	French Pt 2	

2. Minimal use of null values. It is possible to have a number of valid representations of a database, some of which may result in an extensive number of tuples taking null values. In Table 4.3 we have three tuples with a null value for TUTOR. This is because one of the courses (French Pt 2) has no tutor assigned. Apart from the redundancy aspect, null values are a problem in relational databases because we cannot determine their precise meaning. Does this mean that there is no tutor for this course, that there is a tutor but his or her name has not been entered, or that this course is a self-study course that requires no tutor, and this attribute therefore does not apply to these tuples? These difficulties of interpretation make it desirable that the use of null values is minimized.

3. Prevention of loss of information. One of the major problems with the representation in Table 4.3 is that it contains no information for courses which have no students. Moreover, if the second student in the relation (S Abdul) were to leave, that would result in the loss of all information about the course Spanish Pt 3. This is another form of anomaly known as a 'deletion anomaly'.

A better representation of this database is given in Table 4.4.

The potential for redundancy and anomalies in Table 4.3 have been removed. The original relation has been decomposed into two relations with a foreign key COURSENO referencing each a student to a set of course details. Thus all students with the same course number are automatically associated with the same set of course details. If we wish to change the details for a course, then all we need to change is the one tuple in the course relation that describes that course. If a student changes course, all we need to change is the course number; we no longer need to change the course details as well. When inserting a student, we no longer need to insert the course details, just the course number. If we remove all students on a given course, the details for that course still remain in the database in the course relation. Note that

Table 4.4 A 'Better' representation of a relational database

STUDENTS

SNO	SNAME	COURSENO
1	J Smith	1264
4	S Abdul	1564
7	K Chan	1264
11	J Jones	1265
13	M Jones	1265
16	K Sanders	1264
18	J Ngugih	1265

COURSE

COURSENO	COURSENAME	TUTOR
1264	French Pt 1	J LeClerc
1265	French Pt 2	
1266	French Pt 3	P Simpson
1562	Spanish Pt 1	K Lopez
1563	Spanish Pt 2	K Lopez
1564	Spanish Pt 3	K Rodriguez

we are now able conveniently to store information about courses that currently have no students. The use of null values has also been reduced.

Normalization techniques would guide us to the implementation shown in Table 4.4.

4.2.2 A worked example of normalization

We shall now examine the techniques of normalization by applying them to the example database given in Chapter 2. As stated above, normalization tends to be used as a means of refining a database that has already been derived using a semantic modelling methodology such as E/R modelling. However, in order to demonstrate fully its various stages we shall ignore the E/R model and start with the descriptive scenario.

Here is a restatement of the original database description:

The Rock Solid Banking Corporation stores details of its accounts with the following information for each account: Customer details (Reference_ Number, Name, Address, Status), Account_Number, Balance. Accounts may be of two types: deposit and current. Customers may have any number of accounts. Accounts may be shared by a number of customers. Account numbers uniquely identify an account. Each customer has a unique reference

number. Each account is handled at a distinct branch of the bank. Branch
details include Branch Name, Address and Manager. No two branches have
the same name.

First normal form

A relational database designer might intuitively decide to implement this as two
relations: one for BANK containing details of all accounts held at each branch
of the bank and one for CUSTOMER with a foreign key (AccNo) linking a
customer to his or her account details. This would result in the representation
with some sample data as shown in Table 4.5.

We have a problem straightaway with this representation in that it
contradicts one of the basic tenets of a relational database by using multi-
valued attributes (ACCNO in CUSTOMER, ACCNO, BALANCE and TYPE in BANK).
We say that this is a completely unnormalized database. Normalization theory
consists of a number of definitions of what are termed 'normal forms'. The
most basic normal form is first normal form (1NF).

First normal form requires that all attribute domains in a relational database
must include only simple, non-dividable values and that every attribute value in
every tuple must be a single value from its domain. A 1NF representation of
Table 4.5 is given in Table 4.6.

The representation is now valid in terms of basic relational theory, but is a
poor representation with a lot of redundancy and the potential for anomalies as
described in the previous section. A better ('higher') normal form is
required.

Table 4.5 An unnormalized database

BANK

BRANCHNAME	ADDRESS	MANAGER_NO	ACCNO	BALANCE	TYPE
Crawley	1, High Street	1768	{120768, 678453 348973}	(234.56, -456.78, 12567.56)	{'D' 'C' 'C'}
Bugstone	12, Low Street	9823	{987654, 745363}	{789.65, -23.67}	{'C', 'D'}

CUSTOMER

REFNO	NAME	ADDRESS	STATUS	ACCNO
2345	P Abdul	23, High Street	Business	{120768, 348973}
7654	K Peters	45, The Ash	Domestic	{987654}
8764	P Jones	17, Low Street	Business	{745363, 678453, 348973}

Table 4.6 A normalized database in 1NF

BANK

BRANCHNAME	ADDRESS	MANAGER_NO	ACCNO	BALANCE	TYPE
Crawley	1, High Street	1768	120768	234.56	'D'
Crawley	1, High Street	1768	678453	-456.78	'C'
Crawley	1, High Street	1768	348973	12567.56	'C'
Bugstone	12, Low Street	9823	987654	789.65	'C'
Bugstone	12, Low Street	9823	745363	-23.67	'D'

CUSTOMER

REFNO	NAME	ADDRESS	STATUS	ACCNO
2345	P Abdul	23, High Street	Business	120768
2345	P Abdul	23, High Street	Business	348973
7654	K Peters	45, The Ash	Domestic	987654
8764	P Jones	17, Low Street	Business	745363
8764	P Jones	17, Low Street	Business	678453
8764	P Jones	17, Low Street	Business	348973

Functional dependency and second normal form

The concept of functional dependency is central to normalization theory.

Functional dependency is a semantic concept. It is concerned with a particular semantic relationship between the attributes of a relation. If we take a set of attributes ('X') within a relation, we say that an attribute, or set of attributes ('A'), is functionally dependent on X if, and only if, for every combination of values in X, there is one, and only one, corresponding value in A. We denote this in the form:

X ---> A

For example, take the attribute BRANCHNAME in the relation BANK. A bank branch only has one address. Thus each BRANCHNAME value has associated with it one, and only one, ADDRESS. Each branch also has exactly one manager. Thus we can say:

    BRANCHNAME ---> ADDRESS
    BRANCHNAME ---> MANAGER_NO

A more abbreviated form of this is to say:

    BRANCHNAME ---> ADDRESS, MANAGER_NO

A BRANCHNAME value may be associated with any number of ACCNO values, any number of BALANCE values and up to two TYPEs of deposit. These attributes are not therefore functionally dependent (FD) on BRANCHNAME. However, given a particular ACCNO, there will be one BALANCE and one TYPE value. Therefore, we can say:

ACCNO - - - > BALANCE, TYPE

Moreover, because accounts can only be kept at one branch, the following FDs also hold:

ACCNO - - - > BRANCHNAME, ADDRESS, MANAGER_NO

In the CUSTOMER relation, we can readily deduce the following FDs:

REFNO - - - > NAME, ADDRESS, STATUS

If an account can only be owned by one customer, then we might want to establish FDs on ACCNO. However, there is an instance of an account (348973) being owned by two different customers. If this is valid, (i.e. an M–N relationship exists between CUSTOMER and ACCOUNT) then there is nothing in this relation that is functionally dependent upon ACCNO.

An FD may be established on any set of attributes. All of the above examples are on single attribute sets. The following FDs are also valid in the BRANCH relation:

BRANCHNAME, ACCNO - - - > BALANCE, TYPE, ADDRESS, MANAGER_NO

Likewise, in the CUSTOMER relation, we can say:

REFNO, ACCNO - - - > NAME, ADDRESS, STATUS

Even though accounts may be owned by more than one customer, the above FDs hold, because for every combination of REFNO and ACCNO there is one, and only one, NAME, ADDRESS and STATUS value respectively.

FDs are a useful means of identifying candidate keys. To recap, a candidate key is an attribute, or set of attributes, that gives a unique identity to each tuple in a relation. Suppose that we have an FD in the form $X - - - > A$ where the union of X and A comprises the complete set of attributes in a relation. If each tuple is to be unique, each combination of values in X can only occur once as it is tied to exactly one set of values in A which comprises the rest of the tuple. This does not mean that X is necessarily a candidate key. It is what is known as a superkey.

A superkey exists when each combination of values for a particular set of attributes can only occur once. A superkey for any relation is the set of all of its attributes. However, this is not much use as an identifier. We need to extend our definition of candidate key from that already given. A candidate key is a superkey that has no redundancy. By redundancy, we mean a superkey with attributes within it that could be removed but it would still be able to give a unique identity to each tuple. A candidate key is a non-reducible (i.e. minimal) set of attributes that gives a unique identity to a tuple. In order to deduce candidate keys, we need to reduce all superkeys to the minimal sets of attributes required to provide unique tuple identity.

For instance, in the BANK relation, we have a superkey of the form:

```
BRANCHNAME, ADDRESS, ACCNO, BALANCE, TYPE
```

indicating that each row is unique. As stated above, this is not a meaningful key. We can reduce this to:

```
BRANCHNAME, ADDRESS, ACCNO, BALANCE ---> TYPE
```

because each concatenation of the attributes on the left will give one, and only one, TYPE value.

We can further reduce this to:

```
BRANCHNAME, ADDRESS, ACCNO ---> BALANCE, TYPE
```

A given BRANCHNAME, ADDRESS combination can yield many ACCNO, BALANCE, TYPE combinations. Therefore, it cannot be reduced to:

```
BRANCHNAME, ADDRESS ---> ACCNO, BALANCE, TYPE
```

meaning that BRANCHNAME, ADDRESS cannot be a superkey for this relation. All candidate keys are subsets of a superkey. Thus, neither BRANCHNAME nor ADDRESS can be candidate keys. We can reduce BRANCHNAME, ADDRESS, ACCNO to:

```
BRANCHNAME, ACCNO ---> ADDRESS, BALANCE, TYPE
```

and further to:

```
ACCNO ---> BRANCHNAME, ADDRESS, BALANCE, TYPE
```

As we cannot reduce this any further, this indicates that ACCNO is indeed a candidate key for BANK.

With the CUSTOMER relation, we can start with the superkey:

```
REFNO, NAME, ADDRESS, STATUS, ACCNO
```

We cannot reduce this to:

```
REFNO, NAME, ADDRESS, STATUS ---> ACCNO
```

owing to the fact that one customer may hold many accounts at the same branch. In fact, we cannot do any reduction which has ACCNO on one side and

REFNO on the other owing to the M–N relationship between these attributes. We can say:

```
REFNO, STATUS, ACCNO ---> NAME, ADDRESS
```

and further reduce this to:

```
REFNO, ACCNO ---> STATUS, NAME, ADDRESS
```

We cannot reduce this any further as there are attributes which have no FD upon either REFNO or ACCNO. Therefore, neither of these alone can be candidate keys for the relation. This leaves REFNO, ACCNO as the sole candidate key for the relation.

A candidate key is therefore a superkey that cannot be reduced. All attributes that are part of a candidate key are termed 'key' attributes. Attributes that do not form any part of a candidate key are 'nonkey' attributes. In those relations with more than one candidate key, we must designate one of these to be the primary key.

Having identified the primary key for each relation, we can improve our database design by the application of the second normal form (2NF). To be in 2NF, a relation must be: (i) in 1NF; (ii) have no nonkey attributes that are not fully functionally dependent upon the primary key.

A nonkey attribute is an attribute that is not part of a candidate key. Thus in BRANCH, the attributes BRANCHNAME, ADDRESS, MANAGER_NO, BALANCE and TYPE are nonkey attributes. In CUSTOMER, the attributes NAME, ADDRESS and STATUS are nonkey attributes.

Full functional dependence means that when an attribute ('A') is dependent upon a set of attributes ('{X,Y}') thus:

$$\{X,Y\} ---> A$$

there is no dependence of A upon any subset of {X,Y}. Thus, if the following dependence also exists:

$$X ---> A$$

then A is not fully functionally dependant upon {X,Y}.

When a primary key consists of only one attribute, then all other attributes must be fully functionally dependent on it as it cannot be subdivided in any way. However, in the case of a composite key, full functional dependence may be compromised. In the CUSTOMER relation, we have established that REFNO, ACCNO is a candidate key, and NAME, ADDRESS and STATUS are nonkey attributes. We have within this relation the following FDs:

```
REFNO, ACCNO ---> NAME, ADDRESS, STATUS
REFNO ---> NAME, ADDRESS, STATUS
```

REFNO is a subset of the primary key REFNO, ACCNO. This relation is therefore not in 2NF. To reduce a relation to 2NF, we must remove those attributes that are only partially dependent on the primary key and create a new relation consisting of these attributes along with the attribute set on which they are dependent as the primary key. This attribute must also remain in the original relation as part of the original composite key. Thus, we need to decompose CUSTOMER into:

CUSTOMER

REFNO	NAME	ADDRESS	STATUS
2345	P Abdul	23, High Street	Business
7654	K Peters	45, The Ash	Domestic
8764	P Jones	17, Low Street	Business

CUSTOMER_ACCOUNT

REFNO	ACCNO
2345	120768
2345	348973
7654	987654
8764	745363
8764	678453
8764	348973

In the above relations, we have decomposed CUSTOMER into two relations: CUSTOMER and CUSTOMER_ACCOUNT. The CUSTOMER relation now has REFNO as the primary key. As REFNO is a single-attribute key, all nonkey attributes are fully functionally dependent upon it. The new relation CUSTOMER_ACCOUNT has the previous primary key for CUSTOMER (REFNO, ACCNO). All nonkey attributes have been removed from this relation as none of them were found to be fully functionally dependent upon the primary key.

These two relations are now clearly free of redundancy. There is only one tuple in the CUSTOMER relation for each customer and one tuple in the CUSTOMER_ACCOUNT relation for each account/customer relationship. Moreover, if a customer has no accounts, we do not need to lose information on that customer. However, there is still clearly some redundancy in the BRANCH relation. A higher normal form is required to remove this.

Third normal form

The BRANCH relation has a single-attribute primary key (ACCNO). It follows therefore that all non-key attributes must be fully functionally dependent upon it. However, we have a problem with this relation in that BRANCH information is replicated for all accounts at a particular branch. This is due to the FDs upon BRANCHNAME:

BRANCHNAME - - - > ADDRESS, MANAGER_NO

This is an FD between a nonkey attribute and another nonkey attribute. We call this a 'transitive dependency'. A relation in third normal form (3NF) is one with no transitive dependencies. To be in 3NF, a relation: (i) must be in 2NF; (ii) contain no transitive dependencies.

When we find a transitive dependency, we must remove those attributes that have a transitive dependency. We must then create a new relation consisting of these removed attributes along with the attribute upon which they are dependent. The attribute on which the dependence exists becomes the primary key for the new relation and remains as a foreign key in the original relation, allowing the tuples to be reconstituted as before using a natural join. Thus, the BRANCH relation decomposes into:

BRANCH

BRANCHNAME	ADDRESS	MANAGER_NO
Crawley	1, High Street	1768
Bugstone	12, Low Street	9823

ACCOUNT

ACCNO	BALANCE	TYPE	BRANCHNAME
120768	234.56	'D'	Crawley
678453	-456.78	'C'	Crawley
348973	12567.56	'C'	Crawley
987654	789.65	'C'	Bugstone
745363	-23.67	'D'	Bugstone

We now have a database in 3NF where each tuple represents a single, discrete, assertion. The only attributes that are replicated are the foreign keys that enable relationships to be established between the relations. There is inevitable replication of data under foreign key attributes, representing data-defined groupings of tuples, for example all accounts belonging to Crawley will have the foreign key value of Crawley in their tuple.

Boyce–Codd normal form

3NF is concerned with FDs between the primary key and the nonkey attributes and with transitive dependencies. A relation may still have redundancy problems in 3NF as it ignores relationships between or within candidate keys.

In the BRANCH relation, if managers can only manage one branch and no two branches can share the same address, we actually have three candidate keys (BRANCHNAME, ADDRESS, MANAGER_NO) as these must all be unique to each tuple. The following FDs therefore exist:

```
BRANCHNAME - - - > ADDRESS, MANAGER_NO
ADDRESS - - - > BRANCHNAME, MANAGER_NO
MANAGER_NO - - - > BRANCHNAME, ADDRESS
```

As 3NF is only defined in terms of FDs between the primary key and nonkey attributes and transitive dependencies, the above dependencies are of no interest to the database designer aiming for 3NF. In fact, because each of these attributes has to be unique to each tuple, once we have created a tuple with a particular set of attribute values, it is not then possible to associate these values with any other. Unnecessary replication of data will simply not occur. However, a problem can arise when a relation has more than one candidate key and some of these keys are composite.

Let us refer to the courses/tutors database. In Table 4.4, we had a relation COURSE with the FDs:

```
COURSENO - - - > COURSENAME, TUTOR
```

Suppose we wanted to have a scheme whereby the same course can be delivered at different times by different tutors. This could give us the following relation:

```
COURSE
| ----------------------------------------------------------- |
| COURSENO | COURSENAME    | TUTOR       | TIME    |
| ---------------------------------------------------------- |
| 1264     | French Pt 1   | J LeClerc   | 19.00   |
| 1265     | French Pt 2   |             | 18.00   |
| 1266     | French Pt 3   | P Simpson   | 19.00   |
| 1562     | Spanish Pt 1  | K Lopez     | 17.00   |
| 1563     | Spanish Pt 2  | K Lopez     | 18.00   |
| 1564     | Spanish Pt 3  | K Rodriguez | 17.00   |
| 1264     | French Pt 1   | P Simpson   | 18.00   |
| 1264     | French Pt 1   | J LeClerc   | 17.00   |
| ----------------------------------------------------------- |
```

COURSENO would no longer be the primary key for this table. Instead, because a tutor cannot be expected to teach two different courses at the same time, we would have a candidate key of TUTOR, TIME, giving the following FDs:

```
TUTOR, TIME - - - > COURSENO, COURSENAME
```

COURSENO - - - > COURSENAME

The FD of COURSENAME on COURSENO is now transitive, meaning that we need to divide our relation into two thus:

COURSE

COURSENO	COURSENAME
1264	French Pt 1
1265	French Pt 2
1266	French Pt 3
1562	Spanish Pt 1
1563	Spanish Pt 2
1564	Spanish Pt 3

OFFERING

COURSENO	TUTOR	TIME
1264	J LeClerc	19.00
1266	P Simpson	19.00
1562	K Lopez	17.00
1563	K Lopez	18.00
1564	K Rodriguez	17.00
1264	P Simpson	18.00
1264	J LeClerc	17.00

We might now decide to include information regarding the room that a course was delivered in. If every tutor had their own room where they did all of their teaching, we could have the following dataset:

OFFERING

COURSENO	TUTOR	TIME	ROOM
1264	J LeClerc	19.00	E12
1266	P Simpson	19.00	138
1562	K Lopez	17.00	139
1563	K Lopez	18.00	139
1564	K Rodriguez	17.00	E14
1264	P Simpson	18.00	138
1264	J LeClerc	17.00	E12

We now have a problem because rooming information is now replicated. This is because we have an FD of ROOM on TUTOR thus:

TUTOR - - - > ROOM

However, the relation is in 3NF. The combination ROOM, TIME is unique to each tuple, no room being used twice at the same time. Thus the above FD does not contravene 3NF as it does not involve any nonkey attributes.

Boyce–Codd normal form (BCNF) was devised in order to address this sort of problem. In BCNF, we have the concept of a 'determinant'. This is very similar to functional dependency. When we have an FD in the form A - - - > B, we say that A is a determinant.

BCNF is achieved when all determinants in a relation are candidate keys. The above relation contradicts BCNF as it has a determinant TUTOR that is not a candidate key.

When we have a determinant with non-unique values, we must decompose the relation by separating out the non-unique determinant along with those attributes which have an FD upon it, leaving this determinant as a foreign key in the original relation. Thus, we decompose the OFFERING relation into:

OFFERING

COURSENO	TUTOR	TIME
1264	J LeClerc	19.00
1266	P Simpson	19.00
1562	K Lopez	17.00
1563	K Lopez	18.00
1564	K Rodriguez	17.00
1264	P Simpson	18.00
1264	J LeClerc	17.00

TUTOR_ROOM

TUTOR	ROOM
J LeClerc	E12
P Simpson	138
K Lopez	139
K Rodriguez	E14

BCNF subsumes 3NF. The fundamental difference between the two forms is that 3NF allows for an FD of A - - - > B when A is not in itself a superkey and

B is part of a candidate key. In BCNF, A must be a superkey. Thus, BCNF is a stronger form of 3NF.

Most relations that are in 3NF are also in BCNF. The only time that a relation might be in 3NF but not BCNF is when there is more than one candidate key for a relation and at least one of these candidate keys is composite.

4.3 An overview of the relational database design process

Normalization was originally proposed as the defining methodology for designing relational databases. It is severely limited in its semantics. It only really has one semantic concept, that of functional dependency. Moreover, it is not very easy to represent functional dependencies in a diagrammatically convenient form. E/R models on the other hand have a very simple and intuitive form of diagrammatic modelling and are more semantically powerful than normalization models. E/R modelling and relational databases do have common concepts. Indeed, in the very first published paper on relational databases (Codd 1969) states:

> The set of entities of a given entity type can be viewed as a relation . . .
> The remaining relations . . . are between entity types and are . . . called inter-entity relations.

Clearly, the terms 'entity' and 'relation' have a close intuitive linking and it is therefore unsurprising that the process of transforming an entity/relationship diagram into a relational database is relatively straightforward. A properly analyzed and transformed E/R model should result in a relational database that is at least in 3NF. We cannot absolutely guarantee this. Therefore, the most widespread and convenient form of designing a relational database is to use a form of E/R modelling for the original design, transform the E/R model to derive a set of relations and then analyze these to ensure that they minimally meet 3NF, and preferably BCNF.

There do exist higher normal forms which are more difficult to detect and which in practice are seldom checked for. Indeed, occasionally relations are deliberately kept in 2NF. Take a relation that kept addresses for customers with the primary key REFNO and addresses consisting of the attributes STREET, STATE, ZIPCODE. We would have a transitive FD of:

ZIPCODE - - - > STATE

meaning that the relation would not be in 3NF. Strictly speaking, we should separate this out into a separate relation. This would mean that we would have to perform a JOIN of two relations every time we wished to display the full address of a customer. Most designers would not choose to do this and instead run the risk of inconsistent ZIPCODE, STATE combinations for the sake of improved performance. Thus, ironically, there are times when a database is deliberately 'denormalized'.

Summary

- An entity/relationship model of a database can be transformed into a relational database using, at most, eight steps.
- Functional dependencies in a relation must be identified in order that its normal form can be deduced.
- A relational database can be regarded as efficient when all of its relations are minimally in 3NF, and preferably in BCNF.
- Relations that are not in 3NF should be decomposed into this state unless there exists a very good reason not to.

Exercises

1   Here is a restatement of the EverCare County General Hospital Scenario:

At the EverCare County General Hospital, patients are admitted and given a unique Patient Id. We record their name, home address and date of admission. They are assigned to a ward and to a consultant. They may then be diagnosed a set of conditions. Whilst in our care, they will receive a set of treatments. Each treatment will have a date and details of the nurse administering the treatment, the drug being administered and the dosage. Drugs have a unique Drug Id, a name and a recommended dosage (which may not be the same as the dosage given in individual treatments). Nurses have a Nurse Id and a name and are assigned to a ward. Each ward has a Sister (who is a nurse). Consultants have a Doctor Id and a name.

(a)   Identify the functional dependencies in the above dataset.
(b)   Using the functional dependencies that you have identified, produce a set of tables in third normal form to represent this dataset as a relational database.
(c)   Use the E/R diagram that you drew as your answer to Exercise 1(a) in Chapter 2 to derive a set of tables for this dataset in third normal form, using the transformation rules at the start of this chapter. (You should arrive at the same answer as (b)!)

(d) Demonstrate that your answer to (b) and (c) is also in Boyce–Codd normal form.

(e) What difference would it make to your relational database design if:

(i) drugs could be known by more than one name;

(ii) patients could be assigned to more than one consultant?

(f) The hospital wishes to introduce an operations schedule, whereby each operation is performed by one consultant on one patient at a given timeslot for one condition. (Note: A consultant cannot perform more than one operation in a given timeslot and a patient cannot be operated on more than once in a given timeslot!) Extend your database to show this, ensuring that it remains in Boyce–Codd normal form.

Further reading

Date (1995) Chapters 9, 10, 11 and 12
Elmasri and Navathe (1994) Chapter 6
Gardarin and Valduriez (1989) Chapter 5
Hawryszkiewycz (1991) Chapters 3 and 4
Korth and Silberschatz (1991) Chapters 4 and 5
Kroenke (1995) Chapter 6
Ozkarahan (1990) Chapter 6

Reference

Codd, E.F. (1969) 'Derivability, Redundancy and Consistency of Relations stored in Large Data Banks', IBM Research Report RJ599, August

Relational databases 3 – SQL

This chapter introduces the structured query language (SQL). SQL was originally devised in the 1970s as a language for relational databases and has since become the *de facto* industry standard language for relational systems. With SQL, a database user can create and delete data held in relations, enforce the relational integrity rules as described in Chapter 3 and perform the full range of operations required by the relational algebra. It is a relationally complete language, but it is not yet a computationally complete language. It exists purely as an interface to data held in relations. Only some very basic data processing functions are provided. Complete applications usually require SQL calls to be embedded within a computationally complete language such as C, FORTRAN, COBOL, Pascal or Ada.

SQL has undergone a series of standardizations, the most recent at the time of writing being in 1992. Not all relational products that support SQL necessarily support all of the most recent standard. As it is not yet computationally complete most vendors of relational systems tend to provide features that enhance SQL in some way. Such enhancements are ignored in this text which will instead concentrate purely on the major aspects of the most recent standard.

By the end of this chapter, the reader should know how to:

1. Create a simple relational database using SQL.
2. Use SQL to perform the full range of relational operations.
3. Perform some simple data processing tasks with SQL.

5.1 SQL basics

In Chapter 3, we described the use of the relational algebra for retrieving data from a relational database. SQL provides a higher level of interface to a relational system. It is a declarative rather than a procedural language. With the relational algebra, we specify a sequence of operations (i.e. a procedure) for retrieving a given set of data. With a declarative language such as SQL, we provide a description of the data to be retrieved by means of a command. This command is then translated by the underlying system into a series of algebraic operations. As the reader shall see later in the text, certain types of algebraic operation can be invoked directly from an SQL command.

SQL is not just a language for retrieving data from a relational database. It is a complete database language, with provisions for database creation and database security. There are three basic types of SQL command:

1. Data definition commands. These are commands that define the contents of a relational database in terms of tables and views. A table is the equivalent of a base relation. These commands include column definition expressions that define the attributes of a table. A view is defined by using a data manipulation command to specify its data contents.
2. Data manipulation commands. These commands are used to insert, retrieve, update and delete data held in tables and views. They include simple facilities for processing the data held in tables and views.
3. Data control commands. These are used for controlling access to tables and views.

We shall present the normalized database given in the previous chapter (Table 5.1) and give examples of the data manipulation commands before examining how this database can be defined using the data definition commands.

5.2 SQL data retrieval

The SQL data manipulation language has four commands:

```
SELECT: for retrieving data
INSERT: for creating data
UPDATE: for altering data
DELETE: for removing data
```

This section is devoted to the SELECT command.

5.2.1 Simple data retrieval operations

The SELECT command provides the full functionality of the relational algebra. A SELECT command takes a set of relations (tables and/or views) and describes the constraints that must be placed on them to return a given set of rows. SELECT can be thought of as a command that builds a table from the tables or views that exist in a database.

A very informal, and incomplete, syntax of SELECT is as follows:

```
SELECT columns (or '*')
FROM relation(s)
[WHERE constraint(s)] ;
```

Table 5.1 An example database

CUSTOMER

REFNO	NAME	ADDRESS	STATUS
2345	P Abdul	23, High Street	Business
7654	K Peters	45, The Ash	Domestic
8764	P Jones	17, Low Street	Business

CUSTOMER_ACCOUNT

REFNO	ACCNO
2345	120768
2345	348973
7654	987654
8764	745363
8764	678453
8764	348973

BRANCH

BRANCHNAME	ADDRESS	MANAGER_NO
Crawley	1, High Street	1768
Bugstone	12, Low Street	9823

ACCOUNT

ACCNO	BALANCE	TYPE	BRANCHNAME
120768	234.56	'D'	Crawley
678453	-456.78	'C'	Crawley
348973	12567.56	'C'	Crawley
987654	789.65	'C'	Bugstone
745363	-23.67	'D'	Bugstone

'*' is the equivalent of saying 'all the columns in' the given relations. Columns can be defined in a number of ways, examples of which will follow. The top line thus describes the heading of the table that the query is attempting to build. The FROM line lists the set of relations that contain the data necessary for servicing the query. The WHERE constraint part of the SELECT command is optional. Without this, all of the rows in the given relations will be returned.

If we wished to display all of the tuples of a given relation, we would say:

```
SELECT *
FROM CUSTOMER;
```

This would display the entire contents of the CUSTOMER relation. We can constrain this. For instance, to build a table consisting only of those customers with the name P Abdul, we would say:

```
SELECT *
FROM CUSTOMER
WHERE NAME = 'P Abdul';
```

We have now put a constraint on our result. Here we have specified that all rows returned must have the value P Abdul under the column NAME. If we gave the command:

```
SELECT *
FROM CUSTOMER
WHERE NAME = 'J Jones';
```

The result would be an empty table. Note how we have put quotation marks (' ') around the value that we are searching on. This is because this particular column has the data type of a string of characters. If we were searching on numeric columns, we would say, for instance:

```
SELECT *
FROM CUSTOMER
WHERE REFNO = 2345;
```

Constraints may use the full range of comparative ($<, >, !=, >=, <=$) and logical operators (AND, OR, NOT). Thus, we would achieve the same result saying:

```
SELECT *
FROM CUSTOMER
WHERE REFNO = 2345 AND NAME = 'P Abdul';
```

If we said:

```
SELECT *
FROM CUSTOMER
WHERE REFNO = 8764 AND NAME = 'P Abdul';
```

we would get an empty table as there are no tuples that satisfy both of these constraints. However, if we were to say:

```
SELECT *
FROM CUSTOMER
WHERE REFNO = 8764 OR NAME = 'P Abdul';
```

we would get a table with two rows as there are two tuples that satisfy one or the other of these constraints.

The command:

```
SELECT *
FROM CUSTOMER
WHERE REFNO > 1000 OR NAME = 'P Abdul';
```

would return the whole relation as every single tuple satisfies at least the first constraint.

When SELECT * is used with a single relation, it can be regarded as the equivalent of the relational RESTRICT operation.

Attribute values may be retrieved through the specification of columns. The command:

```
SELECT NAME
FROM CUSTOMER;
```

will give:

```
| ----------|
| NAME      |
| ----------|
| P Abdul   |
| K Peters  |
| P Jones   |
| ----------|
```

A set of columns may be specified, for example:

```
SELECT BRANCHNAME, ADDRESS
FROM BRANCH;
```

giving:

```
| ---------------------------------|
| BRANCHNAME  | ADDRESS            |
| ---------------------------------|
| Crawley     | 1, High Street     |
| Bugstone    | 12, Low Street     |
| ---------------------------------|
```

The use of column references provides the functionality of the relational PROJECT operator. Strictly speaking, a PROJECT operation should return a set of tuples with no duplicates. We can achieve this in SQL by use of the DISTINCT constraint on a column:

```
SELECT DISTINCT REFNO
FROM CUSTOMER_ACCOUNT;
```

giving:

```
| --------- |
| REFNO     |
| --------- |
| 2345      |
| 7654      |
| 8764      |
| --------- |
```

Without the DISTINCT constraint, this query would have yielded the following:

```
| --------- |
| REFNO     |
| --------- |
| 2345      |
| 2345      |
| 7654      |
| 8764      |
| 8764      |
| 8764      |
| --------- |
```

We can combine row and column constraints quite easily, for example:

```
SELECT ACCNO, BALANCE
FROM ACCOUNT
WHERE BALANCE > 100.00;
```

giving

```
| ----------------------- |
| ACCNO    | BALANCE      |
| ----------------------- |
| 120768   |   234.56     |
| 348973   | 12567.56     |
| 987654   |   789.65     |
| ----------------------- |
```

In this example, we are constraining the output in two ways: only those columns ACCNO and BALANCE from the ACCOUNT table and only those rows with BALANCE > 100.00.

We can also define constraints using values for columns that do not appear in the result. This is because the WHERE constraint is on the relation referenced in the FROM clause, not on the result. For instance, the following command is perfectly valid:

```
SELECT ACCNO, TYPE
FROM ACCOUNT
WHERE BALANCE > 100.00;
```

giving:

```
| ----------------- |
| ACCNO    | TYPE  |
| ----------------- |
| 120768   | 'D'   |
| 348973   | 'C'   |
| 987654   | 'C'   |
| ----------------- |
```

Note how we have a replicated value in this output ('C' under TYPE). Use of the DISTINCT constraint would not remove this replication. This is because DISTINCT works at the row level, not the column level. It constrains each row in the output to be different, which is the case in this example.

The relational JOIN operation builds a relation from two relations over a compatible attribute from each relation. We implement this in SQL by declaring more than one relation on the FROM line and then placing a constraint in the WHERE clause that compares column values from the different relations. If we wished to JOIN the CUSTOMER relation with the CUSTOMER_ACCOUNT relation, we would say:

```
SELECT *
FROM CUSTOMER, CUSTOMER_ACCOUNT
WHERE CUSTOMER.REFNO = CUSTOMER_ACCOUNT.REFNO;
```

giving:

REFNO	NAME	ADDRESS	STATUS	REFNO	ACCNO
2345	P Abdul	23, High Street	Business	2345	120768
2345	P Abdul	23, High Street	Business	2345	348973
7654	K Peters	45, The Ash	Domestic	7654	987654
8764	P Jones	17, Low Street	Business	8764	745363
8764	P Jones	17, Low Street	Business	8764	678453
8764	P Jones	17, Low Street	Business	8764	348973

In this command, we have the constraint CUSTOMER.REFNO = CUSTOMER_ACCCOUNT.REFNO. This means that we only retrieve rows from these two tables where the REFNO attributes have the same value. Note how we have used column references with qualifiers (CUSTOMER.REFNO, CUSTOMER_ACCOUNT.REFNO). The command would be ambiguous without these.

We can constrain the columns appearing in the result quite easily. For instance, we might only wish to display the NAME, STATUS, ACCNO columns thus:

```
SELECT NAME, STATUS, ACCNO
FROM CUSTOMER, CUSTOMER_ACCOUNT
WHERE CUSTOMER.REFNO = CUSTOMER_ACCOUNT.REFNO;
```

In the output above, the REFNO column appears twice, reflecting the fact that a column by that name exists in both tables. If we wished to display this column just once, we need to qualify the column specification with a table reference thus:

```
SELECT NAME, STATUS, CUSTOMER.REFNO, ACCNO
FROM CUSTOMER, CUSTOMER_ACCOUNT
WHERE CUSTOMER.REFNO = CUSTOMER_ACCOUNT.REFNO;
```

We need to do this whenever column names appear in more than one table. Without the table reference, the column reference becomes ambiguous.

When writing queries using multiple tables, it is convenient to use relation 'aliases' to abbreviate the table references. The above command can be rewritten thus:

```
SELECT NAME, STATUS, C.REFNO, ACCNO
FROM CUSTOMER C, CUSTOMER_ACCOUNT CA
WHERE C.REFNO = CA.REFNO;
```

In this example, we have entered the relation aliases 'C' for the CUSTOMER table 'CA' for the CUSTOMER_ACCOUNT table. These can now be used in the column references on the top line and in any part of the constraining WHERE clause.

JOINs can be implemented over any number of relations. Here is a JOIN involving all of the relations in the example database:

```
SELECT C.REFNO, NAME, STATUS, A.ACCNO, TYPE, B.BRANCHNAME
FROM CUSTOMER C, CUSTOMER_ACCOUNT CA, ACCOUNT A, BRANCH A
WHERE C.REFNO = CA.REFNO
AND CA.ACCNO = A.ACCNO
AND A.BRANCHNAME = B.BRANCHNAME;
```

giving:

REFNO	NAME	STATUS	ACCNO	TYPE	BRANCHNAME
2345	P Abdul	Business	120768	'D'	Crawley
2345	P Abdul	Business	348973	'C'	Crawley
7654	K Peters	Domestic	987654	'C'	Bugstone
8764	P Jones	Business	745363	'D'	Bugstone
8764	P Jones	Business	678453	'C'	Crawley
8764	P Jones	Business	348973	'C'	Crawley

In the command above, we join tuples on the BRANCH relation with those tuples in the ACCOUNT relation that have the same BRANCHNAME value. This is then JOINed with tuples in the CUSTOMER_ACCOUNT relation with the same ACCNO value. Next, this is JOINed with tuples in the CUSTOMER relation with the same REFNO value. The result is constrained to displaying those columns referenced on the top line. We can further constrain the output with row constraints, for example:

```
SELECT C.REFNO, NAME, STATUS, A.ACCNO, TYPE, B.BRANCHNAME
FROM CUSTOMER C, CUSTOMER_ACCOUNT CA, ACCOUNT A, BRANCH A
WHERE C.REFNO = CA.REFNO
AND CA.ACCNO = A.ACCNO
AND A.BRANCHNAME = B.BRANCHNAME
AND BALANCE > 100.00;
```

giving:

REFNO	NAME	STATUS	ACCNO	TYPE	BRANCHNAME
2345	P Abdul	Business	120768	'D'	Crawley
2345	P Abdul	Business	348973	'C'	Crawley
7654	K Peters	Domestic	987654	'C'	Bugstone
8764	P Jones	Business	348973	'C'	Crawley

A further constraint such as AND STATUS = 'D' would result in an output of just one row.

Using aliases, we can JOIN a table with itself. Suppose we wished to discover which accounts were shared by more than one customer. We could do this as follows:

```
SELECT FIRST.REFNO, SECOND.REFNO, FIRST.ACCNO
FROM CUSTOMER_ACCOUNT FIRST, CUSTOMER_ACCOUNT SECOND
WHERE FIRST.ACCNO = SECOND.ACCNO
AND FIRST.REFNO < SECOND.REFNO;
```

giving:

```
-------------------------
| REFNO | REFNO | ACCNO   |
-------  -----------------
| 2345  | 8764  | 348973  |
-------------------------
```

This compares the contents of CUSTOMER_ACCOUNT with itself, effectively duplicating the relation. Where a tuple in the alias 'FIRST' matches the ACCNO value in the alias 'SECOND' a row is returned. We constrain this result with FIRST.REFNO < SECOND.REFNO otherwise we will discover that every customer owns an account that also belongs to themselves. We would also get the row above replicated in reverse order.

JOINs are simply a constrained form of the relational TIMES operation. In SQL, we can implement TIMES simply by declaring an unconstrained join, for example:

```
SELECT * FROM ACCOUNT, BANK;
```

This produces a composite table that pairs every tuple in the ACCOUNT relation with every tuple in the BANK relation, making a table with 12 rows in all.

In this section, we have demonstrated the implementation of RESTRICT, PROJECT and JOIN in SQL. We will demonstrate more advanced operations after a consideration of some further aspects of the language.

5.2.2 Data retrieval with subqueries

With SQL, we can nest a query within a query. For instance, the following query lists the REFNOs for all customers who have an account at Crawley:

```
SELECT REFNO
FROM CUSTOMER_ACCOUNT
WHERE ACCNO IN
        (SELECT ACCNO FROM ACCOUNT
        WHERE BRANCHNAME = 'Crawley');
```

Here we have a subquery that returns a set of tuples representing the ACCNOs in the ACCOUNT relation for accounts kept at Crawley. This is nested in an outer query which compares the ACCNO for each CUSTOMER_ACCOUNT tuple against this set of ACCNOs. If it is found to be a member of this set, the REFNO of that tuple is returned. Note the use of the IN operator to test membership of a set.

Queries may be nested within subqueries. If we wished to find the names and addresses of customers who held accounts at Crawley, we would say:

```
SELECT NAME, ADDRESS
FROM CUSTOMER
WHERE REFNO IN
        (SELECT REFNO FROM CUSTOMER_ACCOUNT
        WHERE ACCNO IN
                (SELECT ACCNO FROM ACCOUNT
                WHERE BRANCHNAME = 'Crawley' ));
```

The previous query returned a set of REFNO values. We now nest this within a query that tests the membership of this set against REFNO values in the CUSTOMER tuples and returns the corresponding NAME and ADDRESS values where membership is found to be true.

We have here a form of JOIN. The above query could have been written thus:

```
SELECT NAME, ADDRESS
FROM CUSTOMER C, CUSTOMER_ACCOUNT CA, ACCOUNT A
WHERE BRANCHNAME = 'Crawley'
AND C.REFNO = CA.REFNO
AND CA.ACCNO = A.ACCNO;
```

The difference between this JOIN and those given previously is that the result is a PROJECTion over attributes from just one of the participating relations. Such JOINs can be conveniently rewritten as subqueries. It is usually the case, however, that it is best to avoid the use of subqueries to implement JOINs as they tend to involve a greater overhead in the use of temporary tables to evaluate the answer. There are certain types of query that are better implemented with a subquery, foremost amongst these being existence type tests. Suppose we wished to retrieve details of customers without an account. Using a subquery, we would say:

```
SELECT * FROM CUSTOMER
WHERE REFNO NOT IN
        (SELECT REFNO FROM CUSTOMER_ACCOUNT);
```

This would return an empty set, indicating that all of our customers own at least one account, which is the correct answer. However, if we tested this with a JOIN, we would be tempted to say:

```
SELECT C.REFNO, NAME, ADDRESS, STATUS
FROM CUSTOMER C, CUSTOMER_ACCOUNT CA
WHERE C.REFNO ! = CA.REFNO;
```

What we would get is the following:

```
-------------------------------------------------------------
| REFNO      | NAME       | ADDRESS          | STATUS         |
-------------------------------------------------------------
| 2345       | P Abdul    | 23, High Street  | Business       |
| 2345       | P Abdul    | 23, High Street  | Business       |
| 2345       | P Abdul    | 23, High Street  | Business       |
| 2345       | P Abdul    | 23, High Street  | Business       |
| 7654       | K Peters   | 45, The Ash      | Domestic       |
| 7654       | K Peters   | 45, The Ash      | Domestic       |
| 7654       | K Peters   | 45, The Ash      | Domestic       |
| 7654       | K Peters   | 45, The Ash      | Domestic       |
| 7654       | K Peters   | 45, The Ash      | Domestic       |
| 8764       | P Jones    | 17, Low Street   | Business       |
| 8764       | P Jones    | 17, Low Street   | Business       |
| 8764       | P Jones    | 17, Low Street   | Business       |
-------------------------------------------------------------
```

This query returns a tuple from the CUSTOMER relation each time it finds a tuple in the CUSTOMER_ACCOUNT relation that it cannot join with. Thus, the tuple for customer P Abdul appears four times as there are four tuples in the CUSTOMER_ACCOUNT relation that it cannot join with. The above is not the kind of answer that we were looking for.

There are other types of query that are better performed with subqueries as we shall see later.

5.2.3 Processing data

SQL provides some simple functions that can be used to derive information from relations as a result of processing the data held. These functions include:

COUNT: returns a count of tuples evaluating to 'true' for a given constraint
MIN: returns the lowest value for an attribute
MAX: returns the highest value for an attribute
SUM: returns the sum of values for a numeric attribute
AVG: returns the average value for a numeric attribute

We can find the number of tuples in a relation quite easily thus:

```
SELECT COUNT(*)
FROM CUSTOMER;
```

giving:

```
| ---------- |
| COUNT(*)   |
| ---------- |
|          3 |
| ---------- |
```

Constraints can be expressed in the usual way. The number of accounts held at Bugstone will be:

```
SELECT COUNT(*)
FROM ACCOUNT
WHERE BRANCHNAME = 'Bugstone';
```

giving:

```
| ---------- |
| COUNT(*)   |
| ---------- |
|          2 |
| ---------- |
```

MIN and MAX can be used on both numeric and alphanumeric columns. The highest balance can be found thus:

```
SELECT MAX(BALANCE)
FROM ACCOUNT;
```

giving

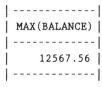

```
| ------------- |
| MAX(BALANCE)  |
| ------------- |
|     12567.56  |
| ------------- |
```

The branch with the lowest name alphabetically would be found thus:

```
SELECT MIN(BRANCHNAME)
FROM BRANCH;
```

giving

```
| ---------------- |
| MIN(BRANCHNAME)  |
| ---------------- |
|        Bugstone  |
| ---------------- |
```

SUM may be used on numeric columns to return the SUM of all values. The command:

```
SELECT SUM(BALANCE)
FROM ACCOUNT;
```

will give:

```
| ------------- |
| SUM(BALANCE)  |
| ------------- |
|     13111.32  |
| ------------- |
```

This represents the total value of all accounts. We could constrain this, for instance, to just an account held at Crawley:

```
SELECT SUM(BALANCE)
FROM ACCOUNT
WHERE BRANCHNAME = 'Crawley';
```

giving

```
| ------------- |
| SUM(BALANCE)  |
| ------------- |
|     12345.34  |
| ------------- |
```

AVG returns the simple arithmetic mean of a numeric column. The average of all account balances is returned using:

```
SELECT AVG(BALANCE)
FROM ACCOUNT;
```

giving

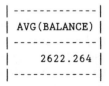

```
| ------------- |
| AVG(BALANCE)  |
| ------------- |
|     2622.264  |
| ------------- |
```

AVG may be constrained in the same way as SUM if we wished to find the average of all accounts at Crawley.

Functions (or strictly speaking 'scalar expressions') may be mixed together on a line in a manner similar to column specifications. The following command is perfectly legal:

```
SELECT MIN(BALANCE), MAX(BALANCE), SUM(BALANCE),
AVG(BALANCE)
FROM ACCOUNT;
```

and gives a row that is a concatenation of previous commands.

Functions may also appear in, or use, subqueries. The following command returns the sum of all balances for accounts held by the customer P Abdul:

```
SELECT SUM(BALANCE)
FROM ACCOUNT
WHERE ACCNO IN
        (SELECT ACCNO FROM CUSTOMER_ACCOUNT
        WHERE REFNO IN
                (SELECT REFNO FROM CUSTOMER
                WHERE NAME = 'P Abdul'));
```

We have a double nested query. The innermost query finds the REFNO for all customers with the name P Abdul. At the next level, ACCNOs are returned for all customer accounts that match this REFNO. At the outermost level we return the sum of all balances that match against these ACCNOs.

We can nest functions within a subquery. We can find the name of the customer(s) with the highest balance thus:

```
SELECT NAME
FROM CUSTOMER
WHERE REFNO IN
        (SELECT REFNO FROM CUSTOMER_ACCOUNT
        WHERE ACCNO IN
                (SELECT ACCNO FROM ACCOUNT
                WHERE BALANCE =
                        (SELECT MAX(BALANCE) FROM ACCOUNT)));
```

We need a further level of nesting here in order that we can start with the highest balance. We then find all accounts with this value and from there work back to the CUSTOMER relation. Note how we find accounts with the highest balance using a test for equality rather than using the IN operator. This is because the innermost query returns exactly one value. An equality test is more sensible in this situation than a test for set membership.

We could rewrite the above query using a series of JOINs thus:

```
SELECT NAME
FROM CUSTOMER C, CUSTOMER_ACCOUNT CA, ACCOUNT A
WHERE C.REFNO = CA.REFNO
AND A.ACCNO = CA.ACCNO
AND BALANCE =
        (SELECT MAX(BALANCE) FROM ACCOUNT);
```

This achieves the same result without the same level of subquery overhead as above. We still need one level of subquery to find the maximum balance value.

The SUM of all balances held by P. Abdul can be completely rewritten with JOINs thus:

```
SELECT SUM(BALANCE)
FROM ACCOUNT A, CUSTOMER_ACCOUNT CA, CUSTOMER C
WHERE C.REFNO = CA.REFNO
AND CA.ACCNO = A.ACCNO
AND NAME = 'P Abdul';
```

The examples we have used up to this point have returned tables with one row to represent the result of a function call. Functions can return multi-row tables using the GROUP BY clause. This causes the results of a function to be grouped according to a common attribute value. If we wished to find the sum of balances on a branch by branch basis, we would say:

```
SELECT BRANCHNAME, SUM(BALANCE)
FROM ACCOUNT
GROUP BY BRANCHNAME;
```

giving:

BRANCHNAME	SUM(BALANCE)
Crawley	12345.34
Bugstone	765.98

By using the GROUP BY clause, we have instructed the system to subdivide the given relation into groups of tuples with the same BRANCHNAME value. The result will now return for each group one row representing the sum of all balances within the same BRANCHNAME value. On the first line of the command, we must now include a reference to the attribute by which the grouping occurs. When using a function, we cannot make column references on the top line unless they exist in a GROUP BY clause. We can group a number of functions together, for example:

```
SELECT BRANCHNAME, SUM(BALANCE), AVG(BALANCE), COUNT(*)
FROM ACCOUNT
GROUP BY BRANCHNAME;
```

giving:

```
| ---------------------------------------------------------|
| BRANCHNAME  | SUM(BALANCE)  | AVG(BALANCE)  | COUNT(*) |
| ------------|---------------|---------------|----------|
| Crawley     |    12345.34   |     4115.11   |        3 |
| Bugstone    |      765.98   |      382.99   |        2 |
| ---------------------------------------------------------|
```

We can constrain the subgroups that appear by using the HAVING clause. The following command will return just the first row of the output above:

```
SELECT BRANCHNAME, SUM(BALANCE), AVG(BALANCE), COUNT(*)
FROM ACCOUNT
GROUP BY BRANCHNAME
HAVING COUNT(*) > 2;
```

The clause HAVING COUNT(*) > 2 means that we are only interested in those subgroups where the COUNT(*) function evaluates to more than 2.

Here is a command that retrieves the sum of all balances for customers with more than one account:

```
SELECT REFNO, NAME, SUM(BALANCE)
FROM CUSTOMER C, CUSTOMER_ACCOUNT CA, ACCOUNT A
WHERE C.REFNO = CA.REFNO
AND CA.ACCNO = A.ACCNO
GROUP BY REFNO, NAME
HAVING COUNT(*) > 1;
```

Here we perform the natural join of customer, customer account and account as in the example in the previous section. However, we are now constraining this join. The GROUP BY clause means that all rows in the output with the same REFNO, NAME value are grouped together for the purpose of calculating a SUM(BALANCE) value. As above, the top line may only contain column references that are part of a GROUP BY clause, in this case a clause that creates a composite of two columns. The HAVING clause further constrains the output to just those groups with more than one row. The result will be:

```
| -------- | ---------- | --------------- |
| REFNO    | NAME       | SUM(BALANCE)    |
| -------- | ---------- | --------------- |
| 2345     | P Abdul    |       12802.12  |
| 8764     | P Jones    |       12087.11  |
| ---------------------------------------- |
```

5.2.4 Data retrieval with set operators

The SELECT command returns a table which is a set of rows. Tables may be combined using the set operators UNION, INTERSECT and EXCEPT. In order that two tables may be combined, they must have the same number of columns and each column must be 'compatible' with its equivalent in the other table. By this, we mean that if the first column in one table contains numeric data, then the first column in the other table must contain numeric data and so on.

The UNION operator combines the result of two SELECT commands and returns a table consisting of all rows satisfying either or both commands. For instance, the UNION of names of all customers with accounts at Crawley and Bugstone would be:

```
SELECT NAME
FROM CUSTOMER
WHERE REFNO IN
        (SELECT REFNO FROM CUSTOMER_ACCOUNT
        WHERE ACCNO IN
                (SELECT ACCNO FROM ACCOUNT
                WHERE BRANCHNAME = 'Crawley'))
UNION
SELECT NAME
FROM CUSTOMER
WHERE REFNO IN
        (SELECT REFNO FROM CUSTOMER_ACCOUNT
        WHERE ACCNO IN
                (SELECT ACCNO FROM ACCOUNT
                WHERE BRANCHNAME = 'Bugstone'));
```

giving:

```
| ---------- |
| NAME       |
| ---------- |
| P Abdul    |
| K Peters   |
| P Jones    |
```

```
| ---------- |
```

Note how the name P Jones only appears once in the output. This is because, although this customer has an account at both branches, the UNION operator removes all duplicate rows from the result. This effect can be negated using UNION ALL:

```
SELECT NAME
FROM CUSTOMER
WHERE REFNO IN
        (SELECT REFNO FROM CUSTOMER_ACCOUNT
        WHERE ACCNO IN
                (SELECT ACCNO FROM ACCOUNT
                WHERE BRANCHNAME = 'Crawley'))
UNION ALL
SELECT NAME
FROM CUSTOMER
WHERE REFNO IN
        (SELECT REFNO FROM CUSTOMER_ACCOUNT
        WHERE ACCNO IN
                (SELECT ACCNO FROM ACCOUNT
                WHERE BRANCHNAME = 'Bugstone'));
```

giving:

```
| ---------- |
| NAME       |
| ---------- |
| P Abdul    |
| K Peters   |
| P Jones    |
| P Jones    |
| ---------- |
```

The INTERSECT operator returns only those rows that appear in both tables. Thus, the command:

```
SELECT NAME
FROM CUSTOMER
WHERE REFNO IN
        (SELECT REFNO FROM CUSTOMER_ACCOUNT
        WHERE ACCNO IN
                (SELECT ACCNO FROM ACCOUNT
                WHERE BRANCHNAME = 'Crawley'))
```

```
INTERSECT
SELECT NAME
FROM CUSTOMER
WHERE REFNO IN
        (SELECT REFNO FROM CUSTOMER_ACCOUNT
        WHERE ACCNO IN
                (SELECT ACCNO FROM ACCOUNT
                WHERE BRANCHNAME = 'Bugstone'));
```

will just return the row P Jones as this is the only row that would be returned by both commands. The EXCEPT operator returns those rows that would appear in the first command with those that would also appear in the second command removed. The command:

```
SELECT NAME
FROM CUSTOMER
WHERE REFNO IN
        (SELECT REFNO FROM CUSTOMER_ACCOUNT
        WHERE ACCNO IN
                (SELECT ACCNO FROM ACCOUNT
                WHERE BRANCHNAME = 'Crawley'))
EXCEPT
SELECT NAME
FROM CUSTOMER
WHERE REFNO IN
        (SELECT REFNO FROM CUSTOMER_ACCOUNT
        WHERE ACCNO IN
                (SELECT ACCNO FROM ACCOUNT
                WHERE BRANCHNAME = 'Bugstone'));
```

would give:

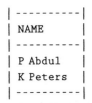

```
| ---------- |
| NAME       |
| ---------- |
| P Abdul    |
| K Peters   |
| ---------- |
```

P Jones has been removed from the result as this row would also appear in the table returned by the second command.

UNION and INTERSECT are the equivalent of the relational algebra operators of the same name. EXCEPT is the equivalent of the algebraic MINUS. Indeed, many dialects of SQL use MINUS rather than EXCEPT.

5.2.5 Data retrieval with EXISTS

SQL provides the EXISTS operator to return a Boolean value from a subquery. A Boolean value is one that is either true or false. For instance, a way of listing all those customers with an account could be:

```
SELECT NAME FROM CUSTOMER C
WHERE EXISTS
          (SELECT * FROM CUSTOMER_ACCOUNT CA
          WHERE AND CA.REFNO = C.REFNO );
```

Here we have a query that returns the names of customers. It is constrained using EXISTS against a subquery. For each tuple in CUSTOMER, the subquery returns the value 'true' if there is at least one tuple in CUSTOMER_ACCOUNT that has the same REFNO value. This is determined by the join CA.REFNO = C.REFNO. What the query is effectively saying is 'Give names of customers where it is true that their REFNO exists in the CUSTOMER_ACCOUNT relation'.

Note how the inner query uses SELECT *. It could be anything in this part of the query (e.g. SELECT 'X'). This is because the subquery returns no data. It simply returns a truth value that is determined by the specified JOIN.

To return a list of customers with no accounts, we simply negate the EXISTS clause:

```
SELECT NAME FROM CUSTOMER C
WHERE NOT EXISTS
          (SELECT * FROM CUSTOMER_ACCOUNT CA
          WHERE AND CA.REFNO = C.REFNO );
```

EXISTS can be used within subqueries. Thus, to find names of all customers who have an account at the branch Crawley, we could say:

```
SELECT NAME FROM CUSTOMER C
WHERE EXISTS
          (SELECT * FROM CUSTOMER_ACCOUNT CA
          WHERE AND CA.REFNO = C.REFNO
          AND EXISTS
                    (SELECT * FROM ACCOUNT A
                    WHERE BRANCHNAME = 'Crawley'
                    AND A.ACCNO = CA.ACCNO));
```

On this occasion, we only get the name of a customer if there is at least one tuple in CUSTOMER_ACCOUNT which has the same REFNO value and which also has the same ACCNO value as a tuple in ACCOUNT with the BRANCHNAME of Crawley.

Using EXISTS, we can implement the DIVIDE operation from the relational algebra. Suppose we wanted to discover which customers had an account at every branch. We need first of all to create a view that JOINs customer accounts with accounts to give the branch where each customer has an account, thus:

```
CUST_BRANCH
-----------------------------------
| REFNO   | ACCNO    | BRANCHNAME  |
| 2345    | 120768   | Crawley     |
| 2345    | 348973   | Crawley     |
| 7654    | 987654   | Bugstone    |
| 8764    | 745363   | Bugstone    |
| 8764    | 678453   | Crawley     |
| 8764    | 348973   | Crawley     |
-----------------------------------
```

(How such views are created is given in section 5.3.5 below.) We now DIVIDE this by the set of branch names in the BANK relation. What we are looking for is those REFNOs that are paired against every possible BRANCHNAME. We can achieve this as follows:

```
SELECT DISTINCT REFNO
FROM CUST_BRANCH CB
WHERE NOT EXISTS
         (SELECT BRANCHNAME FROM BANK
          EXCEPT
          SELECT BRANCHNAME FROM CUST_BRANCH CB1
          WHERE CB1.REFNO = CB.REFNO);
```

This would give the following result:

```
|--------|
| REFNO  |
|--------|
| 8764   |
|--------|
```

The outer query examines each tuple in the CUST_BRANCH relation and returns its REFNO if the inner query evaluates to 'false'. The inner query here builds a set of all possible BRANCHNAME values. From this it removes all BRANCHNAMEs that are paired with the REFNO in a tuple with the same REFNO value for the tuple obtained by the outer query. If this REFNO is paired with every possible BRANCHNAME value, then the result is an empty set and the inner query returns the value 'false', that is there are no BRANCHNAME values that are not paired with this particular REFNO.

To find the names of such customers, we simply nest this in another query:

```
SELECT NAME FROM CUSTOMER
WHERE REFNO IN
SELECT DISTINCT REFNO
FROM CUST_BRANCH CB
WHERE NOT EXISTS
        (SELECT BRANCHNAME FROM BANK
        EXCEPT
        SELECT BRANCHNAME FROM CUST_BRANCH CB1
        WHERE CB1.REFNO = CB.REFNO);
```

We have now demonstrated that the full range of the relational algebra can be implemented in SQL, rendering it a relationally complete language. In the next section, we shall demonstrate how relational databases may be defined using SQL.

5.3 SQL data definition

5.3.1 Creating tables

In order to retrieve data from a relation using SQL, that relation must already exist within the database. We establish the existence of a base relation in SQL using the CREATE TABLE command.

Here is an example of the CREATE TABLE command:

```
CREATE TABLE CUSTOMER
        (REFNO NUMBER,
        NAME CHAR (20),
        ADDRESS CHAR (30),
        STATUS CHAR (8));
```

which shows the basic elements of the command. In the first line, the name of the base relation being created is designated. We then have a declaration of the columns that exist in that relation. Each column has a name and a data type.

In standard SQL, there exists just a restricted range of data types: CHAR, NUMBER, FLOAT and INTEGER. Most commercial implementations of SQL enrich this with types such as MONEY, DATE, STRING and so on. Note how we had to subscript the type CHAR with a number. This indicates the maximum width of character-type columns. We may optionally restrict the width of numeric columns, for example:

```
CREATE TABLE ACCOUNT
        (ACCNO INTEGER (6),
        BALANCE FLOAT (10,2),
        TYPE CHAR (1));
```

In this example, we have limited the ACCNO column to integers of up to six digits in width. The BALANCE column is a decimal number with a maximum width (10 digits) and a precision (two digits). This means that BALANCE may have a decimal part of up to two numbers. Thus we can specify numbers such as 9.75, 20.55, 45.45 as values for BALANCE. The value 9.756 would be stored as 9.75. The value 20 would be stored as 20.00.

5.3.2 Simple constraints

At present, we have created tables rather than relations in the true sense. This is because we have not provided a primary key for these tables. A more correct set of definitions would be:

```
CREATE TABLE CUSTOMER
        (REFNO NUMBER PRIMARY KEY NOT NULL,
        NAME CHAR (20),
        ADDRESS CHAR (30),
        STATUS CHAR (8));
CREATE TABLE ACCOUNT
        (ACCNO INTEGER (6) PRIMARY KEY NOT NULL,
        BALANCE FLOAT (10,2)
        BRANCHNAME CHAR (20),
        TYPE CHAR (1));
```

In these examples, we have added constraints to the columns REFNO in CUSTOMER and ACCNO in ACCOUNT. The constraints are PRIMARY KEY and NOT NULL. PRIMARY KEY indicates that all values for these columns must be unique. NOT NULL is used to designate a column that must have a value for all rows in a table. It may be used for any column for which we wish to debar NULL values.

Primary keys may be composite, consisting of a number of columns. When this happens, we need to use a table constraint thus:

```
CREATE TABLE CUSTOMER_ACCOUNT
        (REFNO NOT NULL,
        ACCNO NOT NULL,
        PRIMARY KEY (REFNO, ACCNO));
```

Here, the PRIMARY KEY constraint is not attached to any particular column but acts as a constraint across the table as a whole. Note that we still place NOT NULL as a constraint on the individual columns that compose the PRIMARY KEY.

Another constraint is UNIQUE. This may be specified for columns that are not part of the primary key but for which we wish every value to be unique. A table with alternate candidate keys should use this constraint to specify such keys.

5.3.3 Foreign keys

The other main type of key in a relational database is the foreign key. We can specify this as a column constraint or, in the case of composite foreign keys, as a table constraint. In CUSTOMER_ACCOUNT, we have two foreign keys (REFNO and ACCNO). These can be specified as follows:

```
CREATE TABLE CUSTOMER_ACCOUNT
        (REFNO NOT NULL REFERENCES CUSTOMER,
        ACCNO NOT NULL REFERENCES ACCOUNT,
        PRIMARY KEY (REFNO, ACCNO));
```

If we had another relation that referenced the CUSTOMER_ACCOUNT relation by means of its composite key, we would require a table constraint declared thus:

```
FOREIGN KEY (REFNO, ACCNO) REFERENCES CUSTOMER_ACCOUNT
```

In the 'live' situation, we would not be able to give multiple CREATE TABLE commands on the same table. Once CREATEd, if we found our definition to be unsatisfactory, we would have to alter the table definition. For instance, we omitted the foreign key reference to BANK when we created the ACCOUNT relation. We can alter its definition thus:

```
ALTER TABLE ACCOUNT
ADD (FOREIGN KEY (BRANCHNAME) REFERENCES BANK);
```

Here we have added a table constraint to the table definition. We can also ADD columns, for example:

```
ALTER TABLE ACCOUNT
ADD (OVERDRAFT_LIMIT FLOAT (10,2));
```

Column definitions may themselves be altered, for example:

```
ALTER TABLE CUSTOMER
MODIFY (NAME CHAR (25));
```

The MODIFY clause has been used here to alter the width of a CHAR column. Numeric columns may be MODIFYed from FLOAT to INTEGER and vice versa or have their width altered. We can also add constraints to columns. The foreign key modification above could have been specified as a column constraint thus:

```
ALTER TABLE ACCOUNT
MODIFY (BRANCHNAME CHAR (20) REFERENCES BANK);
```

When defining a foreign key, we should also specify referencing constraints. These are necessary to preserve referential integrity (see section 3.2.3 above). In SQL, we can specify the constraints RESTRICT, SET NULL and CASCADE on a foreign key. To recap, RESTRICT means that the referenced table may not change a primary key value if there exists a row in a referencing table with that value. For instance, if we placed this constraint on REFNO in CUSTOMER_ ACCOUNT, then we would not be able to change the REFNO for any customer who had an account. SET NULL means that any change to a primary key value will cause the referencing column to have the value NULL entered for those rows with the previous value. If we had this constraint on ACCNO in CUSTOMER_ACCOUNT, then a change to an ACCNO in ACCOUNT would cause the equivalent rows in CUSTOMER_ACCOUNT to have their ACCNO value set to NULL. CASCADE means that any change to the referenced table will be transmitted to the referencing table. Thus, a CASCADE on BRANCHNAME in ACCOUNT will mean that if a branch changed its name, then all ACCOUNTs referencing this branch will have their BRANCHNAMEs updated to the same value.

Thus far we have used the word 'change', meaning an update to a value. Another type of change is the deletion of a row. If RESTRICT is placed on deletions, then a row in a referenced table may not be removed if there are any rows that reference it. CASCADE means that the deletion of a row in a referenced table will result in the deletion of all rows that use its primary key as a foreign key value. SET NULL means that the row in the referenced table may be deleted, whilst the referencing rows remain but have their foreign key value set to NULL.

When specifying a referencing constraint, we must specify not only what type of constraint it is (RESTRICT, SET NULL, CASCADE), but also the action on which this constraint is being placed (UPDATE or DELETE).

In the following definition, we are stating that if a bank changes its BRANCHNAME, then that change will be transmitted to all rows in the ACCOUNT relation with the equivalent value. We are also stating that if a bank is deleted from the BANK relation, then all rows in the ACCOUNT relation with that BRANCHNAME will have that value set to NULL.

```
CREATE TABLE ACCOUNT
        (ACCNO INTEGER (6) PRIMARY KEY NOT NULL,
        BALANCE FLOAT (10,2)
        BRANCHNAME CHAR (20) REFERENCES BANK
                            ON UPDATE CASCADE
                            ON DELETE SET NULL,
        TYPE CHAR (1));
```

The next definition states that when a customer has his or her REFNO changed, then those rows in CUSTOMER_ACCOUNT with that REFNO will be similarly changed. However, we are also stating that if the REFNO of a customer exists in CUSTOMER_ACCOUNT, then that customer may not be deleted from the CUSTOMER relation. For ACCNO, we are stating that an ACCNO may not be altered if it has any references in CUSTOMER_ACCOUNT, but it may be deleted and this deletion will result in all rows referencing it being deleted.

```
CREATE TABLE CUSTOMER_ACCOUNT
        (REFNO NOT NULL REFERENCES CUSTOMER
                ON UPDATE CASCADE
                ON DELETE RESTRICT,
        ACCNO NOT NULL REFERENCES ACCOUNT
                ON UPDATE RESTRICT
                ON DELETE CASCADE,
        PRIMARY KEY (REFNO, ACCNO));
```

5.3.4 Further constraints

The integrity of data in relations may be further preserved using the CHECK clause. This may be used to constrain the set of allowable values for a column thus:

```
CREATE TABLE ACCOUNT
        (ACCNO INTEGER (6) PRIMARY KEY NOT NULL,
        BALANCE FLOAT (10,2)
        BRANCHNAME CHAR (20) REFERENCES BANK
                        ON UPDATE CASCADE
                        ON DELETE SET NULL,
        TYPE CHAR (1)
        CHECK (TYPE = 'D' OR TYPE = 'C')
        );
```

We have entered the constraint CHECK (TYPE = 'D' OR TYPE = 'C') meaning that any attempt to enter a value under this column that is not 'D' or 'C' will be rejected. We can have CHECK clauses that test for a range, for example:

```
CHECK (BALANCE BETWEEN -1000.00 AND 99999999.99)
```

SQL provides limited support for user-defined data types with the CREATE DOMAIN command. For instance, we can specify a general type MONEY thus:

```
CREATE DOMAIN MONEY (FLOAT 10,2)
CHECK (MONEY < = 1000000.00);
```

and then use it in a table definition:

```
CREATE TABLE ACCOUNT
        (BALANCE MONEY
        etc. )
```

When we do this, any constraints placed on the domain will automatically be exported to the base table column. CHECK constraints may also be altered using the ALTER TABLE and ALTER DOMAIN commands.

It is good practice to name constraints when specifying them. A better definition of ACCOUNT would be:

```
CREATE TABLE ACCOUNT
        (ACCNO INTEGER (6) PRIMARY KEY NOT NULL,
    BALANCE FLOAT (10,2)
    BRANCHNAME CHAR (20) REFERENCES BANK
                    ON UPDATE CASCADE
                    ON DELETE SET NULL,
    TYPE CHAR (1)
    CONSTRAINT TYPE_CHECK CHECK (TYPE = 'D' OR TYPE = 'C');
```

If we wished, we can now delete this constraint using ALTER TABLE thus:

```
ALTER TABLE ACCOUNT
DROP CONSTRAINT TYPE_CHECK;
```

or modify it thus:

```
ALTER TABLE ACCOUNT
MODIFY CONSTRAINT TYPE_CHECK (CHECK (TYPE = 'D' OR TYPE =
                                'C' OR TYPE = 'S'));
```

5.3.5 Creating views

A view is a logical relation that derives its contents from already existing relations. We create a view in SQL by means of a SELECT command to specify its contents, for example:

```
CREATE VIEW DEPOSIT_ACCOUNT
AS
SELECT * FROM ACCOUNT
WHERE TYPE = 'D';
```

The above is a simple view that takes a subset of the rows from the ACCOUNT relation. It can now be referenced as a table in SELECT commands, for example:

```
SELECT * FROM DEPOSIT_ACCOUNT;

SELECT ACCNO
FROM DEPOSIT_ACCOUNT
WHERE BALANCE > 100.00;

SELECT MANAGER_NO, REFNO, BALANCE
FROM BANK B, DEPOSIT_ACCOUNT DA
WHERE B.BRANCHNAME = DA.BRANCHNAME
AND BALANCE < 1000.00;
```

Views based on JOINs can be easily specified. Here is a view that displays details of the overall financial position of all customers:

```
CREATE VIEW CUSTOMER_BALANCES
AS
SELECT REFNO, NAME, SUM(BALANCE)
FROM CUSTOMER C, CUSTOMER_ACCOUNT CA, ACCOUNT A
WHERE C.REFNO = CA.REFNO
AND CA.ACCNO = A.ACCNO
GROUP BY REFNO, NAME;
```

The columns that appear in this view will be as specified in the SELECT command. We can provide 'aliases' for these columns. For instance, we could have specified this view as:

```
CREATE VIEW CUSTOMER_BALANCES (REF, NAME, TOTAL)
AS
SELECT REFNO, NAME, SUM(BALANCE)
FROM CUSTOMER C, CUSTOMER_ACCOUNT CA, ACCOUNT A
WHERE C.REFNO = CA.REFNO
AND CA.ACCNO = A.ACCNO
GROUP BY REFNO, NAME;
```

The effect of this is that any SELECT command using this view will display data using the column headings REF, NAME and TOTAL. For instance, the command:

```
SELECT * FROM CUSTOMER_BALANCES
```

will give:

REF	NAME	TOTAL
2345	P Abdul	12802.12
7654	K Peters	987.65
8764	P Jones	12087.11

When referencing this view, we must now use the alias column names, for example:

```
SELECT TOTAL FROM CUSTOMER_BALANCES;

SELECT CUSTOMER.NAME, ADDRESS, TOTAL
FROM CUSTOMER C, CUSTOMER_BALANCES CB
WHERE CB.REF = C.REFNO;
```

5.3.6 Removing database objects

Tables, views and domains may be removed from a database using the DROP command, for example:

```
DROP TABLE CUSTOMER;
DROP VIEW DEPOSIT_ACCOUNT;
DROP DOMAIN MONEY;
```

When a table is removed, then all views that reference that table are logically deleted. Likewise, when a view is removed, if that view is referenced by another view, then the referencing view is also logically removed. (The user has to be careful here. Many systems will retain the definitions of such logically redundant views, meaning that they will continue to 'exist', but any attempts to use them will raise runtime errors.) When a domain is removed, the definitions of any columns using that domain are altered to the data type on which that domain is defined. Any constraints that are part of that domain definition are deleted.

5.4 Altering data using SQL

5.4.1 Inserting data

The SQL INSERT command is used to create tuples. In its simplest form, a tuple can be created thus:

```
INSERT INTO CUSTOMER
VALUES
(2345, 'P Abdul', '23 High Street', 'Business');
```

In this form, the literal values given are assigned to the columns in the order that they appear in the original CREATE TABLE command. Thus, a row with a REFNO of 2345, NAME of P Abdul, ADDRESS of 23 High Street and STATUS of Business is created in the CUSTOMER relation. Note that non-numeric columns require the quotation marks around their assigned values.

The order of assignment can be changed thus:

```
INSERT INTO CUSTOMER (NAME, ADDRESS, REFNO, STATUS)
VALUES
('P Abdul', '23 High Street', 2345, 'Business');
```

Here the values are assigned to the columns in the order given on the top line. This is especially useful in the case of null values. Suppose we had a customer with no address or status. A default assignment would be:

```
INSERT INTO CUSTOMER
VALUES
(7462, 'J Smith', NULL, NULL);
```

An alternative method of assignment would be:

```
INSERT INTO CUSTOMER (REFNO, NAME)
VALUES
(7462, 'J Smith');
```

In this second example, the value NULL is assigned to any non-specified columns.

When INSERT is used, any constraints placed upon a table are checked. In both of the examples above we demonstrate two ways to create the same tuple. If we were to enter this string of commands into an SQL system, the second attempt to create each tuple should be rejected as they both contradict the PRIMARY KEY constraint on REFNO (implying that no two rows may have the same REFNO).

INSERT can also be used to copy a set of data from one table to another. Suppose we had an archive relation OLD_CUSTOMERS which kept details of former customers, and that this relation had the same attributes as the current CUSTOMER relation. To copy a tuple from CUSTOMER to OLD_CUSTOMERS, we can simply say:

```
INSERT INTO OLD_CUSTOMERS
SELECT * FROM CUSTOMER WHERE REFNO = 7654;
```

This does not have the effect of deleting the tuple from CUSTOMER. This requires the use of the DELETE command.

5.4.2 Deleting data

Tuples are removed from a relation using the DELETE command. A simple DELETE would be:

```
DELETE FROM CUSTOMER
WHERE REFNO = 7654;
```

All tuples that satisfy the constraint given in the WHERE clause are removed. Constraints can be relatively complex. For instance, the command:

```
DELETE FROM CUSTOMER
WHERE REFNO IN
        (SELECT REFNO FROM CUSTOMER_BALANCES
        WHERE TOTAL < -1000.00);
```

has the effect of removing all customers whose total balances are overdrawn by more that 1000.00.

When DELETEing, any foreign key constraints will be checked. In section 5.3.3 above, the constraint ON DELETE RESTRICT was placed on the column REFNO in CUSTOMER_ACCOUNT that referenced CUSTOMER from the CUSTOMER_ACCOUNT relation. This means that any customer with an account cannot be removed, causing the above DELETE to be rejected. The correct way to give this command in this context would be in two stages:

```
DELETE FROM CUSTOMER_ACCOUNT
WHERE REFNO IN
        (SELECT REFNO FROM CUSTOMER_BALANCES
        WHERE TOTAL < -1000.00);
```

This would remove all details of the relationships between overdrawn customers and accounts. We can then delete the CUSTOMER tuple thus:

```
DELETE FROM CUSTOMER
WHERE REFNO NOT IN
        (SELECT REFNO FROM CUSTOMER_ACCOUNT);
```

An unconstrained DELETE will remove all tuples from a relation, for example:

```
DELETE FROM ACCOUNT;
```

will remove all accounts. It will also remove all CUSTOMER_ACCOUNT tuples due to the ON DELETE CASCADE constraint placed on ACCNO in CUSTOMER_ ACCOUNT.

5.4.3 Updating data

The UPDATE command is used to alter data held in tuples. A simple example of UPDATE is as follows:

```
UPDATE CUSTOMER
SET NAME = 'S Abdul'
WHERE REFNO = 2345;
```

Here we have changed the value of the attribute NAME in the relation CUSTOMER for all tuples with the REFNO of 2345. As with DELETE, UPDATE commands may be constrained by referential integrity checks. For instance, the command:

```
UPDATE CUSTOMER
SET REFNO = 2346
WHERE REFNO = 2345;
```

will cause rows in the CUSTOMER_ACCOUNT relation also to be changed as we previously specified an ON UPDATE CASCADE constraint on REFNO in this table.

UPDATE can be used with expressions across a number of columns and rows. The command:

```
UPDATE ACCOUNT
SET BALANCE = BALANCE + 1000.00
WHERE BALANCE > 0;
```

will add 1000.00 to all accounts with a positive balance. A multi-column change takes the form:

```
UPDATE CUSTOMER
SET NAME = 'J Smith', ADDRESS = '67, Peter Street'
WHERE REFNO = 7654;
```

As with INSERT, a nested SELECT expression can be used to copy data from one part of the database to another. The command:

```
UPDATE CUSTOMER
SET NAME = (SELECT NAME FROM CUSTOMER WHERE REFNO = 2345);
```

will cause all customers to have the same name as the customer with the REFNO of 2345.

Data may be updated in views as long as the view is a simple subset of tuples from one relation. Thus, in the above examples, DEPOSIT_ACCOUNTS is updateable, but CUSTOMER_BALANCES is not. Data can only be updated in this second view by altering data in the relations that service it. Any UPDATE to a base relation will obviously alter the data held in views that it supports.

5.5 Data control in SQL

Access to data in a multi-user system is implemented using the GRANT and REVOKE commands. Each command requires a user to be specified, an object (table or view) on which a privilege is to be specified and a privilege. The following command GRANTs a user 'X' to be given the ability to SELECT data from the table CUSTOMER:

```
GRANT SELECT ON CUSTOMER TO X;
```

'X' can now retrieve data from the CUSTOMER relation, but cannot alter it in any way. 'X' would need the UPDATE privilege to be given:

```
GRANT SELECT, UPDATE ON CUSTOMER TO X;
```

If we wished to give 'X' full access to all operations on this relation, we would say:

```
GRANT ALL ON CUSTOMER TO X;
```

In all SQL systems, there is a special user PUBLIC which means all users of the database. The following command provides retrieval powers to everyone on the BANK relation:

```
GRANT SELECT ON BANK TO PUBLIC;
```

Views are a specially useful form of providing data security. If we wished users to be able to access deposit accounts only, we would give them privileges on the view DEPOSIT_ACCOUNTS rather than on the base relation ACCOUNT:

```
GRANT SELECT, UPDATE ON DEPOSIT_ACCOUNTS TO Y;
```

REVOKE is the inverse of GRANT. It is used to remove privileges. Here are some examples of REVOKE:

```
REVOKE UPDATE ON DEPOSIT_ACCOUNTS FROM Y;
REVOKE ALL ON CUSTOMER FROM X;
REVOKE SELECT ON BANK FROM PUBLIC;
```

When REVOKEing a privilege, some groups will subsume others. By REVOKEing a privilege from PUBLIC, this removes this privilege from all users, including those who have had it specifically GRANTed. When we say REVOKE ALL, this revokes all privileges currently GRANTed to the given user.

Summary

- SQL is a relationally complete language which has become the *de facto* standard language for relational systems.

- The SQL SELECT command provides the full functionality of the relational algebra.
- Relations that conform to the rules of entity and referential integrity can be created using SQL.
- Data held in relations can be inserted, amended and deleted using the SQL INSERT, UPDATE and DELETE commands.
- SQL provides some simple aggregate functions that assist with the task of processing data held in relations.
- GRANT and REVOKE are used to control access to relations in a multi-user database system.

Exercises

1 Here is the flights/reservation database originally shown in Chapter 3:

```
CUSTOMERS                          FLIGHTS
--------------------    ------------------------------------------------
| CUSTNO  |CUSTNAME  |   | FLIGHTNO | DESTINATION  | DAY     | TIME  | COST  |
--------------------    ------------------------------------------------
| 1       | P Jones  |   | FL2X     | Paris        | Tuesday | 1400  |  78.95|
| 2       | H Chan   |   | HK101    | Hong Kong    | Sunday  | 0900  | 525.00|
| 4       | S Abdul  |   | JX74     | Bahrain      | Monday  | 1300  | 275.75|
| 6       | K Smith  |   | ------------------------------------------------|
| 7       | N Le Mer |
| -------------------|


RESERVATIONS
--------------------
| CUSTNO  |FLIGHTNO  |
--------------------
| 1       | FL2X     |
| 1       | HK101    |
| 2       | HK101    |
| 6       | JX74     |
| 7       | JX74     |
| 1       | JX74     |
| -------------------|
```

1 Write the SQL commands to:
   (a) Display all rows in the CUSTOMERS table.
   (b) Display all customer names.
   (c) Display the details of flight HK101.
   (d) Display just the destination of flight HK101.

(e)   Display, without using a subquery, the names of customers booked on flight JX74.

(f)   Display, without using a subquery, the names of customers who have booked a flight to Paris. (Assume, in this instance, that the user does not know the FLIGHTNO of this flight.)

(g)   Get the same results for (e) and (f) using subqueries.

(h)   Display the COST, FLIGHTNO and DESTINATION for the most expensive flight.

(i)   Display the COST, FLIGHTNO and DESTINATION for the cheapest flight.

(j)   Display the total cost of all reservations made.

(k)   Display for each customer, the CUSTNO, CUSTNAME and the cost of all reservations that the customer has made.

(l)   Display the CUSTNAME, FLIGHTNO and DESTINATION of all reservations made by any customers who have made a reservation for all available flights.

(m)   Change the destination for FLIGHTNO JX74 to Pittsburgh.

(n)   Increase by 50% the cost of all flights for which the customer N Le Mer has made a reservation.

2   (a)   Write the CREATE TABLE commands for the above tables, specifying any primary keys.

(b)   Amend your answer to (a) to include foreign key references. Incorporate the following constraints:

(i)   A flight cannot be deleted or altered if it has any reservations.

(ii)   When a customer is deleted, the reservation references are set to null. When a customer has his or her CUSTNO altered, all foreign key references to this CUSTNO must be similarly changed.

(iii) No flights may cost more than $10,000.00.

(c)   Write a command to add a new column (DEPARTURE_POINT) to the FLIGHTS table, consisting of strings of up to 20 characters.

3   What SQL commands would be required to populate this database?

4   Write the SQL commands to:

(a)   Create a view (FLIGHT_INFO) that joins the rows in the RESERVATIONS table with the relevant rows in the FLIGHTS and CUSTOMERS table so that all of the information for a given reservation may be conveniently accessed.

(b)   Write a constrained version of this view (PARIS_FLIGHT_INFO) so that it applies to Paris flights only.

(c)   Grant a user called JULES the facility to retrieve data from the view PARIS_FLIGHT_INFO.

(d)   Grant the user JULES the facility to create, delete and retrieve rows from the CUSTOMERS table.

(e)   Remove all privileges from JULES.

Further reading

Date (1995) Chapter 8
Date and Darwen (1993) Chapters 7, 8, 9, 12, 13, 14 and 15
Elmasri and Navathe (1994) Chapter 7
Korth and Silberschatz (1991) Chapter 4
Kroenke (1995) Chapter 10
Ozkarahan (1990) Chapter 5
Rolland (1992) Chapters 3 and 6
Rolland (1996) Chapters 2, 3, 4, 5, 6, 7 and 8
Ryan and Smith (1995) Chapter 14
Van der Lans (1993) Chapters 6, 7, 8, 9, 10, 11, 12, 14, 15, 16, 18, 21, 24 and 25

CHAPTER 6

Traditional database models

In this chapter, we shall briefly examine the hierarchic and network database models. These models dominated the DBMS market in pre-relational days. There are still many large corporate database systems that are built upon these models and which will continue to exist for many years to come owing to the large amount of data that is effectively 'locked up' within them.

By the end of this chapter, the reader should be able to:

1. Describe the main features of the hierarchic and network database models.
2. Be able to design a simple database upon hierarchic and network lines.
3. Explain how data is retrieved from these types of system.
4. Assess the shortcomings and advantages of these types of database model.

6.1 Hierarchic database design principles

A hierarchic database system is one that is built as a tree of related record types. All hierarchic databases have one, and only one, 'root' record type. This root record type may participate in one-to-many relationships with any number of 'child' record types. Each child may itself have child record types.

In Figure 6.1, we have the start of a hierarchic model for our bank database, with BANK as the root record type and ACCOUNT and EMP as child record types, indicating that each bank may have many accounts and many employees,

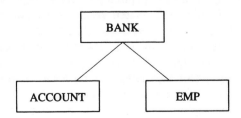

Figure 6.1 A root record with child records.

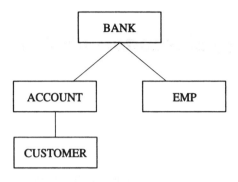

Figure 6.2 Child record types with descendants.

whereas each account and employee instance 'belongs to' exactly one bank. We describe this as an ownership relationship, whereby BANK 'owns' EMP and ACCOUNT.

As stated above, child record types may in themselves own many child records. In Figure 6.2, we attach CUSTOMER to ACCOUNT, indicating that an account may have many customers.

This immediately brings us up against one of the major shortcomings of the hierarchic model, in that it is only capable of showing one type of relationship (1–M) and that all relationships must work in one direction only towards a single root entity. If a customer was only allowed to have one account, then this would not be a problem. However, our scenario in Chapter 2 indicated that a customer may have many accounts. In the hierarchic data model given in Figure 6.2, this means that when a customer has more than one account, then his or her record will have to appear under every account that the customer owns. Moreover, if the customer has accounts at more than one branch, then the record will have to make multiple appearances under different roots.

Figure 6.3 shows how the data held in the relational database in Chapter 5 would have to be stored using the hierarchic model we have devised. Note how the implementation of a hierarchic system results in a set of trees, each starting with the root record type. Thus, a hierarchic database is an ordered set of trees. For each tree, we have links ('pointers') between a parent record and its child records. We also have pointers that go across the trees that link all records of the same type together. This facilitates data retrieval. Note the replication of customer details amongst the customer records.

Replication in a hierarchic system can be overcome by various devices which are complex and beyond the purposes of this text. For now, we shall examine how our example hierarchic database can be implemented.

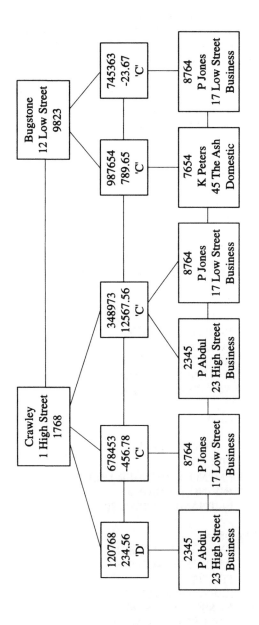

Figure 6.3 Hierarchic database example.

6.2 Implementing a hierarchic schema

A hierarchic database schema consists of a simple series of record descriptions, each of which includes a reference to the 'owner' of that record. In Figure 6.4, we have a segment of code that defines the model devised above. This is a 'pseudo-coded' definition which is the not the precise language of any particular product.

This definition shows some important features of all hierarchic definitions. Apart from the root, every record type has one parent. Data typing is typically very primitive. There is no need to declare foreign keys as with a relational

```
DBNAME = BANKSYSTEM

RECORD
        TYPE    = BANK
        FILDS
        BRANCHNAME = CHAR20
        ADDRESS = CHAR 30
        MANAGER_NO = INTEGER

RECORD
        TYPE    = ACCOUNT
        PARENT  = BANK
        FIELDS
        ACCNO   = INTEGER UNIQUE
        BALANCE = FLOAT
        ACC_TYPE = CHAR 1

RECORD
        TYPE  = EMP
        PARENT = BANK
        FIELDS
        EMPNO  = INTEGER UNIQUE
        INS_NO = CHAR 9
        EMPNAME = CHAR 30

RECORD
        TYPE  = CUSTOMER
        PARENT  = ACCOUNT
        FIELDS
        REFNO  = INTEGER
        NAME  = CHAR 20
        ADDRESS = CHAR 30
        STATUS  = CHAR 8
```

Figure 6.4 A hierarchic database definition.

system; the concept does not exist as such. Each record may only have one parent. Thus, when it is created, it is physically attached (typically by means of a pointer, or a chain of pointers) to its parent. The idea of relating two records together in a database schema by means of common data values is simply not present in a hierarchic system. This has the following implications for data integrity in a hierarchic system:

1. No child record may exist without a parent.
2. When a parent record is removed, then all of its child records are automatically removed.
3. Any changes to a parent record are, by implication, cascaded to the information that is stored about its child records.

Points 1 and 2 above have great implications regarding potential loss of information. In our database, we cannot store any information regarding customers who do not presently have an account opened. It may be a semantic point that the definition of a customer is 'someone who has an account', but it does raise problems such as storing information regarding customers who have temporarily suspended their accounts.

6.3 Hierarchic data manipulation

The examples given in this section are very loosely based on DL/1, the data query language for the IMS (Information Management System) product from IBM. This was the foremost hierarchic system.

6.3.1 Hierarchic data retrieval

Operators in a hierarchic system work on a 'record at a time' basis, meaning that each activation of an operator retrieves just one record. To retrieve a set of records requires a retrieval operation to be applied repetitively. In the original hierarchic systems, data retrieval operations were embedded within a host language (such as COBOL or FORTRAN). The implementation of a program-ming loop in order to retrieve a set of records would be encoded in the host language. In this section, we will informally use 'while' loops to demonstrate routines that retrieve sets of records.

Relationships between record types in hierarchic databases are implemented by means of pointers that connect sets of records together. In order to implement a retrieval operation, a hierarchic system needs to keep track of where it has read to within each participating set of records. This is done by maintaining a 'read' pointer for each record set, which indicates the next available record from that set.

The simplest retrieval operation is GET FIRST, meaning 'get the first record'. To find the name of a branch with a given address, we would say:

```
GET FIRST bank
WHERE bank.address = '12 Low Street';
PRINT bank.branchname;
```

This operation reads all BANK type records until it finds one satisfying the given condition. This operation examines the root set of records in our system. It is possible to perform a direct access operation on records below the root. The details of an account could be retrieved thus:

```
GET FIRST account
WHERE account.accno = 678543;
PRINT account.balance, account.type;
```

This second command will examine all of the account records starting from the first account under the first branch and read all account records from that point onwards until it finds an account with the given ACCNO value.

To retrieve a set of records, we require the GET NEXT operator. This retrieves literally the next record available. As the language only works on a 'record at a time' basis, we need to set up a loop to retrieve a set of records. For instance, to find all accounts with a positive balance, we would say:

```
GET FIRST account
WHERE account.balance > 0;
WHILE DB_STATUS_OK
      PRINT account.accno;
      GET NEXT account
      WHERE account.balance > 0;
END-WHILE
```

Here we find the first account with a balance of more than zero. We then check a flag DB_STATUS_OK. This flag sets to false when the end of a record set is encountered. In this case, this means when the 'accounts' pointer is at the end of all account records in the database. If this is not yet true, we get the next record with a positive balance and so on until the flag indicates that there are no more account records available.

With the above command, we can only display the data held in the account record. We cannot print details of the branch where that account is held as we have not retrieved it. This is done quite simply by including the root record in each retrieval:

```
GET FIRST bank, account
WHERE account.balance > 0;
WHILE DB_STATUS_OK
      PRINT account.accno ;
      PRINT bank.branchname;
      GET NEXT bank, account
      WHERE account.balance > 0;
END-WHILE
```

With this command, data will be displayed in bank account groups as each set of account records is stored 'under' its owning bank record.

If we wished to constrain the retrieval to the accounts for just one branch, we would use the GET NEXT WITHIN PARENT operator thus:

```
GET FIRST bank
WHERE bank.branchname = 'Crawley';
GET NEXT WITHIN PARENT account;
WHILE DB_STATUS_OK
    PRINT account.balance;
    GET NEXT WITHIN PARENT account;
END-WHILE
```

With this code, we initially set the database to point at the tree with 'Crawley' as its root. We now use the GET NEXT WITHIN PARENT to retrieve the next available record under that root. The DB_STATUS_FLAG now equates to false when there are no more records available within that tree, not within the database as a whole.

To display the details of the customers who own a particular account, we would start the search at a level lower. This command retrieves customer details for the account 678543:

```
GET FIRST account
WHERE account.accno = 678543;
GET NEXT WITHIN PARENT customer;
WHILE DB_STATUS_OK
    PRINT customer.name;
    GET NEXT WITHIN PARENT customer;
END-WHILE
```

6.3.2 Hierarchic data updating

To insert data into a hierarchic database, it is necessary to build a data record with the required values and then insert it under the required owner record. For instance, to insert a new account at the Crawley branch, we need to do the following:

```
account.accno = 929292;
account.balance = 0.00;
account.type = 'C';
INSERT account
WHERE bank.branchname = 'Crawley';
```

To enter a customer for this account, we would say:

```
customer.refno = 2394;
customer.name = 'LA Parath';
```

```
customer.address = 'Box 456, Kellysville';
customer.status = 'Business';
INSERT customer
WHERE account.accno = 929292;
```

Both of these INSERT operations would fail if there was no parent record with the existing search condition.

To update a record, we need to find the record to be updated and then change the relevant values. To change the address of a customer, we would say:

```
GET HOLD FIRST customer
WHERE refno = 2345;
customer.address = 'PO Box 457, Kellysville';
REPLACE;
```

We use GET HOLD FIRST rather than GET FIRST so that the database pointer remains at the record retrieved rather than at the start of the next record. The REPLACE command now causes a new record to be written into the position occupied by the old one.

To delete a record, we locate it and then simply give the DELETE command, for example:

```
GET HOLD FIRST customer
WHERE customer.refno = 2345;
DELETE;
```

This would simply delete the first customer with this reference number. If this customer was attached to many accounts and we wished to delete all record of their existence, we would need a loop:

```
GET HOLD FIRST customer
WHERE customer.refno = 2345;
WHILE DB_STATUS_OK
    DELETE;
    GET HOLD NEXT customer
    WHERE
    customer.refno = 2345;
END-WHILE
```

We have no requirement to use a loop for deleting child records. The command:

```
GET HOLD FIRST bank
WHERE branchname = 'Crawley';
DELETE;
```

will cause all accounts at that branch to be removed as well as details of all customers holding these accounts. Only details of customers holding accounts elsewhere will be retained.

6.4 Network databases

A major disadvantage of hierarchic databases is that they are only capable of representing 1–M relationships that emanate in a single line from a root record type. This means that they are extremely inflexible both in terms of the data models that they can represent and the data queries that can be conveniently formulated. Mainly in response to the perceived shortcomings of the hierarchic model, an alternative model (DBTG, 1971) was proposed and developed, originally termed the CODASYL model, but more informally known as the network model.

A network database consists primarily of a collection of record types. Record types are associated together by links. A link represents a 1–M relationship between a record of one type ('the owner') and a set of records of another type ('the members'). The major difference between hierarchic and network systems is that there is no constraint on the number and direction of links that may be established between record types. The need for a root record type is removed and record sets are free to participate in any number of 1–M relationships.

In Figure 6.5, we have a network database where BANK is participating in a 1–M relationship with ACCOUNT. This is indicated by the direction of the arrow from BANK to ACCOUNT. We also have an arrow going from CUSTOMER to REGISTRATION, indicating a 1–M relationship, and likewise from ACCOUNT to REGISTRATION. Note how each of these links is given a name. This is because links are in themselves a form of entity in a network database. Each time we associate, for instance, a set of accounts with a bank, we are creating an instance of the BANK-ACCOUNT link. No record may participate in more than one instance of a given link. Thus, the BANK-ACCOUNT link means that all accounts may only belong to one bank. We have no need of the foreign key concept in a network system. M–N relationships cannot be implemented directly using links. Instead, we have to have a record set that is owned by two other record sets. In Figure 6.5, if REGISTRATION did not already exist as a weak entity, we would have to 'invent' it as a record type that indirectly linked CUSTOMER and ACCOUNT together in an M–N relationship.

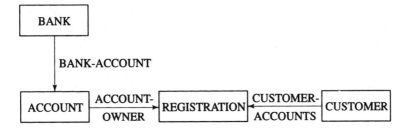

Figure 6.5 A simple network database.

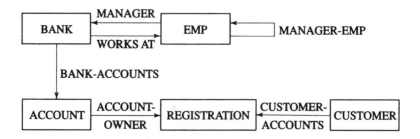

Figure 6.6 A network database with multiple link types.

Although record types are constrained to participating in just one instance of a given link, they may participate in more than one type of link. In Figure 6.6 we show BANK and EMP participating in two links: WORKS-AT and MANAGER. WORKS-AT associates each bank with a distinct set of employees. MANAGER associates an employee with a set of banks, meaning that in this database an employee may manage more than one bank.

In Figure 6.6, we have a link on EMP from itself labelled MANAGER-EMP. This indicates a link between one EMP and a set of EMPs reflecting a recursive relationship between a manager (who is an employee) and a set of employees. It is possible to implement most facets of standard E/R modelling on a network database. (In fact, in some respects, such as multi-valued attributes, it is easier to implement an E/R model in a network system than in a relational system.) In Figure 6.7, we demonstrate a network implementation of the relational data given in Chapter 5. Note how we have removed the duplication and redundancy of the hierarchic implementation.

6.5 Implementing a network schema

A network database schema consists of a series of record type declarations and set declarations that establish the links between between record types. The code segment given in Figure 6.8 is a pseudo-coded representation of a network schema of the system modelled in Figure 6.5 and populated with data in Figure 6.7. It is not representative of the language of any particular product.

The most important difference between this code and that used to implement the hierarchic system is the absence of any ownership references within the record declarations. Instead, we have 'set' declarations to represent the relationships between record types. The OWNER IS X MEMBER IS Y syntax establishes a 1–M relationship between X and Y which is physically implemented as a chain of connecting pointers between an owner record and its 'ownees'. The MANDATORY phrase indicates that every member type record must have an owner. Thus, in our schema, all accounts must belong to a branch.

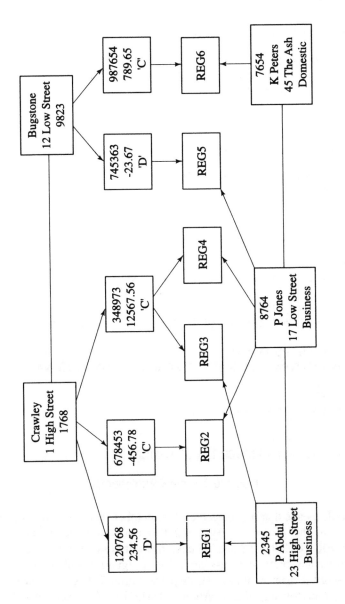

Figure 6.7 A network database example.

SCHEMANAME BANKSYSTEM.

RECORD BANK.
FLD BRANCHNAME   CHAR(20) DUPLICATES NOT ALLOWED.

FLD BANK-ADDRESS   CHAR(30).

RECORD ACCOUNT.
FLD ACCNO   INTEGER(6) DUPLICATES NOT ALLOWED.
FLD TYPE   CHAR(1).
FLD BALANCE   FLOAT(10.2).

RECORD CUSTOMER.
FLD REFNO   INTEGER(4) DUPLICATES NOT ALLOWED.
FLD NAME   CHAR(20).
FLD CUST-ADDRESS   CHAR(30).
FLD STATUS   CHAR(8).

RECORD REGISTRATION.
FLD DATE-ACCOUNT-OPENED   CHAR(6).

SET BANK-ACCOUNTS.
OWNER IS BANK MEMBER IS ACCOUNT MANDATORY AUTOMATIC.

SET ACCOUNT-OWNER.
OWNER IS ACCOUNT MEMBER IS REGISTRATION MANDATORY AUTOMATIC.

SET CUSTOMER-ACCOUNTS.
OWNER IS CUSTOMER MEMBER IS REGISTRATION OPTIONAL MANUAL.

SET BANK-FILE.
OWNER IS SYSTEM MEMBER IS BANK.

SET CUSTOMER-FILE.
OWNER IS SYSTEM MEMBER IS CUSTOMER.

Figure 6.8 A network schema.

OPTIONAL means that it is possible for a member record to exist that does not participate in the given set. By using this phrase on the definition for the CUSTOMER-ACCOUNTS set, we have made it possible for an account not to be owned by any particular customer. The designation MANUAL means that when a record is inserted into a set, its place within that set is controlled by the programmer performing the insertion. AUTOMATIC means that the system takes care of the insertion operation (see section 6.6.2 below).

Note the special sets BANK-FILE and CUSTOMER-FILE. These are both owned by SYSTEM. SYSTEM owned sets provide entry points to the database.

Any record type that is part of a SYSTEM-owned set must belong to it. Thus, the MANDATORY/OPTIONAL clause is redundant. All sets that are not SYSTEM owned can only be accessed via a SYSTEM-owned set (see section 6.6.1 below).

The designation of OPTIONAL and MANDATORY AUTOMATIC has implications for data integrity. When set membership is MANDATORY, then when the owner of a record set is removed, all of its members are removed. Thus, removing a branch of the bank in our schema will result in the removal of all of its accounts. Removal of a customer will not result in the disappearance of all registrations owned by a customer owing to the OPTIONAL membership of the CUSTOMER-ACCOUNTS set. Instead, the removal of all registrations owned by a deleted customer will have to be implemented by the database user.

6.6 Network data manipulation

The examples of code given in this section are purely 'pseudo-coded' program segments that are very loosely based on the original CODASYL definitions.

6.6.1 Network data retrieval

Network data retrieval operators work on a 'record at a time' basis. As with a hierarchic system, an operation has to be applied repetitively to retrieve a set of records. Network data retrieval operations are classically embedded within a host language that takes care of programming loops. As with our hierarchic examples, we shall informally use 'while' loops to demonstrate routines for retrieving sets of records.

The retrieval of data in a network system is best described as a process of navigation. The programmer has to be able to 'navigate' the database to the actual record that is required. This record will be within a set of records of the given type, and the process of navigation may require following ownership and membership links between different record sets and within a set of records. As stated above, network operations work on a 'record at a time' basis. Each time an operation is activated, the result is that, hopefully, one particular record is 'pointed at' within the database. The record currently pointed at is known as the 'current of run unit' (CRU). The process of retrieving a record consists of two stages:

1. Use the FIND operator to navigate the database to a particular record. The address of this record becomes the CRU.
2. Use the GET operator to retrieve the record located by the CRU.

The simplest form of retrieval is the location of a single record within a SYSTEM-owned set. For instance, to retrieve the name of a bank with a given address, we require the following routine:

```
BANK.ADDRESS : = '12 Low Street';
FIND ANY BANK USING ADDRESS;
IF DB_STATUS_OK
    GET BANK;
    PRINT BANK.BRANCHNAME
END-IF;
```

The FIND ANY operator locates the first record within the given set that satisfies the given constraint. A DB_STATUS flag is required in case the operation has failed to locate any such record, leaving the CRU in an undetermined state. If the CRU does have a determined state (that is, a record has been located), then the GET operator is activated to return the record located via the CRU.

The navigation above was straightforward. To locate a record within a set that is not SYSTEM owned is more problematic. The record set ACCOUNT is such an example. In order to get to a particular account in the schema described above, we must access it via its owning branch. The navigation is a two-stage process. We need to examine the set of banks and, for each bank, examine the set of accounts until we locate the required account. This may be encoded thus:

```
ACCOUNT.ACCNO = 678453;
FIND FIRST BANK WITHIN BANK-FILE;
WHILE DB_STATUS_OK
    FIND ANY ACCOUNT WITHIN BANK_ACCOUNTS USING
    ACCNO;
    IF DB_STATUS_OK
        GET ACCOUNT;
        PRINT ACCOUNT.BALANCE, ACCOUNT.TYPE;
        EXIT
    END-IF;
    FIND NEXT BANK WITHIN BANK-FILE
END-WHILE
```

In this program, we start by setting a search value (ACCOUNT.ACCNO = 678453). We then proceed to examine the set of BANK records with the command FIND FIRST WITHIN BANK-FILE. The FIND FIRST operator locates the CRU at the first record within a given set. Here we make reference to the set BANK-FILE, the SYSTEM-owned set of bank records.

Having set the CRU to the first bank, we then use a loop to examine all accounts within all banks until the required account is located. We do this firstly by using the FIND ANY ... WITHIN operator. This is used for examining a given set of records.

When the CRU is set, not only do we get the address of the most recently located record, but we also get the start addresses of any record sets that it participates in as the owner. Thus, when the first bank is retrieved, we also retrieve the start point of the set of accounts that it owns. The FIND ANY ACCOUNT WITHIN BANK-ACCOUNTS operation will retrieve the set of accounts associated with that bank and find any within the given account number. If that account is found, then it is returned and the program is exited.

If no such account is found within the set of accounts for a bank, then the FIND NEXT WITHIN BANK-FILE operation is activated. There is a slight problem here in that the CRU at this point will be addressing the last record in the set of accounts for the previous bank. The address of the previous bank will have been overwritten. Network systems get around this by keeping a copy of the address of the most recently located record for each currently active set. Thus, the FIND NEXT WITHIN BANK-FILE will retrieve the address of the most recently retrieved BANK, overwrite the CRU with this value and then, from this, locate the next bank record within the BANK-FILE set.

Thus, in order to implement the navigation process, a network system not only needs to maintain a CRU that points to the currently located record, but must also maintain a 'currency indicator' for each active set that stores the address of the most recently located record in that set.

The above command uses a loop, though it still only retrieves one record. Retrieval of a set of records requires a similar set of operations. Here we will print branch and account details for all accounts with no money:

```
ACCOUNT.BALANCE : = 0.00
FIND FIRST BANK WITHIN BANK-FILE;
WHILE DB_STATUS_OK
   GET BANK
   FIND FIRST WITHIN BANK-ACCOUNTS USING BALANCE;
   WHILE DB_STATUS_OK
      GET ACCOUNT
      PRINT ACCOUNT.NUMBER
      PRINT BANK.BRANCHNAME
      FIND NEXT ACCOUNT WITHIN BANK-ACCOUNTS USING
      BALANCE
   END-WHILE
   FIND NEXT BANK WITHIN BANK-FILE
END-WHILE;
```

Here we have two loops which cause every account within every bank to be examined for a zero balance. In the outer loop, we use GET BANK to retrieve the details of each bank. This effectively saves the details of a bank in memory while we examine its set of accounts. In the inner loop, we use GET ACCOUNT to retrieve details of each account with a zero balance. Note how we retrieve the set of such accounts for each bank by finding its first such account. If we find an account, we then enter a loop finding all remaining accounts within that bank that satisfy the condition. Having done this, we are then back into the outer loop. Here we overwrite the CRU with the currency indicator for the BANK-FILE set and find the next bank.

The FIND FIRST ... WITHIN operator moves from an owner record to the first member of its owned set. We may wish to move from a set member to its owner. To retrieve details of the customers who own an account, we need to move from that account to its set of registration records and then from each of these registration records, to the customer that owns it. This is done using the FIND OWNER operator as follows:

```
ACCOUNT.ACCNO = 678453;
FIND FIRST BANK WITHIN BANK-FILE;
WHILE DB_STATUS_OK
    FIND ANY ACCOUNT WITHIN BANK_ACCOUNTS USING
    ACCNO;
    IF DB_STATUS_OK
        FIND FIRST REGISTRATION WITHIN ACCOUNT_OWNER
        WHILE DB_STATUS_OK
        FIND OWNER WITHIN CUSTOMER-ACCOUNTS
        GET CUSTOMER
        PRINT CUSTOMER.NAME
        FIND NEXT REGISTRATION WITHIN ACCOUNT-OWNER
        END-WHILE
            EXIT
    END-IF;
    FIND NEXT BANK WITHIN BANK-FILE
END-WHILE
```

As in the previous query, we find the members of a set by finding its first member and then entering a loop to find any remaining members. This time we have two loops, the outer one to retrieve a particular account within the bank system and the inner one to retrieve its set of registrations. For each registration, the FIND OWNER WITHIN CUSTOMER-ACCOUNTS operation will locate its owning customer.

6.6.2 Network updating

The updating of data in a network database requires a record to be built and then navigation to the point where the update must take place.

With SYSTEM-owned sets, this is relatively straightforward. For instance, to create a new customer record, we can simply say:

```
CUSTOMER.NAME : = 'K Chan';
CUSTOMER.ADDRESS : = '57, Peterlee Road';
```

```
CUSTOMER.REFNO : = '9182';
CUSTOMER.STATUS : = 'Domestic';
STORE CUSTOMER;
```

The STORE operator automatically causes the insertion of the given customer into the SYSTEM-owned set CUSTOMER-FILE. Navigation as such is not necessary here. To change the details of a customer, some navigation is required. For instance, the alteration of a customer's address would require the following:

```
CUSTOMER.NAME = 'P Jones'
FIND FOR UPDATE ANY CUSTOMER WITHIN CUSTOMER-FILE
USING NAME;
GET CUSTOMER;
CUSTOMER.ADDRESS : = '23, Pipe Hayes';
MODIFY CUSTOMER;
```

Here we locate a particular customer, get the record, overwrite part of it with a new value and then use the MODIFY operator to write it back in the position indicated by the CRU.

The insertion and updating of records within non-SYSTEM-owned sets is more problematic. This is because we need to navigate to the appropriate point of update. Also, we may need to use CONNECT and RECONNECT operators to insert records into a set and remove them from a set.

To create a new account, we need to find the set of accounts belonging to a branch and then insert it into that set thus:

```
BANK.BRANCHNAME : = 'Crawley';
ACCOUNT.ACCNO : = 929292;
ACCOUNT.BALANCE : = 0.00;
ACCOUNT.TYPE : = 'C';
FIND ANY BANK WITHIN BANK-FILE USING BRANCHNAME;
IF DB_STATUS_OK
    FIND LAST WITHIN BANK-ACCOUNTS;
    STORE ACCOUNT
END-IF;
```

With this command, we set the CRU to point at the last record in the set of accounts for a bank and store it at that point. All accounts must belong to a bank, membership of the BANK-ACCOUNTS set being MANDATORY AUTOMATIC. When this is the case, the STORE operator will automatically connect a member to its ownership set. This account should also have at least one owning customer. An account is connected to a customer via a registration link. We need to create a registration and STORE it. This will automatically connect it to its owning account. Membership of a CUSTOMER-ACCOUNTS set is OPTIONAL MANUAL. This means that when a registration is created, it will not be automatically connected to a customer. Instead, we will need to connect it explicitly using the CONNECT operator:

```
BANK.BRANCHNAME : = 'Crawley';
ACCOUNT.ACCNO : = 929292;
ACCOUNT.BALANCE : = 0.00;
ACCOUNT.TYPE : = 'C';
REGISTRATION.DATE : = '01-JAN-97';
CUSTOMER.REFNO : = 2309;
CUSTOMER.NAME : = 'LA Parath';
CUSTOMER.ADDRESS : = 'Box 456, Kellysville';
CUSTOMER.STATUS : = 'Business';
STORE CUSTOMER;
FIND ANY BANK WITHIN BANK-FILE USING BRANCHNAME;
IF DB_STATUS_OK
      FIND LAST WITHIN BANK-ACCOUNTS;
      STORE ACCOUNT;
      STORE REGISTRATION;
      CONNECT REGISTRATION TO CUSTOMER-ACCOUNTS;
END-IF;
```

In the above example, the CONNECT command connects a record to a set. The owner of that set is the one located by the currency indicator for the owner record type. The owner record type for CUSTOMER-ACCOUNTS is CUSTOMER. Its currency indicator will be pointing at the record inserted by the STORE CUSTOMER command issued before the account and its registration were stored.

If we wished to change the owner of an account, we need to locate its registration via its owning customer, DISCONNECT it from the set of CUSTOMER-ACCOUNTS owned by that customer and reconnect it to a different set. The following code moves account number 929292 from customer 2309 to customer 2345:

```
CUSTOMER.REFNO : = 2309;
FIND ANY CUSTOMER WITHIN CUSTOMER-FILE USING REFNO;
IF DB_STATUS_OK
      FIND FIRST REGISTRATION WITHIN CUSTOMER-ACCOUNTS;
      WHILE DB_STATUS-OK
            FIND OWNER WITHIN ACCOUNT-OWNER;
            GET ACCOUNT
            IF ACCOUNT.ACCNO = 929292
                  DISCONNECT REGISTRATION FROM CUSTOMER-
                  ACCOUNTS;
                  CUSTOMER.REFNO : = 2345;
                  FIND ANY CUSTOMER WITHIN CUSTOMER-FILE
                  USING REFNO;
```

```
        IF DB_STATUS_OK
            CONNECT   REGISTRATION   TO   CUSTOMER-
            ACCOUNTS
        END-IF;
        EXIT;
        END-IF;
        FIND  NEXT  REGISTRATION  WITHIN  CUSTOMER-
        ACCOUNTS;
    END-WHILE;
END-IF;
```

With this code, we locate customer 2309 and from there we locate the first registration owned by that customer. We scan the customer's set of registrations, using FIND OWNER to retrieve the details of the account to which each registration is applied. If we find the account with the relevant account number (929292), we disconnect its registration from its current CUSTOMER-ACCOUNTS set, thus removing its link to the given customer. We then locate customer 2345, thus resetting the currency indicator for the customer record type. The CONNECT command will now connect the registration to the set of records owned by the newly located customer.

Deleting a record is performed using the ERASE operator:

```
CUSTOMER.NAME = 'P Jones'
FIND FOR UPDATE ANY CUSTOMER WITHIN CUSTOMER-FILE
USING NAME;
ERASE CUSTOMER;
```

This will only delete the first customer found with this name. If we wished to delete all customers with this name, we require a loop:

```
CUSTOMER.NAME = 'P Jones'
FIND FOR UPDATE FIRST CUSTOMER WITHIN CUSTOMER-FILE
USING NAME;
WHILE DB_STATUS_OK
    ERASE CUSTOMER;
    FIND FOR UPDATE NEXT WITHIN CUSTOMER-FILE USING
    NAME
END-WHILE;
```

Each of these examples will only succeed if the given customers did not currently own any registrations. ERASE needs to be qualified in order to specify what should be done in the case of a record that 'owns' other records:

ERASE PERMANENT: deletes a record along with all records that belong
    to sets that it owns whose membership is MANDATORY. Members of
    sets that it owns whose membership is OPTIONAL are disconnected but
    not deleted.

ERASE SELECTIVE: deletes a record, all records in sets that it owns whose membership is MANDATORY and all records in sets that it owns whose membership is OPTIONAL and which do not participate in any other sets.

ERASE ALL: deletes a record along with all records in all sets that it owns, regardless of whether membership is OPTIONAL or MANDATORY.

Summary

- Hierarchic and network databases implement a database as a collection of record types associated together in a series of 1–M relationships.
- In a hierarchic system, the terminology 'parent' and 'child' is used to describe the 1–M tie between record types.
- In a hierarchic system, there exists one root record type. All other record types must have exactly one parent and must be linked either directly or indirectly to the root record type.
- In a network system, 1–M relationships are characterized by sets which connect an 'owner' with its 'members'. There is no restriction on the number of set connections that may be established between and within record types.
- In a network system, record types that are the approximate equivalent of weak entities may be established to represent M–N relationships between record types.
- Hierarchic and network systems both manipulate data on a 'record at a time' basis. Hierarchic operations are characterized by tree handling, network operations are typically navigational in character.

Exercises

Here is a restatement of the EverCare County General Hospital scenario:

At the EverCare County General Hospital, patients are admitted and given a unique Patient Id. We record their name, home address and date of admission. They are assigned to a ward and to a consultant. They may then be diagnosed a set of conditions. Whilst in our care, they will receive a set of treatments. Each treatment will have a date and details of the nurse administering the treatment, the drug being administered and the dosage. Drugs have a unique Drug Id, a name and a recommended dosage (which may not be the same as the dosage given in individual treatments). Nurses have a Nurse Id and a name and are assigned to a ward. Each ward has a Sister (who is a nurse). Consultants have a Doctor Id and a name.

1 Using this and the E/R diagram that you drew for Exercise 1(a) in Chapter 2, draw a diagram of record sets and links to show how this would be represented as a network database.

2 Write a network database schema to implement your answer to quesiton 1 above.

3 Write commands based on your schema to:
   (a) Find the name of the patient with ID '12345';
   (b) List the conditions diagnosed for patient '12345';
   (c) Find the names of patients assigned to the consultant with the name 'Dr Fleischman';
   (d) Find the names of all drugs administered to patients assigned to 'Dr Fleischman'.

4 (a) What difficulties would be encountered if we tried to implement this as a hierarchic database?
   (b) What artificial restrictions would have to be imposed in order that the above scenario might be implemented as a hierarchic database? Using these restrictions, show how the queries for question 3 above might be implemented in a hierarchic system.

Further reading

Elmasri and Navathe (1994) Chapters 10 and 11
Hawryszkiewycz (1991) Chapters 13 and 14
Kroenke (1995) Chapters 13 and 14
Ozkarahan (1990) Chapters 3 and 4

CHAPTER 7

Object-oriented databases

Object oriented database systems currently only have a minor presence in the world of 'live' database systems. However, this is likely to change radically within the next few years. The majority of the database research effort now is in the object-oriented field and there is a major growth in the types of database application that would benefit most from the use of object-oriented techniques.

In this chapter, we shall explain the motivation behind the development of object-oriented database technology, provide a definition of what an object-oriented database is and present examples of how one can be designed and implemented.

At the end of this chapter, the reader should be able to:

1. List the main benefits and drawbacks of object-oriented databases.
2. Define the main characteristics of an object-oriented database system.
3. Outline the main stages in designing and implementing a simple object-oriented database.

7.1 The motivation behind object-oriented database systems

The database examples given up to this point in the text are all drawn from the field of traditional 'data processing'. A data processing application is characterized by the use of files of data that are manipulated to meet a given set of requirements. The hierarchic, network and relational technologies all represent different approaches to the integration of what are, in essence, simple files of data to satisfy a mix of applications. The elegance and power of relational systems have rendered them predominant in the database field. However, the increasing sophistication of the types of data that are now stored on and manipulated by computer systems tends to highlight the limitations of relational technology. These can be summarized as follows:

1. Semantic range. Relational theory only supports a small set of semantic concepts. Many of the semantic notions outlined in Chapter 2 are not supported at all in the relational model, meaning that there is a very

wide range of types of information that cannot be meaningfully represented in a relational database.

2. Data structures. Relational systems are very limited in terms of their data structures. In a relational system, all data is held in relations composed of simple attributes. There are many types of information that are not conveniently represented in such a way.

3. Passive data. The data in a relational system is, in most respects, passive. Application programs are required in order that the data is given some sort of active meaning. As we shall see, in an object-oriented database, it is possible to capture the idea of how data 'behaves' as well as its structure.

4. Semantic integrity. This can be defined as 'the preservation and consistency of database semantics across different applications'. In a relational system, the behaviour of the data is governed by its use in application programs. The same data may behave differently, and thus acquire a different meaning, according to the application that is using it, thus depriving it of any consistent meaning. The types of situation where relational databases are perceived to be weak are those where the data objects are complex and require a large amount of semantic information to be encapsulated within them. Typical application areas include:

   (a) Multimedia databases which require the storage of segments of sound, pictures and text and the ability to associate them together in a consistent manner.

   (b) Geographic information systems which require the storage of different types of mapping and statistical data which may be subdivided into and collated from overlapping regions.

   (c) Design databases which store diagrams and data regarding complex components which may be associated together into further complex components. A given design may itself mutate through various versions and stages.

It is possible to implement such systems using relational techniques. However, the result is often something that is not a very 'natural' or effective representation of the user requirements. Take, for instance, a simple design database consisting of diagrams that may be associated together into more complex diagrams. Suppose we had a data type ('Graphic') that provided the required primitives for storing, manipulating and retrieving a simple diagram. As a starting point, we might implement a table with three attributes: DiagramID (the primary key), Creation_Date and Drawing (with the data type 'Graphic') (Table 7.1).

We could use a graphics package to draw some simple diagrams and store them in this table with the DiagramIDs '1', '2', '3' and '4'. We could, in theory, then use the same package to retrieve some of these diagrams to create

Table 7.1 A relational table for storing diagrams

```
Diagrams
- - - - - - - - - - - - - - - - - - - - - - - - - - - - - - - - - - - - - -
| DiagramID   | Creation_Date   | Drawing |
- - - - - - - - - - - - - - - - - - - - - - - - - - - - - - - - - - - - - -
```

a new diagram and save this with a new `DiagramID` ('5'). However, some important information would be lost using this schema, namely that diagram 5 is composed of, say, diagrams 1, 2 and 3. Also, what if diagrams 1 and 2 have certain characteristics in common, for instance that they are both triangles? Again, this would not be captured in our schema. Clearly, we need to extend our database design.

One area into which we need to extend our design is that of subtyping. We can retain our original table to represent a diagram 'supertype' and then have additional tables for each different type of diagram stored. Thus there will be a table for triangles, a table for squares, a table for rectangles and so on, each with `DiagramID` as the primary key and extra attributes for anything that is particular to that type of diagram (Table 7.2). With a one-level subtyping, there is no real problem. However, with a multi-level subtyping chain such as a square IS-A rectangle IS-A diagram, we need to perform a three-table join to retrieve all of the information about one particular diagram.

Table 7.2 Diagrams database with subtyping

```
Diagrams
- - - - - - - - - - - - - - - - - - - - - - - - - - - - - - - - - - - - - -
| DiagramID   | Creation_Date   | Drawing |
- - - - - - - - - - - - - - - - - - - - - - - - - - - - - - - - - - - - - -

Triangles
- - - - - - - - - - - - - - - - - - - - - - - - - - - - - - - - - - - - - - - - - - -
| DiagramID   | Base_Length   | Angle1   | Angle2 |
- - - - - - - - - - - - - - - - - - - - - - - - - - - - - - - - - - - - - - - - - - -

Equilaterals
- - - - - - - - - - - - - - - - - - - - - - - - - -
| DiagramID   | Base_Length |
- - - - - - - - - - - - - - - - - - - - - - - - - -

Rectangles
- - - - - - - - - - - - - - - - - - - - - - - - - - - - - - - - - - - - -
| DiagramID   | Base_Length   | Side_Length |
- - - - - - - - - - - - - - - - - - - - - - - - - - - - - - - - - - - - -

Squares
- - - - - - - - - - - - - - - - - - - - - - - - - -
| DiagramID   | Base_Length |
- - - - - - - - - - - - - - - - - - - - - - - - - -
```

```
Function Area (N : Base_Length);
Begin
        Return N * N
End;
```

Figure 7.1 A function to return the area of a square.

Our design in Table 7.2 is still very weak in terms of semantics. There is nothing in it that makes explicit the fact that square is a subtype of rectangle which is a subtype of diagram and so on. There is therefore nothing to stop application programmers from treating them as if they were entirely unrelated. Moreover, we cannot prevent an application programmer from treating them in an 'incorrect' manner. Suppose we wished to calculate the area of a square. This is performed quite simply by taking the Base_Length and squaring it. A function 'Area' could be coded as in Figure 7.1, taking a parameter of type 'Base_Length'. There is nothing to stop this function being used to calculate the area of a triangle, which would be quite inappropriate.

Another area into which we would need to extend our design is that of 'complex' diagrams – diagrams that are composed of other diagrams. We could have a table for a general subtype 'Complex' which has DiagramID as the primary key and then a series of non-key attributes (Diagram_1, Diagram_2, Diagram_3, etc.) which are foreign keys to the DiagramIDs for those diagrams of which the complex diagram is composed. The problem with this is that we would not know how many of these non-key attributes to assign to this table. A more sensible mechanism would be that each time we create a new type of complex diagram, we also create a new table with a fixed number of attributes representing foreign keys to the diagrams of which it is composed. We can then store multiple instances of this new type of diagram (Table 7.3).

There is still a lot of semantic information missing here. Although we can now capture the idea of a diagram associating together a series of other diagrams, we are not necessarily capturing the manner in which they are associated together. Complex_Diagram_Type_1 may consist of a circle, a square and a triangle. This is simply not represented in our schema. It becomes the responsibility of the applications programmer to enforce this, which cannot

Table 7.3 Complex diagrams of differing types

```
Complex_Diagram_Type_1 (composed of 3 diagrams)
------------------------------------------------------------
| DiagramID | Diagram_ID_1 | Diagram_ID_2 | Diagram_ID_3 |
------------------------------------------------------------
Complex_Diagram_Type_2 (composed of 2 diagrams)
--------------------------------------------------
| DiagramID | Diagram_ID_1 | Diagram_ID_2 |
--------------------------------------------------
```

be guaranteed. Moreover, different types of diagram are characterized not just by their attributes but also by the operations that can be performed on them. A complex diagram would require a 'decompose' operation which would differ according to the complexity of the diagram. As in the example above, an 'area' operation on a triangle would be different to that on a square.

We see that the implementation of a simple database that is outside the field of traditional data processing can cause problems using relational techniques. Proposals have been made to extend relational technology to address such problems, for example:

1. The introduction of explicit subtyping and supertyping (e.g. table_1 IS-A table_2 and so on).
2. Abstract data typing. The relational model supports the concept of user-defined domains and functions. This can be easily extended to encompass the concept of abstract data typing. One could, for example, create and abstract data type 'Circle' and define functions (e.g. 'Area', 'Radius', 'Circumference') that could be applied to values of this type. We can then have tables that use attributes of this type. The correct behaviour of values assigned to such attributes is guaranteed as the only operations which may be performed on them are those supplied with their abstract data type.
3. The relaxation of normal form to allow nested relations. Attributes could be of type 'Relation', allowing tables of values to be stored within tables. By this mechanism, sets of values can be assigned to individual attributes. In our example above, we could have a single attribute of type 'Relation' to record the set of `DiagramIDs` that comprise a complex diagram. This does require an extension to the relational algebra.

Object-oriented databases are an alternative, though not necessarily conflicting, means of addressing such difficulties.

7.2 Object-oriented concepts

7.2.1 What is an object?

The concept of an object comes from the field of object-oriented programming (OOP). In an OOP environment, the 'world' consists of objects. An object has the following characteristics:

1. It has a unique, unchanging identity.
2. It belongs to a class.
3. It may send messages to other objects.
4. It has an internal state.

Take, for instance, two objects called 'J Smith' and 'M Abdullah'. In order for them to exist, they must belong to a class. Let us say that they both belong to a class 'Person'. These two objects may communicate through messages. Messages take the form of operations that are applied to objects (strictly speaking, 'Methods'). Suppose we had a method 'Spouse' which, when applied to a person, yields the person to whom they are married. If these two people are not married, then the 'Spouse' method applied to either of these objects would yield an empty value. However, we could have a 'Marry' method which could be used by one Person object to marry themselves to another. If we were to apply the 'Marry' method to 'J Smith' with the object value 'M Abdullah' (i.e. in OOP terms, send a message from Abdullah to Smith that they are 'Marry'ing them), this should have the effect of changing the internal state of both objects (resetting their marital status). The application of the 'Spouse' method should now return the name of the Person object to which they are married. Moreover, a further attempt to apply the 'Marry' method should now fail.

The behaviour and structure of an object in an OOP environment is determined entirely by its class. Class is such a fundamental concept that we shall examine it further.

7.2.2 Object classes

An object class has an interface and a private area.

The interface of an object is that which is visible to other objects. It consists of two parts:

1. Class properties. To a very limited extent, these are analogous to the attributes of a relation, for example a person has a name, address, telephone number, marital status and so on. However, they can also include things like explicit links to other objects, or they could even be virtual properties (e.g. 'Age' being derived from 'Date_of_Birth'). There is no limitation placed on how properties may be structured or associated together. Properties may in themselves be objects, allowing for the building of composite objects. The property values of an object cannot be manipulated directly. They can only be accessed via the methods associated with its class.
2. Class methods. Messages are passed to an object class via its methods of its class. These usually take the form of operations and functions which may be parameterized. Objects in a given class may only be accessed or operated on via its methods. At the interface level, all that is visible is the name of each method and its required parameters.

The private area is that part of the class definition which is not visible to other objects. It contains the code that makes the methods work. It may contain additional structural details of the object class that are deliberately shielded. For instance, a property may be presented in the class interface as a set of values.

This may be privately encoded as a stack, a queue, a tree and so on. There may exist extra properties with hidden values. There may also be hidden links and messages to other objects. This shielding of information about the internal workings and values of an object is known as 'information hiding'. An object user is only given details of how to use an object through its methods. How it actually works is completely and deliberately hidden from that user.

· An important OOP concept is that of 'encapsulation'. Briefly, this means that everything about an object is encapsulated within its class definition. It can only be accessed through its interface and its behaviour is entirely defined by its class.

7.2.3 Instantiation

Instantiation is the process by which objects in an object-oriented environment come into existence. Each object is an instance of a class. To make an object exist, we must generate an instance of ('instantiate') a given class.

7.2.4 Inheritance

This is a very important OOP concept. It is somewhat analogous to subtyping and supertyping. We can say that an object class is 'inherited from' another object class. For instance, we may define the classes 'Male' and 'Female' as inherited from 'Person'. This means that everything that characterizes the Person class also exists in the Male and Female classes; thus they have a common set of properties and methods. We may add further properties and methods to these classes that extend their definition beyond that of a person. We can also 'overload' 'person' methods. For instance, the 'Marry' method on the class 'Female' may be rewritten to assign a married surname and a maiden name.

Multiple inheritance is where a class inherits from more than one class, for example a 'Technical Manager' inheriting from the classes 'Technician' and 'Manager'.

Moving on from this brief overview of the object-oriented paradigm, we shall examine what is meant by the term 'object-oriented database'.

7.3 What is an object-oriented database?

An object-oriented database management system (OODBMS) is a database system that allows objects to be stored and shared between different applications.

This is a significant extension of the usual implementation of the OOP paradigm where objects are effectively program variables that only exist during the lifetime of the program that creates and uses them. In an object-oriented database system, objects may be 'persistent'. By 'persistent', we mean that an object has a life that extends beyond the program that creates it. Other programs may retrieve and use such objects and even destroy them. An object-oriented database system must minimally have the following features:

1. A database language that enables the declaration of object classes as described above and the subsequent creation, storage, retrieval and deletion of objects.

2. An object store that may be accessed by different applications. In order that stored objects may be uniquely identified, every object in the object store must have an object identifier (OID). This is different to the primary key concept in relational databases. A primary key is a collection of attributes that uniquely identify a tuple. A primary key value may change (e.g. an employee changing his or her EMPNO). In an object-oriented system, the OID is typically a 64- or 128-bit string that never changes once assigned to an object. An object may still have a set of properties that behave like a primary key in a relational database. This depends entirely on how its class is defined. The handling of OIDs is entirely governed by the OODBMS. The OODBMS relates objects to OIDs and is responsible for their storage and retrieval.

   The object store is the data repository on which an object-oriented database is built. An OODBMS must provide the standard DBMS facilities such as concurrency, transaction control, security, data integrity and so on. In particular, as with a standard DBMS, the object store must only be accessible via the OODBMS software.

There still exists much confusion over what exactly an object-oriented database is or should be and how it is best implemented. This partly reflects the ongoing debate about the precise meaning of the object oriented paradigm itself. When applied to database systems, the implications of the paradigm become increasingly open to differing interpretations. In order to bring some sort of ordered framework to the field, a number of initiatives have been instigated, the main one being ODMG-93 (Cattell 1993). ODMG-93, in outline, takes an OOP environment based on C++ and recommends how it can be extended to support an object-oriented database. In parallel, SQL is currently undergoing revision in order, amongst other things, that object-oriented features may be added to the language. These two strands of development summarize the two general approaches to implementation that have been pursued to date:

1. Take an OOP language (e.g. C++) and extend it with controlled object persistence.

2. Take a relational system and add object-oriented features, including an extended form of SQL.

These two strands are coming together. ODMG-93 includes an object query language that is SQL-like. Proposals exist for a form of object SQL that can be embedded in a C++ environment (Blakely 1995) and there do already exist commercial C++ object-oriented database systems that have an OSQL dialect included. For simplicity, we shall present the two approaches to implementation separately within this chapter.

In order that we can examine the implementation of an object-oriented database, we shall first present an example of how an object-oriented system can be designed.

7.4 Object-oriented database design

As explained above, an object-oriented database consists of objects, all of which must belong to a class. In order to build a conceptual model of an object-oriented database, we must identify its set of classes.

In order to identify an object class, we must determine its properties and its methods. We must also identify its interaction with other objects. The concept of an object class is similar in many ways to the concept of a 'type' as described in Chapter 2. The semantic modelling concepts of generalization, specialization and aggregation as described in that chapter are especially useful in the design of an object-oriented database. The starting point, however, is the process of classification.

7.4.1 Classification

The process of classification is concerned with the identification of objects with similar properties and behaviour and the grouping of such objects into classes. With the diagrams database above, we started by identifying objects called diagrams which all have a date of creation and a drawing. Common operations would be processes such as 'Store', 'Retrieve', 'Amend_Drawing' and so on. From this we can build a simple Class interface definition (Figure 7.2).

In Figure 7.2, we have a pseudo-coded class interface definition. Under 'properties', we have a simple list of fields and data types applicable to all diagrams. We then have a list of methods. Each method has a name and a parameter list. Note how we have the methods 'New' and 'Delete'. These, or their equivalent, are required by all object classes in an object-oriented database. They are what are known as constructor and destructor operations. A constructor instantiates an object and a destructor destroys an object instance. In this example, 'New( )' is used to create an instance of a Diagram object. Separate from 'New( )', we have the method 'Store( )'. This takes an existing Diagram object and stores it in the database. The 'Retrieve( )' method is what is known as an accessor operation. This takes a 'DiagramID' as an argument and returns any stored diagram type object with that ID. 'Drawing' is also an

Class Diagram

properties:
>   DiagramID : integer;
>   Date_of_Creation : Date;
>   Drawing : Graphic;

methods:
New( );
Store( );
Retrieve(DiagramID : integer) : Diagram;
Retrieve_Drawing( ) : Graphic;
Delete( );
Amend_Drawing(New_Drawing : Graphic);

end Diagram.

Figure 7.2 A simple class interface definition.

accessor that returns a graphic representing the Drawing property. We have no argument for this operation, meaning that we simply call it using a diagram type object. 'Amend_Drawing' is a transformer operation, allowing us to change the drawing associated with a diagram type object.

All object class interface definitions must include constructor and destructor operations and should include accessor and transformer operations for all of their properties.

The process of classification can quickly yield objects that may have certain properties and methods in common, but some which are distinct. This is where the concepts of generalization and specialization become useful.

7.4.2 Generalization and specialization

Generalization is the process by which we identify object classes with similar properties and from these similarities abstract a superclass. With our diagrams database, we might have started by identifying classes for triangles, squares, rectangles and circles and from these abstracting a diagram superclass consisting of those properties common to all diagrams.

Specialization is the converse of generalization. Starting with 'Diagram' as a superclass, we may then identify subclasses for different types of diagram, each sharing the common properties and methods of a diagram but having additional properties and/or methods that are unique to each class.

Whichever process we use, the result is a generalization hierarchy as shown in Figure 7.3. Such a hierarchy is highly significant in an object-oriented database as it indicates an inheritance chain. When declaring such classes, we

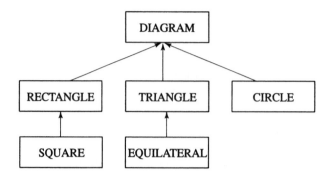

Figure 7.3 A simple generalization hierarchy.

must make their participation in the inheritance chain explicit as in Figure 7.4.

These two class definitions both contain a reference to a superclass using an 'inherit' statement. The class 'Triangle' inherits all the properties and methods of a diagram. Additional properties are declared. The 'New' method is

```
Class Triangle

inherit Diagram

properties:
     Base_Length : Real;
     Angle_1 : Real;
     Angle_2 : Real;

methods:
     New( );
     Area(Base_Length, Angle_1, Angle_2) : Real;

end Triangle.

Class Equilateral

inherit Triangle

methods:
     New( );
     Area(Base_Length) : Real;

end Equilateral.
```

Figure 7.4 Class definitions in an inheritance chain.

redeclared as it would now need to take account of the additional properties 'Base_Length', 'Angle_1' and 'Angle_2'. An additional method 'Area' is declared for returning the area of a triangle. The class 'Equilateral' is declared as inheriting from 'Triangle'. This means that it inherits the properties and methods of 'Triangle' and also the properties and methods of everything that 'Triangle' inherits from 'Diagram'. There are no additional properties. The method 'New( )' is again redefined. This is because there is no need to take account of the angles of an equilateral triangle (they are all the same), unlike with a standard triangle. The 'Area' method is similarly redefined as only the Base_Length property is required for calculating the area of an equilateral triangle.

7.4.3 Aggregation

Aggregation is the process whereby object classes may be associated together to form an 'Aggregate' class. Take, for instance, our bank database consisting of customers, accounts and branches and the relationships between them. When implementing this using relational techniques, we created separate relations for each entity and we used foreign keys to represent 1–M relationships. We also had to implement a separate relation using foreign keys to represent the M–N relationship between CUSTOMER and ACCOUNT. To build a view of all the details relating to a given account we must join the four base tables. An object-oriented database would allow us to encapsulate this within a single aggregate object class. We could create a class 'Registration' (Figure 7.5) which explicitly associates together the customer, account and branch type objects. Each Registration object will associate a customer with an account, with an extra property indicating the date when this registration was made.

The pseudo object code for creating this class is given in Figure 7.6.

Aggregate object classes are also useful for modelling the IS-PART-OF semantic as described in Chapter 2. This is where we can have an object that is actually 'composed of' objects, for example a car being composed of an engine, a gearbox, a set of wheels and so on. This is sometimes referred to as a composite object. This is slightly different to the associative semantic where

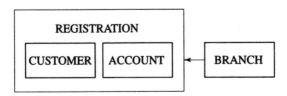

Figure 7.5 An aggregate object.

Class Registration

properties:
Customer_Owner : Customer;
Registered_Account : Account;
Date_of_Registration : Date;

methods:
New( );
Store( );
Retrieve_Branch_Details( ) : Branch;
Retrieve_Customer_Details( ) : Customer;
Retrieve_Account_Details( ) : Account;
Delete( );

Figure 7.6 Implementing an aggregate object.

we create an object class that represents the association of otherwise independent objects. In an object-oriented database, this subtle differentiation can be lost.

7.4.4 Object-oriented data modelling summary

The derivation of an object-oriented database schema relies on the processes of classification, generalization, specialization and aggregation. Though presented here serially, they can take place in parallel. In this chapter, we have not presented a transformation algorithm for deriving an object-oriented database from an E/R model as there is no straightforward analogy between entities and relationships on the one hand and object classes on the other. Moreover, E/R modelling is almost entirely data oriented and tells us nothing about the behaviour of entities beyond the cardinalities of the relationships in which they participate. A more straightforward transformation can be made using the semantic object modelling techniques described in Chapter 2.

The transformation of a semantic object model into an object-oriented database is as follows:

1. For each semantic object, create an object class.
2. Where a parent/subtype relationship is identified between two semantic objects, implement an inheritance connection between the object class representing the subtype and the object class representing the parent.
3. Implement aggregate and association type semantic objects as aggregate object classes.
4. Maintain the integrity of cardinalities between semantic objects, the grouping of semantic objects and disjoint subtyping using methods.

Semantic object modelling remains more of a data-structure-oriented rather than a behaviour-oriented technique. A full object-oriented schema requires data behaviour to be identified in order that methods may be specified. The addition of methods to object classes from a semantic model may cause further refinement to the class design. Classes that have common properties and methods may be abstracted together into superclasses with associated inheritance chains.

Having built our data model of object classes, we then need to implement this. As explained in section 7.3 above, there are two basic approaches: use an object-oriented programming language such as C++ that has been extended with persistence, or use a form of SQL that has been extended with object-oriented features.

7.5 Implementation of an object-oriented database

In this section, we shall demonstrate the implementation of part of our banking database using object-oriented techniques. The design for this database will be based on the semantic object diagrams that model the banking database in Chapter 2. These show some basic semantic objects (BRANCH, ACCOUNT, CUSTOMER and EMP), an associative object REGISTRATION that associates customers with accounts and MANAGER which is a subtype of EMP.

7.5.1 A C++ implementation

The C++ implementation presented here is based on ONTOS, an object-oriented database management system that supports a C++ dialect that provides for a persistent object store.

In C++, the code for implementing an object class consists of two parts: a header file and a methods file. The header file encodes the object interface as defined above. The methods file contains the program code that implements the methods and governs the behaviour of all objects belonging to a class.

In Figure 7.7, we have the ONTOS C++ header code for declaring the object class for BRANCH. This is a considerably simplified version with some details deliberately omitted for the sake of clarity.

In this code, we 'include' the header code for the class `Object`. In an ONTOS database, all persistent object classes are required to inherit either directly or indirectly from the superclass 'Object'. This provides a set of methods for handling persistence. We therefore declare the class `Branch` to be a `public Object`, meaning that it inherits directly from the class `Object`.

In the next part of the code, we have a `private` section where we declare the properties of `Branch`. Here we declare the simple string type attributes `priv_branchName`, `priv_address` and `priv_manager`. This part is private

```
//Branch.h
#include <Object.h>

class Branch : public Object
{
private :
    char* priv_branchName;
    char* priv_address;
    int priv_manager;
public:
    // Constructor
    Branch(char *BranchName, char* Address,
            int Manager);

    //Accessors

    char* Address();
    void Address(char* newAddress);
    char* Manager();
    void Manager(int newManager);
    void display();
    char* get_branchname();
};
```

Figure 7.7 C++ header code for object class for BRANCH.

as we cannot directly access the properties of an object. We can only do this via the methods associated with its class. These are declared in the `public` section of the header file.

We start the public section with constructor methods. We have a constructor with the name of the class. This takes parameter values that can be assigned to its private properties. We do not require a 'Store' method. This is because the superclass 'Object' has a 'putObject( )' method which stores an object instance in the database. This method is automatically inherited by 'Branch'. Similarly, there is no need for a 'Delete' method. The Object superclass has a 'deleteObject( )' method for the purpose of removing an object from the database.

Next come the accessor methods. We have two methods for 'Address', the first used for returning the address of a branch, the second for assigning an address. We also have two methods for 'Manager', the first to retrieve a branch manager, the second to assign a manager for a branch. The 'display' method is used to display the values pertaining to a Branch object.

In Figure 7.8, we have the header files for the ACCOUNT and CUSTOMER classes.

In the class definition for `Account`, we have included `Branch.h` in our declarations. This is because one of our properties (`priv_branchname`) is

```
// Account.h
#include Object.h
#include Branch.h

class Account : public Object;
{
 private:
 int priv_accno;
 int priv_balance;
 Branch* priv_branchname;

 public:
   Account (int accno, char* branchname);

   void deposit (int amount);
   void withdraw (int amount);
   int displaybalance();
   Branch* retrieve_branch_details();
   void change_branch (char* newbranch);
   void add_customer (char* Refno);
   void remove_customer (char* Refno);
   void RemoveAccount ();
}

//Customer.h

#include Object.h

class Customer : public Object
{
private:
    int priv_Refno;
    char* priv_Name;
    char* priv_Address;

public:
    Customer (int Refno, char* name, char* address);

    char* name();
    void name(char* newname);
    char* address();
    void address (char* newaddress);
    void open_account (int accno);
    void display_account_details();
    void RemoveCustomer();
}
```

Figure 7.8 Class definitions for ACCOUNT and CUSTOMER.

declared as a branch type object. We also have a method (`retrieve_branch_details`) which returns a branch type object. This object can then use the methods associated with the Branch class. Thus, to find the name of a branch holding an account, an application program will require two lines of code as follows:

```
branch = account --> retrieve_branch_details();
branchname = branch --> get_branchname();
```

The first line finds the Branch object associated with an account. The second line uses the 'get_branchname' method using the object returned by the first line to return a string representing the name of the branch.

Note how we have not troubled ourselves with a parameter value for balance in our constructor method. This is because the code for this method will automatically set the balance for any new account to zero. Figure 7.9 shows how the Account constructor may be encoded.

In Figure 7.9, the first thing we do is to declare this method as a function that returns a persistent object. The object is itself parameterized by the `accno` value. This means that the `accno` value will serve as the object identifier (OID) which will never change during the lifetime of the object. The code then checks the database for the existence of a Branch object with the given `branchname` value as its OID. This is done using the `OC_lookup` function. If no such object exists, then the constructor returns a null value, otherwise it will assign relevant values to the private properties.

The code for this method acts to preserve the referential integrity concept, ensuring that accounts are not assigned to non-existent branches. However, referential integrity is a relational concept, not an object-oriented concept, and its enforcement is down to the coding of individual methods, rather than enforced at the system level.

Figure 7.10 demonstrates the code for declaring the class for REGISTRATION.

```
Account::Account (char* branchname) : Object (accno);
{
Branch* thebranch;

thebranch = (Branch*)OC_lookup(branchname);
if thebranch == NULL return NULL
    else
    priv_accno = accno;
    priv_balance = 0;
    priv_branchname = thebranch;
}
```

Figure 7.9 Code for Account constructor method.

```
// Registration.h

#include Customer.h
#include Account.h
#include Object.h

class Registration : public Object;
{
private:
    Customer* priv_RefNo;
    Account* priv_AccNo;
    char* priv_date;

public:
    Registration(char* RefNo, char* AccNo, char* Date);
}
```

Figure 7.10 Header file for object class for REGISTRATION.

This class has no requirement for any methods other than its constructor. This is because it simply represents the association between objects of two other classes. Instances of this class will in fact be created, retrieved and used by methods of the associating classes. For instance, the 'open_account' method for Customer will use the Registration constructor to record the association between a customer and a new account. The 'add_customer' method for Account will use the Registration constructor to add a customer to the set of customers associated with an account. As with the Account constructor, the Registration constructor should incorporate code that checks for considerations of referential integrity. The 'display_account_details' method for Customer will find all Registration objects containing the relevant customer RefNo and from these find details of the associated Account objects.

In a system based on C++, the code for implementing is stored entirely separately from the header code, and is not made generally available to the database users. How methods actually work is deliberately hidden. The methods associated with an object may affect the values associated with other objects and may even create or destroy other objects. For instance, the 'RemoveCustomer( )' and 'RemoveAccount( )' methods associated with customer and account respectively have been included in order that all Registration objects associated with a given customer or account are deleted when a customer or an account is removed. We need to encode this directly in methods in an object-oriented database owing to the absence of the inbuilt concept of referential integrity.

Up to this point, all of our objects have inherited directly from the superclass 'Object'. In Figure 7.11, we have header files for EMP and MANAGER. Note how EMP inherits from 'Object', while MANAGER inherits from EMP. This

```
// Emp.h
#include <Object.h>
#include <Branch.h>

class Emp : public Object
{
private:
    int priv_EmpId;
    char* priv_Insurance_No;
    char* priv_emp_Name;
    Branch* priv_Employed_At;

public:
    Emp (int EmpId, char* Insurance_No, char* Emp_Name,
    char* Employed_At);

    char* Insurance_No();
    void Insurance_No (char* newNo)
    char* Emp_Name();
    void Emp_Name (char* newName);
    Branch* Employed_At();
    void Employed_At (char* Branch);
    void display();
};


// Manager.h
#include <Emp.h>
#include <Branch.h>

class Manager : public Emp;
{
private:
    int priv_grade;
    Branch* priv_Manages;

public:
    Manager (int EmpId, char* Insurance_No, char* Emp_Name,
    char* Employed_At, int Grade);

    int grade ();
    void grade (int newgrade);
    Branch* Manages();
    void Branch(char* Branch);
}
```

Figure 7.11 Header files for the classes of EMP and MANAGER.

means that MANAGER is a subtype of EMP which is itself a subtype of 'Object'. Thus, all of the object persistence methods inherited by EMP are passed on to MANAGER as well as all EMP methods and properties.

7.5.2 An OSQL implementation

OSQL (Object SQL) aims to combine the declarative simplicity of SQL with the computational completeness of an object-oriented language. It is highly influenced by the functional database approach as described in Chapter 2. Again, we present a highly simplified form of the language.

An OSQL database consists of types, functions and objects. Objects are instances of types. Their behaviour is determined by the functions associated with their type. A type declaration has a superficial similarity to the SQL CREATE TABLE command. However, instead of attributes, a type has associated with it a series of functions. Figure 7.12 shows the code for declaring some simple types.

The use of functions rather than attributes is important. To create an object, the system-supplied 'CreateObj' function is supplied. This creates an object and allows values to be assigned to functions of that object, for example:

CreateObj(Customer, Refno(1), Name(P.Abdul), Address(12, Low Street))

```
create type customer
functions
(Refno Number,
Name Char (var 30),
Address Char (var 30));

create type account
functions
(AccNo Number,
Balance Number,
Branch char (var 20));

reate type registration
functions
(AccNo Number,
CustId Number,
Date_of_Registration Char (var 9));

create type branch
functions
(BranchName char (var 30),
Address char (var 30),
Manager Number);
```

Figure 7.12 OSQL type definitions.

This will generate and store a Customer object along with a system-generated object ID (OID) that is permanent. Retrieval and update is performed using the relevant function(s) using the OID argument. For instance, in order to find the name of a person, we would say:

```
select Name(001);
```

This applies the function 'Name' to the object with an OID of '001'.

Of course, users are unlikely to know OIDs and will more naturally use literal values. OIDs can be retrieved within OSQL commands and passed as implicit arguments, as the following example demonstrates:

```
select Name(c)
for each Customer c
where Address(c) = '12 Low Street';
```

Here we use a variable 'c'. In the 'where' part of the command it is used to return the OID of all Customer objects whose address function returns the given value. This is then used to return the result of the name function applied to the same object.

'CreateObj' is a general purpose function. We can have functions for particular types. When creating a registration, we would wish to check its referential integrity. Thus, a special function 'CreateReg' would have to be encoded:

```
create function CreateReg (Ref Number, Acc Number,
                          Date_of_Reg Char(9) ) - - > void
as osql
begin
declare reference_valid boolean;
reference_valid : = checkCustExists(Ref) and checkAccExists(Acc);
if reference_valid
     CreateObj(Registration, RefNo(Ref), AccNo(Acc),
                          Date_of_Registration (Date_of_Reg) );
endif;
end;
```

The above code assumes the existence of two user-defined functions 'check-CustExists' and 'checkAccExists' which respectively check for the existence of given key values in the sets of Customer and Account objects. In the given code, we declare a Boolean value 'reference_valid'. We assign it to be 'true' if the functions 'checkCustExists' and 'checkAccExists' both evaluate to true. If both of these functions are 'true', then this means that we can now create a Registration object with the given argument values assigned to its functions.

Subtype declarations can be made using the create type command thus:

```
create type emp
functions
```

```
(EmpId number,
Insurance_No Char (var 9),
Name Char (var 20),
BranchName Char (var 20) );
```

```
create type manager subtype of emp
functions
(grade number);
```

In this example, the manager type inherits all of the functions of an emp type. Functions may be redeclared and overwritten. Queries may themselves be stored as functions which effectively become methods if they are tied to one particular type. A function for listing all of the employees at a bank would be:

```
create function list_employees (Branch b) - - >  BagType(Char (20))
as osql

begin
declare BagType (Char (20)) r;
declare cursor c as
                select name(e)
                for each Emp(e)
                where BranchName(e) = BranchName(b);
        open cursor c
        while true
                r: = r+fetch(c);
        end; (*while*)
        close (c);
        return r;
    end;
```

The above code is a considerably simplified form of an OSQL function. It has the following salient features:

- It takes a parameter argument (b) of type Branch.
- It returns a 'Bag' of strings (a 'Bag' is similar to a set, except that it is allowed to contain duplicate values).
- A Bag type variable 'r' is created to hold the result.
- It builds a query to find all employee names from the database based on a classic SQL-type join of Branch and Emp.
- A cursor is created to hold each value returned by the query.
- A loop is used that 'fetch'es each cursor value (a string representing an employee name) and adds it to 'r'.
- When the cursor seeks to return a value, the loop is terminated and 'r' is returned as the result.

As with an ONTOS database, functions can be created using object arguments that can affect the state of other objects. Unlike an ONTOS database, functions in an OSQL database are objects in themselves that are not necessarily tied to a given object class. An OSQL database is weak on encapsulation.

7.6 A short critique of object-oriented database systems

The object-oriented database paradigm has been extensively researched and developed in recent years, mainly as a response to the perceived shortcomings of relational databases. However, there are still relatively few successful implementations of object-oriented database systems and the suitability of the paradigm has been strongly criticized by various authors, in particular Date (1995). Briefly, the shortcomings can be summarized as follows:

1. The absence of a well-defined unifying field of theory. Relational databases benefit from having a relatively precise definition of what it means to be 'relational'. Object-oriented databases, being an adaptation of a programming paradigm, are not so precisely defined, leaving many implementors coming up with varying interpretations of what an object-oriented database actually is. This presents confusion regarding terminology. The users of object-oriented databases frequently find that they are confronted by a raft of new concepts every time they come to a new system. Database interoperability is a major problem for object-oriented systems.
2. The absence of a formally defined database design methodology such as normalization. There is very little to guide the designer of an object-oriented system as to the optimal way of designing an object-oriented database, resulting in potentially highly inefficient systems.
3. The absence of *ad hoc* querying facilities. Objects can only be accessed through pre-defined methods. If the method does not exist for building a particular dataset, then the 'casual' user cannot access such a dataset, even though the data may exist within the database objects. Contrast this with an SQL-based relational database where a user with SQL knowledge (or, more typically, using a tool that provides a 'user-friendly' front end for generating SQL queries) can build any dataset from that part of the database to which the user is granted access.
4. An absence of general integrity rules. Data integrity can be enforced in an object-oriented system, but this relies entirely on individual programmers being able to write the appropriate methods. All data integrity becomes *ad hoc*. System-wide integrity rules such as entity and referential integrity which can be consistently understood by users and supported by the underlying DBMS simply do not exist.

5. Navigational queries. In the section on ONTOS, we did not present an example of a data query method. This is because the reader would have had to understand a considerable amount of C++ in order to make sense of such a method. Object-oriented languages such as C++ typically access sets of stored objects using loops retrieving 'one object at a time'. Connections between objects are usually established via chains of pointers. The programmer writing such a method has therefore to 'navigate' along pointer chains that connect the objects that contain the data to satisfy a given query. This leads to a navigational form of database querying that is highly reminiscent of the worst features of network databases. This is clearly a giant step backwards.

6. The handling of object identifiers (OIDs). Again, this suffers from a lack of consistent interpretation. Locating objects via OIDs rather than by key values adds a significant querying overhead.

At present, object-oriented database systems are characterized, in the main, by complexity and have thus been slow to make a significant commercial impact. However, they have a huge potential. There is, in principle, no limit to the type of data that they can represent and manipulate and the range of semantics that they can support.

Summary

- Object-oriented database systems represent an attempt to apply the object-oriented programming paradigm to database technology.
- An object-oriented database consists of objects belonging to classes.
- An object's behaviour is entirely governed by its class membership.
- The process of object-oriented database design is based around the identification of object classes.
- Object-oriented systems tend to be based around an extended form of C++ or an extended form of SQL.

Exercises

Here is a restatement of the scenario at the EverCare County General Hospital as set out in Chapter 2:

At the EverCare County General Hospital, patients are admitted and given a unique Patient Id. We record their name, home address and date of admission. They are assigned to a ward and to a consultant. They may then be diagnosed a set of conditions. Whilst in our care, they will receive a set of treatments. Each treatment will have a date and details of the nurse administering the treatment, the drug being administered and the dosage. Drugs have a unique Drug Id, a name and a recommended dosage (which may not be the same as the dosage given in individual treatments). Nurses have a Nurse Id and a name and are assigned to a ward. Each ward has a Sister (who is a nurse). Consultants have a Doctor Id and a name.

1   Identify the object classes that can be derived from the above scenario.
2   For each object class identified, list the properties of that class.
3   For each object class identified, list the functions that would be required to establish relationships between classes (e.g. a function 'Patients_ assigned' that yields the patients assigned to a consultant).
4   Introduce into your object schema the refinement that consultants may be either surgeons or physicians.

(Note: For the above four questions, the semantic object diagrams that you drew for the exercises at the end of Chapter 2 should prove helpful.)

5   Write C++ type header files to specify the object classes that you have identified in questions 1–4.

Further reading

Annevelink *et al.* (1995)
Brown (1991) Chapters 2, 3 and 4
Cox (1986) Chapters 3, 4 and 5
Date (1995) Chapters 22, 23, 24 and 25
Delobel *et al.* (1995) Chapters 9, 10 and 11
Elmasri and Navathe (1994) Chapter 22
Gardarin and Valduriez (1989) Chapter 11
Hawryszkiewycz (1991) Chapter 15
Hughes (1991) Chapters 2, 3, 4 and 5
Korth and Silberschatz (1991) Chapter 13
Ozkarahan (1990) Chapter 11
Paton *et al.* (1996) Chapter 5
Ryan and Smith (1995) Chapter 16

References

Blakely J.A. (1995) 'OQL[C++]: Extending C++ with an Object Query Capability' in W. Kim (ed.) *Modern Database Systems*, Addison-Wesley
Cattell, R. (ed.) (1993) *The Object Database Standard: ODMG-93*, Morgan Kaufmann
Date, C.J. (1995) *An Introduction to Database Systems*, 6th edn, Addison-Wesley

CHAPTER 8

Internal management (1)

In Chapter 1, we explained how a database system requires an internal layer that maps the logical database structures into structures that can be physically stored on a computer system. The precise workings of this will vary according to the database system and host system involved. However, there are general principles that apply across a host of operating environments. In this chapter, we shall outline such general principles.

At the end of this chapter, the reader should be able to:

1. Describe the various components of a computer system that provide data storage facilities to a database management system.
2. Explain the ways in which a database management system and its host computer system intercommunicate.
3. Outline means by which the internal database structures may be tuned to enhance database performance.

8.1 Computer file management and a DBMS

Computer files are stored on external media such as disks and tape. Disk drives are known as direct access devices. This means that data can be directly retrieved from any part of a disk once its position on the disk is known. Tape drives are serial access devices, meaning that data can only be retrieved by searching for it from the start of the tape until the required data is found. Database systems by their very nature require the direct access facilities of disk-based storage.

The handling of the input and output of data to and from external devices is one of the tasks of a computer's 'operating system'. An operating system is a set of semi-permanent programs that provide an interface between application programs and the computer hardware. It provides to the programs a range of services such as memory management and input/output. To an operating system, the DBMS is simply another application program to which it provides services. The main service that a DBMS will use is that of physical file handling.

The parts of the operating system that are relevant to file handling are the file manager and the disk manager.

When a computer reads data from, or writes data to, a disk, it does not read it as a simple stream of bytes. Instead, it retrieves it and writes it in fixed size segments. These segments are called 'pages' (or sometimes 'sectors', 'blocks' or 'buckets'). A page is thus a 'unit of I/O' (Input/Output). Typically, such units are 2 or 4 kilobytes in size. A given system will have its own fixed pagesize. Thus, when data is written to a disk in a system using a 4K pagesize, 4K of data is transferred from the computer memory to disk. Likewise, performing a read from disk will result in 4K of data being transferred from the disk to the main memory. In such an environment, reading a 48K file will therefore require 12 'reads'.

Each page stored on disk has a PageID, indicating where it is stored on the disk. This enables an updated page to be written back to disk in the precise location from where it was read. The disk manager is responsible for the management of PageIDs and has within it the device-specific code that enables the reading and writing of specific pages on disk.

A file is a collection of pages. The management of files is the task of the file manager. When a computer file is created, it requires a set of pages. For instance, in a 4K page environment, a 48K file will require 12 pages of storage. When a file is created, the file manager needs to request a set of pages from the disk manager. This set of pages is given a PageSetID. Each page is given a logical ID within its page set. By 'logical' we mean an ID that simply refers to its position within its page set. A file consisting of 12 pages will simply have its pages numbered 1 to 12. The file manager has no knowledge of where pages are physically stored. Instead it communicates with the disk manager, issuing read and write requests for particular (logical) pages within particular page sets (Figure 8.1).

It is the task of the disk manager to translate logical page requests into physical PageIDs that can be used to access particular pages. Typically, the disk manager will maintain a directory with all of the PageSetIDs with pointers

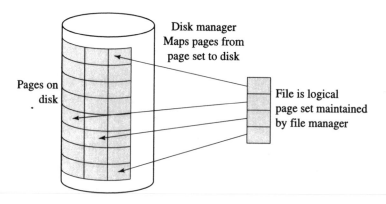

Figure 8.1 Pages, page sets and files.

to the pages belonging to each page set. All code pertaining to the control of the disk device ('device-specific code') can be entirely encapsulated within the disk manager.

The DBMS communicates with the file manager. The logical data objects of the system, be they relations, objects, record sets and so on, need to be converted by the DBMS into requests for data from particular host system files. The file manager maps these into page requests from a given page set. When the file manager provides the database system with a given page, the database system is required to convert the data from that page into the logical form required by the database users. This logical form is the lowest form of representation available to the database user. These internal communications are shown in Figure 8.2.

The neat separation of the file manager from the DBMS does not always exist in practice. Many types of operating system do not provide file management facilities that are suitable for database applications. Many products instead bypass the file manager and communicate directly with the disk manager.

Let us look at the internal management of a particular product.

The ORACLE DBMS is a relational system which fully conforms to the requirement that the lowest level of representation given to users of the database is that of a relational table. Schematically, everything is stored in tables.

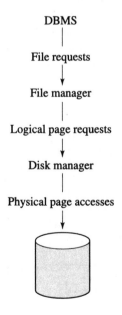

Figure 8.2 DBMS/host system intercommunication.

ORACLE tables are associated together in an ORACLE tablespace. A tablespace is a purely logical structure consisting of ORACLE data blocks. An ORACLE data block is of a fixed size, usually 2K or 4K depending on the operating environment. An ORACLE database may have more than one tablespace. Each tablespace will occupy one or more physical files (Figure 8.3).

When a user or an application creates a table, a given number of ORACLE data blocks are assigned from a tablespace to that table. When a row is inserted into a table, it is stored in the first available data block for that table. Depending on the size of a row, a data block may contain many rows. For example, in a table where each row took up 1K of data, each data block assigned to that table would contain up to four rows. When no more data can be fitted into the first data block assigned to a table, then it is marked 'full', and the next data block is assigned as the 'first available block'. When all of the data blocks assigned to a table are full, then the ORACLE system may assign another set of data blocks to that table.

As stated above, an ORACLE data block is a purely logical structure. It is maintained and managed entirely by the ORACLE DBMS software. The underlying operating system has no 'knowledge' of tables, tablespaces and ORACLE data blocks. The only thing that the operating system 'sees' is the set of physical files in which the ORACLE system stores its logical data blocks. An ORACLE data block may not even be the same size as the underlying system page. A tablespace may span more than one physical file. In this situation, it is even possible for a user's table to span more than one physical file. It is the task of the ORACLE system to translate user table and row requirements into internal ORACLE data block requests and then to translate these data block requests into page requests from host system files that can be

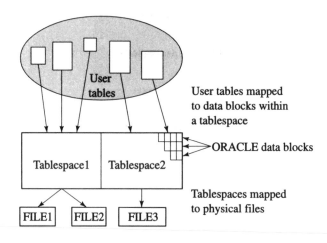

Figure 8.3 ORACLE tablespaces.

'understood' by the host system file manager. Thus, with an ORACLE system, Figure 8.2 is expanded as in Figure 8.4.

The DBMS now has two levels of intercommunication, one with the database user, the other with the underlying host system. The user is only able to view and use the database as if it were a set of tables. Users do have the facility to determine which tablespace a table is stored in and to request an initial allocation of data blocks. Beyond this, the system is opaque to the user. The precise management of tables and data blocks within a tablespace is the task of the ORACLE system itself (we shall exclude details of this). Tablespaces and data blocks are themselves logical structures which must be translated into a form that can be communicated to the underlying file manager. In certain environments, it is possible to 'fine-tune' an ORACLE database so that it can translate its data block requests directly into logical page requests that can be communicated directly to the underlying disk manager, thus bypassing the file manager software.

We have outlined details of the internal workings of a particular relational database system. This is not to suggest that this is the only way a relational system works at this level. Some systems work completely differently. For

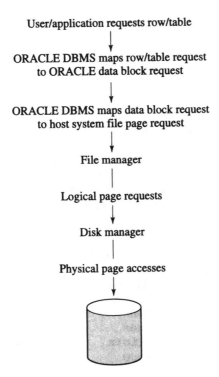

User/application requests row/table

↓

ORACLE DBMS maps row/table request
to ORACLE data block request

↓

ORACLE DBMS maps data block request
to host system file page request

↓

File manager

Logical page requests

↓

Disk manager

Physical page accesses

↓

Figure 8.4 Host system intercommunication in an ORACLE environment.

instance, certain systems assign a separate host system file to each table created. Others create a host system file for each set of tables belonging to a different user. The important thing is that they all 'look like' a relational database to their users. In theory, this should mean that they are capable of providing the same set of user facilities. However, their differing internal arrangements do affect the ways they can be used, especially in terms of the 'tuning' facilities that can be offered.

Database tuning concerns the arrangement of a database system in order that it performs at its maximum speed. Database tuning can be very difficult in a multi-user system with a mix of applications. Configuring the database in a particular way may be beneficial to one set of applications, but can make things worse for another set. At this level, tuning can become as much of a political decision as a purely technical one.

8.2 Tuning at the internal level

8.2.1 Indexes

Database indexes are an important means of speeding up access to sets of records. They are especially useful in relational systems where rows are stored in random sequence within a table. Take the set of rows in Figure 8.5.

Imagine that each record required one 'read' operation. Take the following query:

```
SELECT * FROM EMP
WHERE BRANCH = 'Amersham';
```

To find the data to service this query would require all of the seven rows to be read, checking each one in turn for 'BRANCH = Amersham'. The result will be a single row. This could be considerably speeded up by the use of an index over the attribute BRANCH. An index is an ordered set of values. It is somewhat

EMP

EMPNO	NAME	BRANCH
1	Sharif	Crawley
6	Peters	Dorking
4	Chan	Crawley
3	Jones	Crawley
7	Elliott	Dorking
12	Mason	Amersham
11	Simpson	Dorking

Figure 8.5 An employee relation.

analogous to an index in a book, which is an ordered set of words. In order to find a word in a book, the quickest way is to find it in the index. This will indicate the pages in the book where the word occurs. A database index will list the values for an attribute with pointers to the database pages containing the rows where each value occurs. If each row in our example relation took up exactly one page of I/O, a schematic index for BRANCH will look as follows:

```
BRANCH_INDEX
Amersham 6
Crawley 1,3,4
Dorking 2,5,7
```

To service the query above now only requires two rows to be read, the first one from the index, which points us directly to row 6 in the relation, which we then retrieve. In fact, in this simple example using the index will reduce the number of reads required for any set of branch rows. Finding all Crawley employees will require two reads of the index followed by three reads of the relation.

The above example is slightly unrealistic in that such a small set of data will typically be contained on one page of data and would therefore be obtained simply by retrieving the one page on disk containing the relation and reading the data in main memory to find the rows with the desired value. Reading data in main memory is fast; reading data from disk is slow. The purpose of all database tuning is to reduce the amount of disk access required by the system. A large relation will typically cover many pages of disk. Scanning an entire relation to retrieve any set of rows will, regardless of the size of the set, involve reading all of the pages assigned to that relation, unless there is an index available. An index will be much smaller than the relation itself. Loading and reading the index will be much quicker than reading the relation. Having read the index, the system will then be able to retrieve only those pages containing the rows relevant to servicing the query. The smaller the set of records involved, the greater the saving.

As well as their relative size, the sorted nature of indexes makes them quicker to read. Once we have found a value in the index and retrieved the set of page addresses containing that value, we know that the search is finished and that we require no further reads of the index.

With a large file, the indexes themselves will span a number of pages. With a large index file, it is usual to have an index over the index itself, indicating where values within a certain range can be found. Such indexes may be layered. In Figure 8.6, we have a special form of layered index known as a 'balanced tree' ('B-tree').

In a B-tree, the index is arranged in a tree with two types of page. At the lowest level is the 'sequence set' of pages. These contain pointers to the data blocks containing records with the given index values. Above the sequence set is the 'index set' of pages. These act as an 'index to the index'.

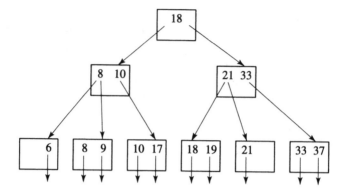

Figure 8.6 A B-tree index.

In the example given, each page contains just two addresses (realistically, thousands of addresses would be stored on each page – the important thing is that each page will have a limit to the number of addresses that can be stored). At the top level, we have a 'root' page with a root value and two pointers, one to the pages in the index set containing values higher than the 'root' value and the other to pages containing values lower than the root value. The next level represents a set of index pages, each with two values. By having two values, each page can maintain three pointers, one to a page containing values lower than the lower value, one to a page containing values between the lower and the higher value and a third to a page containing values equal to or more than the higher value. At the lowest level, we have the sequence set which directly indexes the data file itself. To find a record with a given value, the root is first examined and then the chain of pointers is followed to the page in the sequence set containing that value. This will point at the block in the data file containing the desired record. For example, to find record 17, this value is first compared with the root value. Being lower than the root value, we are guided to the first page in the index set. As 17 is higher than the higher value in this page, we thus follow the rightmost pointer, which guides us to the third page in the sequence set. This contains the value 17 and a pointer to the page on disk holding record 17.

We call this a balanced tree because there are as many index values to the left of the root as there are to the right. This ensures that all parts of the index are layered to exactly the same 'depth'. In this example, every indexed value in the sequence set is two levels below the root, meaning that all record values are located by reading the index exactly three times. We say that this index has a 'depth' of three. If we were indexing a large set of values, the depth of the tree would inevitably grow. In our example index, each page only contains two values. This means that some pages below the root are 'full'. If we were to introduce extra values into a full page in an unconstrained manner, we could

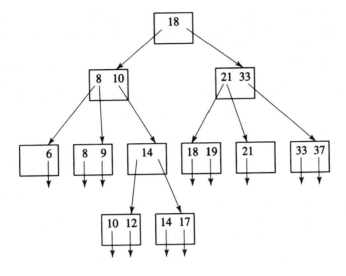

Figure 8.7 An unbalanced tree.

end up with an unbalanced tree (Figure 8.7). In an unbalanced tree, there may be more values to one side of the root than to the other, meaning that some parts of the index are of a greater depth than others. In Figure 8.7, finding the value 17 now requires four reads of the index, whereas locating the value 21 only requires three reads. There exists a B-tree algorithm which is applied in order that when insertions are made which result in extra pages being added to the index, the entire index is rearranged to maintain its balanced nature. This is shown in Figure 8.8. Under this organization, all values are still stored at the same depth, meaning that they are all accessed using the same number of index reads.

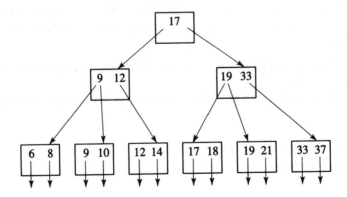

Figure 8.8 A properly balanced tree.

One particular advantage of indexes is their application in existence tests. If a value does not exist in a file, it is far quicker to search for that value and establish its non-existence using an index rather than reading the entire file. Retrieving data of a sorted nature is also performed much more quickly using an index. Without an index, the entire file may have to be read many times over in order that its data may be displayed according to the order of some attribute value. Using an index, records may be simply retrieved in the order indicated in the index.

Indexes do have drawbacks. They do in themselves take up space on disk. A file which has indexes on all of its attributes will effectively take up twice as much space on disk. More seriously, they incur an update overhead. Each time a record is inserted into or altered in a file, not only will the page holding that record have to be updated, but also the indexes will have to be updated. Take, for instance, the altering of the BRANCH value for EMPNO 4 from Crawley to Dorking. This would involve three updates:

1. Change the row in the EMP relation for EMPNO 4.
2. Change the entry in the Branch index for Crawley to remove the pointer to the row for EMPNO 4.
3. Change the entry in the Branch index for Dorking to add the row address for EMPNO 4 to the list of addresses holding this value.

In the case of a B-tree index, inserting a new value into the index may result in a massive reorganization of the index. Similarly, deleting or altering index values may also have drastic effects.

Indexes are therefore not recommended for all situations. Indexes should usually be created for the following types of attribute in a relational database:

1. Primary keys.
2. Foreign keys (in order to speed up joins).
3. Attributes that are frequently queried to yield a small set of records.
4. Attributes that are frequently used for displaying data in a sorted manner.

Indexes should be avoided over attributes where the data values are subject to frequent alteration.

SQL provides the CREATE INDEX command for declaring indexes, for example:

```
CREATE INDEX EMP_BRANCH_INDEX
ON EMP (BRANCH);
```

In most systems, once an index is created, its use is transparent to the user. That is, the system will automatically use it to service any query that refers to the attribute over which the index was built without any intervention on the part of the database user.

8.2.2 Hashing

Hashing is a means of directly determining a page address for a given record without the overhead associated with indexes.

With hashing, we use the data values associated with an item to determine where it is stored. Typically, a candidate key value will be used. Take, for instance, a file of employees, each with a unique six-figure identifying number. We could use this number to determine which page of the file an employee should be stored at, for example:

Emp 100100 - - > store at Page 100100 in the Emp file
Emp 342987 - - > store at Page 342987 in the Emp file

The problem with this scheme is that it forces us to reserve 999,999 pages for this file. All the unused employee numbers will result in unused pages.

A more typical arrangement is to perform some sort of 'hash function' on the key. A hash function is where we process the key to yield an address. Suppose we know that we will have approximately 1000 employees on file. This means that we will need at most 1000 record page addresses. We could take each key above and divide it by 1000 to yield a page address:

Emp 100200 - - > stored at Page 100
Emp 342910 - - > stored at Page 342

One of the disadvantages of this scheme is that, by allocating 1000 pages to the file, we are implicitly assuming that each page will contain exactly one record. If we know that each page can hold up to five records, then this means we only need 200 pages to store the entire file. We should therefore divide each employee key by 5000 to yield a page address in the range 1–200 thus:

Emp 100200 (divide by 5000) - - > stored at Page 20
Emp 342910 (divide by 5000) - - > stored at Page 68

Hash functions are usually rather more subtle than this. In the above two examples, dividing by a constant to yield a record address will cause records to be stored more or less sequentially according to their key value. We can achieve a more random spread by using the remainder rather than the actual value returned. Also, prime number division is more commonly used. To map the key values above to one of 200 page addresses, we might divide the key by 199 and use the remainder to determine the page address (the remainder will always be in the range 0–199):

Emp 100200 (divide by 199 = 503 remainder 103) - - > stored at Page 103
Emp 342910 (divide by 199 = 173 remainder 23) - - > stored at Page 23

When finding individual records in such a file, all we need is the key value. From this we can directly determine the logical PageId of the page containing the required record and issue a direct request for this page. This is the most rapid form of data retrieval and is highly suited to files where the location of individual records according to key value is frequently required. Hashed key mechanisms are widely used in object-oriented databases, where rapid storage and retrieval of individual objects becomes a function of the ObjectID.

Hashing does not come cost free. In the first place, a suitable hashing function must be determined. It must take into account the likely record sizes, the likely file size and the probable distribution of the keys. Moreover, fast direct access will only be available via the key on which the hashing function is performed. It is not feasible to store records according to two different hashing functions performed on alternate keys. Fast access on all other keys will still require indexes to be maintained.

The main problems associated with hashed key files are those of overflow and underflow. A hash function such as prime number division will map more than one record to a page. There will be occasions when more records will be mapped to a page than can be held on that page. The typical solution to this is to set up an 'overflow' page containing records that cannot fit onto the page where they were originally assigned. When a record cannot be fitted onto a page, a pointer is left indicating the overflow page where it is actually stored. When retrieving such a record, the system performs the hash function to retrieve the page where it should be stored. On examining the page, it will discover that the record is actually on the overflow page. The system must then retrieve the overflow page to obtain the record. It may be the case that the overflow page itself fills up, leaving pointers to a further overflow page. Sometimes, retrieving a record may involve a series of overflow page retrievals.

Underflow is the converse of overflow. Just as some pages will get too full, other pages may be only partially full or even empty. This would be as a result of too few keys being generated that are mapped by the hash function to certain pages. The result of this is a wasted disk allocation. It is not uncommon for hashed files to have a mixture of overflowed and underflowed pages within them. This will result in 'pointer chasing' for many of the record retrievals alongside a large amount of unused disk space.

8.2.3 Clusters

Database clustering is a technique whereby the data is physically stored in a manner that reflects some sort of logical arrangement.

Using our employee relation, we might anticipate that we will usually require the employees to be retrieved in branch order. We can achieve this efficiently by physically storing all of the employee rows in branch sequence. The result of this will be that the page set used to store the relation will effectively become a series of subsets, with each page subset containing employees belonging to the same branch. We call each of these subsets a 'cluster'. The clusters themselves will be in branch sequence (Figure 8.9).

When we have a clustered file such as this, the database can maintain a 'sparse' index (Figure 8.10). This is where, instead of an index entry for every occurrence of a given data value (technically, a 'dense' index), we only need an entry for the first occurrence of a given data value. The sorted nature of the file will mean that all pages up to the first occurrence of the next value will have the same value.

We call this form of clustering 'intra file' clustering, meaning that a file is clustered within itself. In the example above, we would call the Branch attribute the 'cluster key', meaning that it is the key that determines which cluster a given row will be stored in. In object-oriented database systems, objects tend to be clustered according to their class.

Intra file clustering is relevant when records from a logical file will be retrieved overwhelmingly in accordance with the cluster logic. It incurs overheads. When a record is created, it must be placed in a page from its relevant cluster, rather than simply being added to the current last page containing data for the logical file. When a record has its cluster key value altered, then it has to be physically moved from one page to another so that it

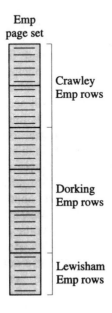

Emp
page set

Crawley
Emp rows

Dorking
Emp rows

Lewisham
Emp rows

Figure 8.9 Clustered pages.

Emp page set
clustered on
branch name

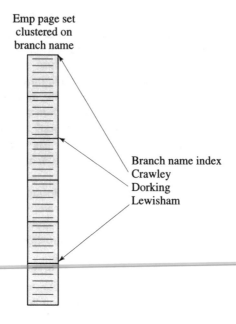

Branch name index
Crawley
Dorking
Lewisham

Figure 8.10 A sparse index.

is in the correct cluster. It is therefore unwise to create a cluster around a key value that is likely to be subject to frequent updates.

Another form of clustering is 'inter file' clustering. This is where we store records from more than one logical database file in the same physical page.

Taking our banking database, we may anticipate that we will frequently wish to perform a JOIN of the EMP and BRANCH relations. If we store these relations separately, then to perform the join, we will need to retrieve two separate page sets. We can speed up the servicing of this join by storing the relations in an interleaved manner, whereby each branch row is followed by the set of employee rows pertaining to that branch. In this way, when the system retrieves the pages for a set of rows from the employee relation, it is also retrieving the data for the joining rows from the BRANCH relation.

In the same database, we could create another inter file cluster using the customer REFNO as the cluster key, whereby each set of rows from the ACCOUNTS relation is stored in a page with the joining customer row. This will speed up joins of CUSTOMER and ACCOUNTS. However, to join this with branch data will now take much longer. This is because the rows that comprise the BRANCH relation are physically dispersed across a number of pages with interleaving employee rows. This is the main problem with an inter file cluster. It will speed up the servicing of the join for which it was devised. It will, however, slow down all other queries using the relations involved in the cluster.

In particular, full table scans of relations that have had their individual rows dispersed across a number of pages will now be considerably slower.

In general, clusters should only be implemented when there is a type of query that they can improve which is overwhelmingly dominant in the use of the database. A set of database files can only be clustered in one way. This is because clusters are physically, rather than logically, implemented. It is not possible to store a file physically in more than one clustered format.

Summary

- Database files are stored in logical page sets. A database management system must communicate with the underlying host system in order that its page set requirements are serviced.
- The underlying physical files that store a database need not equate directly to the internal file representations of the database system. It is the task of the DBMS to map its own internal page set handling to that of the underlying host system.
- Indexes are a useful means of speeding up access to small sets of records from large database files. They incur update overheads.
- Hashed key functions provide fast direct access to individual records. They incur overflow and underflow overheads.
- Intra file clustering concerns the physical arrangement of records within a file according to some logical criteria. It will speed up record access according to the given criteria. It incurs update overheads.
- Inter file clustering concerns the physical interleaving of associated records from different files. It will speed up join queries using these files. It will slow down other types of query.

Exercises

1   What is meant by the term 'a unit of I/O'?
2   Explain the process by which a relational database management system is able to retrieve a tuple for a particular relation from disk.
3   List the types of situation where database indexes are of most use.
4   List the pitfalls associated with the use of database indexes.
5   Outline the advantages and disadvantages of hashed key retrieval.
6   Here is the flights/reservation database originally shown in Chapter 3:

CUSTOMERS

```
------------------------
| CUSTNO  |CUSTNAME    |
------------------------
| 1       | P Jones    |
| 2       | H Chan     |
| 4       | S Abdul    |
| 6       | K Smith    |
| 7       | N Le Mer   |
|---------------------|
```

FLIGHTS

```
-------------------------------------------------------------------------
| FLIGHTNO | DESTINATION   | DAY       | TIME  | COST   |
-------------------------------------------------------------------------
| FL2X     | Paris         | Tuesday | 1400  |  78.95 |
| HK101    | Hong Kong     | Sunday  | 0900  | 525.00 |
| JX74     | Bahrain       | Monday  | 1300  | 275.75 |
|----------------------------------------------------------------------|
```

RESERVATIONS

```
------------------------
| CUSTNO  |FLIGHTNO   |
------------------------
| 1       | FL2X      |
| 1       | HK101     |
| 2       | HK101     |
| 6       | JX74      |
| 7       | JX74      |
| 1       | JX74      |
|---------------------|
```

(a) Suggest which of these attributes should be indexed. Justify your
     answer.
(b) What clusters could be built with this database? For each one,
     outline its advantages and disadvantages.
(c) Airline reservation systems typically require very fast access to
     individual records. In the light of this, explain the advantages and
     disadvantages of providing hashed key retrieval to any of these
     tables.

Further reading

Date (1995) Appendix A
Elmasri and Navathe (1994) Chapters 4 and 5
Gardarin and Valduriez (1989) Chapter 2
Hawryszkiewycz (1991) Chapter 10
Hughes (1991) Chapter 8
Korth and Silberschatz (1991) Chapters 7 and 8
Rolland (1992) Chapter 2
Ryan and Smith (1995) Chapter 8

CHAPTER 9

Internal management (2)

In the previous chapter, we considered aspects of how a database is actually stored and how its storage may be tuned for improved performance. In this chapter, we shall consider other internal management considerations, namely the interrelated topics of transaction management and concurrency and the techniques involved in query optimization. We shall also give an overview of some of the technical issues involved with database administration.

At the end of this chapter, the reader should be able to:

1. Explain what a database transaction is, and how individual transaction integrity may be maintained.
2. Outline the problems encountered by database concurrency and how they may be tackled.
3. Explain how database queries may be optimized.
4. Describe the main tasks of a database administrator.

9.1 Database transactions

A transaction is a 'logical unit of work'. A simple database transaction is one that involves the creation, alteration or deletion of one record within one file. There are many transactions, however, that are a lot more complex than this.

Suppose we had two bank accounts in a database and we wished to transfer money from one account to another. This involves reducing the balance in one account by the given amount and increasing the balance in the other account by the same amount. This requires two separate operations. In an SQL-based database, this would require two commands:

```
UPDATE ACCOUNTS
SET BALANCE = BALANCE - 100
WHERE ACCNO = 1234;

UPDATE ACCOUNTS
SET BALANCE = BALANCE + 100
WHERE ACCNO = 4567;
```

The two commands above would have the effect of transferring 100.00 from account 1234 to Account 4567. Together, they comprise a single transaction.

We have a potential problem with this transaction in that the database may 'crash' between the execution of the two commands. This would leave the data in an inconsistent state. The second account will not have been increased, even though the first account has been decreased. The logical integrity of the transaction as a whole will have been compromised. It would be better if neither of the commands had been executed. Transaction integrity demands that the effects of a transaction should be either complete or not enacted at all.

The COMMIT/ROLLBACK protocol exists to support transaction integrity.

A COMMIT is when changes to a database are made permanent. When a database crashes, any changes that have not been COMMITted will be lost. With the above transaction, we can issue an explicit COMMIT command when both of these update commands have been issued thus:

```
UPDATE ACCOUNTS
SET BALANCE = BALANCE - 100
WHERE ACCNO = 1234;

UPDATE ACCOUNTS
SET BALANCE = BALANCE + 100
WHERE ACCNO = 4567;

COMMIT;
```

This means that the first update is transitory. It is not made permanent until the second update has been executed. Now if the database crashes between the two commands, the effects of the first UPDATE will be lost.

ROLLBACK is a mechanism to undo the effects of a transaction. When a ROLLBACK is issued, all of the database changes since the last COMMIT are undone. To demonstrate its effects, take the following sequence of commands:

(1)   SELECT NAME FROM CUSTOMERS WHERE REFNO = 1; (Returns 'P Abdul')
(2)   UPDATE CUSTOMERS
      SET NAME = 'J Jones'
      WHERE REFNO = 1;
(3)   SELECT NAME FROM CUSTOMERS WHERE REFNO = 1; (Returns 'J Jones')
(4)   ROLLBACK;
(5)   SELECT NAME FROM CUSTOMERS WHERE REFNO = 1; (Returns 'P Abdul')

The ROLLBACK command in (4) undoes the effect of the UPDATE in (2). This is because this UPDATE has not been committed, meaning that it is only a transitory update. However, suppose we were to issue a COMMIT command thus:

(1)   SELECT NAME FROM CUSTOMERS WHERE REFNO = 1; (Returns 'P Abdul')
(2)   UPDATE CUSTOMERS
      SET NAME = 'J Jones'
      WHERE REFNO = 1;
(3)   COMMIT;
(4)   SELECT NAME FROM CUSTOMERS WHERE REFNO = 1; (Returns 'J Jones')
(5)   ROLLBACK;
(6)   SELECT NAME FROM CUSTOMERS WHERE REFNO = 1; (Returns 'J Jones')

The COMMIT command in (3) makes the change permanent. Any subsequent ROLLBACKs will only roll back changes made since the most previous COMMIT, thus leaving this change intact.

The above can be modified by the use of 'savepoints'. A savepoint can be thought of as a 'snapshot' of a transaction at a given time. When a ROLLBACK command is issued, it may make reference to a savepoint. If no COMMITs have been issued since that savepoint, then the database will be rolled back to the condition it was in at the savepoint, rather than at the most recent COMMIT. For instance, take the following sequence of commands:

(1)   SELECT NAME FROM CUSTOMERS WHERE REFNO = 1; (Returns 'P Abdul')
(2)   UPDATE CUSTOMERS
      SET NAME = 'J Jones'
      WHERE REFNO = 1;
(3)   COMMIT;
(4)   SELECT NAME FROM CUSTOMERS WHERE REFNO = 1; (Returns 'J Jones')
(5)   UPDATE CUSTOMERS
      SET NAME = 'P Smith'
      WHERE REFNO = 1;
(6)   SAVEPOINT1;
(7)   UPDATE CUSTOMERS
      SET NAME = 'A Sharif'
      WHERE REFNO = 1;
(8)   ROLLBACK TO SAVEPOINT1;
(9)   SELECT NAME FROM CUSTOMERS WHERE REFNO = 1; (Returns 'P Smith')

The final command retrieves the data that reflects the state of the database at SAVEPOINT1. This is because we rolled back to this point, undoing the effects of the UPDATE in command (7) only. An unconditional ROLLBACK will have undone both of the UPDATEs since the COMMIT of command (3).

In order to support the COMMIT/ROLLBACK protocol, a database system must maintain log files.

The ROLLBACK protocol is supported by maintaining a 'before image' log. This records data values as they are read from the database. During a transaction, values will be directly changed in the computer memory. If a ROLLBACK is issued, then the values saved in the before image log will be used to set the values in memory to what they were when they were first read in. When a COMMIT is issued, the before image values are flushed from the before image log and the new, updated, values are written to the database files.

In order to support savepoints, a database must maintain some form of 'after image' (or 'redo') log. This records the effects of all operations on the data, whether committed or not. The operations must all be timestamped, along with any savepoints. Rolling back to a savepoint can be done in two ways:

1. Retrieve the necessary values from the before image log and then use the operations recorded in the after image log to change these values to the condition they were in at the savepoint. The process of repeating a set of previously performed operations on a database is known as a 'rollforward' as opposed to a rollback. Rolling forward a transaction is referred to as 'redoing' that transaction.
2. Apply in reverse the effects of the operations saved in the after image log since the savepoint. This is known as 'undoing' a transaction.

In order to minimize input/output operations, copies of large sections of the before image and after image logs are usually kept in main memory. After image logs are especially useful in assisting with database recovery (see section 9.4 below).

9.2 Concurrency control

Concurrency control is a major concern in a multi-user database system. Database concurrency is the simultaneous access of database objects (e.g. relations, rows, attributes, views) by a number of users and applications. We do this in order that transactions can be processed in an interleaved manner, with the system servicing the operations that comprise a transaction in parallel with the operations necessary for other transactions. This enables a much more efficient use of the computer resources, resulting in an improved database performance.

Without certain controls, concurrency threatens database integrity. The following are some of the problems that can arise from the concurrent execution of transactions.

The lost update

Suppose we had two transactions ('TA' and 'TB') that consisted of the following commands:

```
TA: UPDATE ACCOUNTS
SET BALANCE = BALANCE + 100
WHERE ACCNO = 1234;

TB: UPDATE ACCOUNTS
SET BALANCE = BALANCE + 200
WHERE ACCNO = 1234;
```

The net effect of these two transactions should be to add 300 to the balance of Account 1234. However, if these transactions were to be enacted concurrently, a problem might occur. A simple update command in SQL comprises three operations: fetch the relevant row, alter its value in main memory, write back the amended row. Each of these transactions will need to find the record for Account 1234, ascertain its current value for the balance and then alter this value accordingly. By operating in an interleaved manner, the following situation might arise:

1. TA reads Account record 1234. Value of balance is 150.
2. TB reads Account record 1234. Value of balance is 150.
3. TA increases balance to 250 (150 + 100).
4. TB increases balance to 350 (150 + 200).
5. TA writes back balance of 250.
6. TB writes back balance of 350.

The account should have a balance of 450, not 350. The update performed by TA has been 'lost'.

The uncommitted dependency

This problem can occur when an update has not yet been committed by a transaction. Another transaction may start using data that has not yet been committed. If a rollback occurs, then the second transaction will be proceeding on the basis of false information. For instance, take the following two transactions:

```
TA:  UPDATE ACCOUNTS
     SET BALANCE = BALANCE - 100
     WHERE ACCNO = 1234;
     IF BALANCE < 0.00 THEN ROLLBACK ELSE COMMIT;

TB:  DELETE FROM ACCOUNTS
     WHERE BALANCE < 0.00;
```

The first of these two transactions reduces the balance in Account 1234 by 100. If this results in a negative balance, then the transaction is rolled back. The second one checks all accounts and deletes them if the balance is negative. It might access Account 1234 in the middle of its update thus:

1. TA retrieves Account 1234. Value of balance is 50.
2. TA reduces balance by 100, leaving it as -50.
3. TA writes back value of -50.
4. TB retrieves Account 1234. Balance is -50.
5. TB deletes Account 1234 as it has a negative balance.
6. TA rolls back update. Too late – the account has been deleted!

We call this an uncommitted dependency. The actions of transaction TB have been rendered dependent on data that has not yet been committed. This is a dangerous situation as the above example demonstrates.

Inconsistent analysis

This can occur when one transaction is accessing a set of records, some of which are being updated by another transaction. Take these two transactions:

```
TA:  SELECT SUM(BALANCE)
     FROM ACCOUNTS;

TB:  UPDATE ACCOUNTS
     SET BALANCE = BALANCE + 100
     WHERE ACCNO = 3;
     UPDATE ACCOUNTS
     SET BALANCE = BALANCE - 100
     WHERE ACCNO = 1;
```

The second transaction should have a neutral effect on the sum of all balances as it is simply transferring a balance from one account to another. However, the following situation might occur:

1. TA retrieves Account 1. Balance is 100. Running total 100.
2. TB retrieves Account 3. Balance is 100.
3. TA retrieves Account 2. Balance is 100. Running total 200.
4. TB updates Account 3 balance to 0.
5. TA retrieves Account 3. Balance is 0. Running total 200.
6. TB retrieves Account 1. Balance is 100.
7. TA retrieves Account 4. Balance is 100. Running total 300.
8. TB updates Account 1 balance to 200.

Transaction TA at this point would report that the sum of all account balances is 300, when in fact it is 400. This is an inconsistent analysis.

Database systems avoid these sorts of problems by the use of locks.

When a transaction requires a database object, it must place a 'lock' on that object. When an object is locked, it may not be accessed by other transactions.

When a transaction is finished with an object, it releases the lock, meaning that another transaction may now place a lock on and use that object.

This means that when two transactions are using the same object, one of them will have to 'wait' until the first transaction that has placed a lock has released it. In this way, 'lock queues' can build up for objects required by a number of transactions.

It is not necessary for all locks to be total. When two transactions are simply reading the same set of data without updating any part of it, no purpose is served by locking the data. We simply get an lock queue. We therefore have two types of lock: shared (S) and exclusive (X).

A shared (S) lock is placed on an object that is being accessed for read purposes only. An exclusive (X) lock is placed on an object that is being altered in some way (i.e. being updated or deleted). We have the following protocol:

When an object has an S lock, other S locks may be placed. A transaction
   requiring an X lock must wait until all S locks have been released.
When an object has an X lock, no other lock may be placed. All
   transactions requiring a lock (either X or S) must wait until the X lock
   has been released.

The protocol basically means that when a 'read-only' operation is being performed (e.g. the SQL SELECT command), other read-only operations may be performed on that object. When an updating operation is being performed, no other operation may. be performed. This protocol avoids the problems outlined above. The lost update is avoided because transaction TA will place an X lock on Account 1234 before it starts the update. This means that transaction TB will not be able to start its update until TA has finished its own update. The uncommitted dependency is similarly avoided because TA will lock TB out from Account 1234 until it has completed the rollback. In the inconsistent analysis, TA will place an S lock on all of the account records. This means that the X lock required by TB will not be granted until TA has completed its analysis.

There are occasions when different types of lock are required on the same object during the course of an individual transaction. The system must be careful as to when locks may be released. Take the following lock requirements by two transactions:

TA:	S lock on Object 1	TB:	S lock on Object 1
	S lock on Object 2		X lock on Object 1
	X lock on Object 1		S lock on Object 2

Both transactions are going to require an X lock on Object 1. If TA is the first 'logical' transaction, then it is important to ensure that it acquires this lock before TB. However, suppose we simply released locks immediately we were finished with them. We would get the following sequence of events if the transactions proceed concurrently:

1. TA places S lock on Object 1.
2. TB places S lock on Object 1.
3. TA releases S lock on Object 1. Places S lock on Object 2.
4. TB places X lock on Object 1 (TA has released its S lock on this object, allowing other transactions to lock it).
5. TA releases S lock on Object 2. It now has to wait for an X lock on Object 1.
6. TB releases X lock on Object 1. Places S lock on Object 2.
7. TA places X lock on Object 1.
8. TB releases S lock on Object 2.
9. TA releases X lock on Object 1.

The effect of this is that transaction TB has updated Object 1 before transaction TA. This is an error because transaction TA is the first 'logical' transaction. This means that its effects should be committed to the database before those of transaction TB. The above schedule of events contradicts the principle of 'serialization'.

The serialization principle ensures, in outline, that when two transactions operate in an interleaved manner, then their effects should be the same as if they operated in a purely serial manner, with one transaction not starting till the previous one has completely finished. More precisely, serialization is concerned with 'conflicting requests'. We have a conflicting request above with both transactions requiring an X lock on Object 1. A schedule of events for a set of transactions is said to be 'serializable' when the conflicting requests are presented in the same order as if the transactions were enacted consecutively. In other words, the X lock for Object 1 should be requested by TA before it is requested by TB.

We can guarantee serializable schedules by using the 'two-phase locking' protocol. This states that a transaction may not acquire any locks on an object when it has released a lock on that object.

In the scenario above, TA will not be allowed to acquire an X lock on Object 1 if it has already released an S lock on that object. It will therefore not release its S lock. The schedule of events will therefore be altered thus:

1. TA places S lock on Object 1.
2. TB places S lock on Object 1.
3. TA places S lock on Object 2.
4. TB requests X lock on Object 1. Request denied. TB waits.
5. TA places X lock on Object 1.
6. TA releases all locks.
7. TB places X lock on Object 1.
8. TB places S lock on Object 2.
9. TB releases all locks.

Two-phase locking is so called because transactions inevitably enter two phases: a phase when they are acquiring locks and a phase when they are

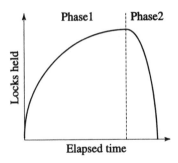

Figure 9.1 Two-phase locking cycle for transactions.

releasing locks (Figure 9.1). In most systems, the second phase is 'put off' until the very end of the transaction when it is ready to commit or roll back. Locks are only released at this point, as in the example above. This is not completely necessary. In the above scenario, TA could have released its S lock on Object 2 before placing an X lock on Object 1. However, leaving the release of locks until a transaction is finished saves the system from having to 'look ahead' for lock requirements.

9.3 Query optimization

Query optimization is concerned with the efficient processing of database queries. When a user enters a database query, there may exist a number of ways of putting together the required data. Query optimization techniques can be used to determine the 'best way' to service a given query. The best way is the way that involves the least amount of input/output.

By way of example, let us take the following query:

```
SELECT CUSTOMER.NAME, CUSTOMER.ADDRESS
FROM CUSTOMER, ACCOUNT, BRANCH
WHERE CUSTOMER.REFNO = ACCOUNT.REFNO
AND ACCOUNT.BRANCHNAME = BRANCH.BRANCHNAME
AND BRANCH.BRANCHNAME = 'Bombay';
```

Let us suppose that there are approximately 10,000 customer rows, 50,000 account rows and 100 branch rows. All accounts have one corresponding customer. About 1% of accounts are from Bombay.

The above query will require a series of algebraic Joins, Restricts and Projects. The order in which these operations are executed will be critical. Let us do the operations in the order presented in the query:

1. Join customers with accounts over REFNO.

   In the worst case, in the absence of aids such as indexes or clusters, this will involve reading the 10,000 customer records, and, for each one, reading all of the 50,000 accounts records to see if a join can be performed, resulting in $10,000 \times 50,000$ (500 million) record reads.

   The result will be a temporary table (R1) comprising the 50,000 account rows joined with the corresponding customer rows.

2. Join R1 with BRANCH over BRANCHNAME.

   We now need to read the 50,000 R1 rows, and for each one check each of the 100 branch rows to see if a join can be made, resulting in $50,000 \times 100$ record reads (5 million reads).

   The result is a temporary table (R2) consisting of all R1 customer/account data joined with the branch data. The table will still be 50,000 rows long. (Each row will itself be very long as it will now contain all of the attributes from all of the tables.)

3. Restrict R2 to rows with branch name Bombay.

   Read the 50,000 R2 rows and reduce this to a temporary table (R3) containing only those rows for Bombay, resulting in 500 rows.

4. Project R3 over CUSTOMER.NAME and CUSTOMER.ADDRESS to give the result.

   Read the 500 rows from R3 and return the projected result.

   The total number of record reads involved in this form of servicing strategy will be 500 million + 5 million + 50,000 + 500, equalling 505,050,500 reads in all.

We could have serviced the first three steps in reverse order to achieve exactly the same result:

1. Restrict BRANCH to rows with BRANCHNAME = 'Bombay'.

   This gives 100 reads of BRANCH, resulting in a temporary table (R1) of 1 row.

2. Join R1 with accounts.

   For the one row in R1, read the 50,000 account rows, resulting in 50,000 reads to produce a temporary table (R2) of 500 rows.

3. Join R2 with customers.

   For each of the 500 rows in R2, read the 10,000 customer rows, resulting in 5 million reads giving a temporary table (R3) of 500 rows of joined customer/account/branch information.

4. Project R3 to give the result.

   Read to 500 rows in R3 and perform the Project to return the result.

This second strategy will result in 100 + 50,000 + 5 million + 500 record reads, giving a total of 5,050,600 reads. This is only slightly more than one-hundredth of the reads required by the first strategy. In other words, an approximate 99% saving in reads has been achieved. We can see that query optimization is a very important issue. The example above demonstrates that even a simple database can run 100 times faster using the correct strategy to service a given query.

The saving above was achieved by changing the order in which the database operations were performed. In a relational system, one set of operations can be transformed into an equivalent set of operations using 'transformation rules'. A transformation rule takes a given sequence of operations and demonstrates that the same result may be achieved by a different sequence of operations. Such sequences are said to be 'equivalent' (using the $<=>$ operator).

Suppose we had three tables A, B and C. They have the attributes A.X, A.Y, A.Z, B.I, B.J, B.H, C.L, C.M and C.N. We can apply the following transformation rules to sequences of operations involving these tables:

1. Join (A,B) where A.X = B.I - - > R1
    Restrict (R1) on R1.Y
    $<=>$
    Restrict A on A.Y - - > R1
    Join (R1,B) where R1.X = B.I

This states that when a Join of two tables is followed by a Restrict on the resulting table, the same result is achieved by performing Restrict on the relevant table first, and then performing the Join using the Restricted table.

2. Join (A,B) where A.X = B.I - - > R1
    Project (R1) on R1.Y
    $<=>$
    Project (A) on A.Y, A.X - - > R1
    Project (B) on B.I - - > R2
    Join (R1,R2) where R1.X = R2.I - - > R2
    Project (R3) on R3.Y

This states that when a Join is followed by a Project, the same result is achieved by Projecting out the required column(s) from the given tables along with the joining key, and then performing the Join on the Projected tables. The temporary result will then have to be further Projected to remove the joining key. This last step does not apply if the joining key is required as part of final Projected result.

3. Restrict (A) on A.X - - > R1
    Restrict (R1) on R1.Y
    $<=>$
    Restrict (A) on A.X and A.Y

This states that a sequence of Restricts using attribute values from the same table may be grouped together into a single Restrict.

4. Restrict (A) on A.X - - > R1
    Project (R1) on R1.Y
    $< = >$
    Project (A) on A.X, A.Y - - > R1
    Restrict (R1) on A.X - - > R2
    Project (R2) on R2.Y

This states that a Restrict followed by a Project on a table may be achieved using a Project followed by a Restrict. If the attribute over which the Project is being performed is not part of the final result, then this attribute must be included on the original Project and then subsequently excluded by a final Project.

5. Join (A,B) where A.X = B.I
    $< = >$
    Join (B,A) where B.I = A.X

This states that when two tables are joined, it makes no difference which order the tables are presented to the Join operation.

6. Join (A,B) where A.X = B.I - - > R1
    Join (R1,C) where R1.I = C.L
    $< = >$
    Join (B,C) where B.I = C.L - - > R1
    Join (R1,A) where R1.I = A.X

This states that when three or more tables are joined, the joins may be performed in any sequence.

These transformation rules allow a system to devise a number of alternative strategies to service a given query. Broadly speaking, the best strategies are those that perform Joins as late as possible. This is because Joins are expensive operations, potentially involving many repetitive reads of the same table to find matching attribute values. The smaller the tables to be Joined, the quicker a Join can be achieved. The main reason why the second of the two strategies was so much more efficient was because the Restrict on BRANCH was performed before any of the Joins. Because only one branch record out of 100 was relevant, this had the effect of reducing the Join of BRANCH with ACCOUNT by 99%, giving a temporary table to be Joined with CUSTOMER that was 99% smaller than the temporary table produced by Joining CUSTOMER with ACCOUNT. It is also usually best to do Projections before joins because these will reduce the width of any temporary tables, meaning that fewer pages of temporary storage will be required to hold them. In the example above, further savings in I/O would probably be achieved if CUSTOMER.NAME, CUSTOMER.ADDRESS, CUSTOMER.REFNO, ACCOUNT.REFNO, ACCOUNT.BRANCHNAME and BRANCH.BRANCHNAME were Projected out at the start, making the temporary tables much smaller, so small that they may even be stored completely in main memory, eliminating transitory I/O altogether.

Truly efficient optimization can only be achieved using statistical information about the database. Suppose we had three tables A, B and C. A has 1000 rows, B has 1000 rows, C has 10 rows. The 1000 rows in A can each join with one of the 1000 rows in B. The 10 rows in C can only join with 10 rows in B. Using transformation rule 6 above, there are two ways in which these three tables may be joined:

1.   Join A,B - -> R1 (1000 rows built from 1000×1000 reads)
     Join R1,C - -> Result (10 rows built from 1000×10 reads)

2.   Join B,C - -> R1 (10 rows built from 1000×10 reads)
     Join R1,A - -> Result (10 rows built from 10×1000 reads)

The first strategy requires in all 1,010,000 reads, the second requires 20,000 reads, a saving of 98%. Joins should be performed in the order that reduces the set of rows as quickly as possible. A database system can only take this into consideration if it maintains statistical information on file sizes, row sizes and the proportion of foreign key matches between tables. In this way, 'guesstimates' can be performed on the likely I/O costs of different sequences of operations.

Other things that a database system should take into account when optimizing queries are the existence of database objects such as clusters and indexes.

When two tables are clustered, they are already physically joined. Any sequence of operations involving these tables should start with the Join of these tables as it has already 'happened'.

Joins over foreign keys are greatly influenced by the use of indexes. Take for example a join of two tables (A, B) where A.X = B.X, X being the primary key of A and a foreign key for B. If an index exists over the attribute X in B, then the speed of the Join is considerably enhanced. For each row in A, the B.X index is searched and the joining rows retrieved. Without the B.X index, a full table scan has to take place to find the matching set of B rows for each A row. Rule 5 states that the order of presentation of tables to a Join does not effect its result. Presuming that there is a primary key index on A and there is no foreign key index on B, then it would probably be quicker instead to examine table B and for each row in B, use the A.X index to find the joining row in A.

Complex queries may generate a large number of alternative sets of equivalent operations. Rather than generating a large set of operation sequences and 'costing' each one in terms of I/O, the majority of systems tend to use the simple guideline of 'do all Joins last', without attempting to cost the different Join sequences. This may not necessarily generate the best strategy for servicing individual queries, but it frees the system from the overhead incurred by in-depth evaluation of queries using statistical information. Such an overhead can cost more than any query servicing benefits gained.

The reader may note that this section has used examples entirely based on relational systems. This is because a relational system services queries using a restricted collection of set type operators, rendering their queries susceptible to optimization techniques. Systems that work on a 'record at a time' and/or 'pointer chasing' level cannot be so easily optimized, the efficiency of queries being mainly determined by the skill of the programmer that writes them.

9.4 Database administration

A multi-user database system requires a Database Administrator. The role of the Database Administrator (DBA) is to protect the integrity of the database whilst maximizing its performance. This is not a purely technical task. In a multi-user system, the user requirements will frequently conflict. Configuring the system in a particular way may benefit one set of users at the expense of another set. Database resources are always finite, meaning that quotas of things like disk space must be fixed for different types of user. The DBA is required to prioritize and manage the conflicting demands on the system. Thus, management skills are as important as technical expertise.

In this section, we shall examine the technical issues of recovery, security, performance and data administration which are the overwhelming concern of a DBA.

9.4.1 Database recovery

Database recovery concerns the restoration of a database to a consistent state after a system failure. As stated above in section 9.1, a database system should keep log files that record all operations on the data. When a database 'crashes', log files may be used to restore the database. The DBA should ensure that a complete copy of the database is stored at regular intervals in an archive file. In this way, when a database suffers a system crash, it can be restored by retrieving the archive file and then using the after image log to roll forward all transactions that have been successfully committed since the archive was taken. In this way, the database can be restored to a consistent and up-to-date condition.

It is not economic to have an infinite series of after image files. After a certain amount of time they are 'logically' discarded by having their oldest transactions overwritten with fresh after image data. Old rollforward data thus gradually becomes lost to the system. The DBA must ensure that archives are taken frequently enough so that the data necessary for a successful rollforward has not been partially lost from the after image files.

Many systems incorporate a 'checkpoint' facility. A checkpoint is similar in concept to a savepoint as previously described (section 9.1), except that it applies to an entire database rather than to an individual transaction. To support checkpoints, the database must periodically: (i) write all before image and after image records currently in memory to an archive store; (ii) write all modified database values to the database; (iii) record in the archive the date and time of the checkpoint. This streamlines the rollforward process described above. When a database crashes, we do not need to restore the database in its entirety from an archive file and then do a complete rollforward as described above. Instead, we can use the database in its crashed state. The database can be rolled back from this state to its checkpoint state using log information on all operations executed since the checkpoint. This has the effect of undoing all transactions started since the checkpoint. It will also undo all transactions that had started but which had not yet been completed at the checkpoint. Operations for transactions that committed successfully before the checkpoint can be ignored as their effects are reflected in the state of the database at the checkpoint. Those transactions that committed successfully after the checkpoint may now be redone using the log information. Transactions which started but which were then rolled back can be discarded. The remaining transactions (those which had started, but which had reached neither a commit nor a rollback stage) may be restarted once the database system is itself restarted.

Database systems may incorporate checkpoints activations systems that are enacted every so many seconds, or every so many transactions. These may be parameterized in some environments. In this case, the DBA is responsible for choosing the best checkpoint/archiving strategies for ensuring efficient, timely and economic database recovery.

9.4.2 Database security

Database security exists on two levels: security against catastrophe and security against unwarranted use.

Catastrophe includes things like fire, theft, earthquake and so on. The DBA must have contingency plans for such events. A classic contingency is to mount the database on two separate machines that are in different locations, with one machine acting as a 'shadow' of the machine that is actually communicating with the users. If one machine suffers irrecoverable damage, then the system can switch to the 'shadow' machine, and a new 'shadow' can be installed.

Unwarranted use concerns infiltration by unwelcome users as well as legitimate database users having access to database objects that should be guarded from them. The DBA must use the system-provided facilities to control access to the system. This includes the enrolment and removal of users, the setting of passwords and the granting of privileges to users. Privileges include the ability to read, create, delete and alter individual database objects. Objects include files, views, applications, tools and users. All privileges on all objects must ultimately be controlled by the DBA. In this respect, the most useful tools for a DBA are those which allow the DBA to define given sets of privileges on given sets of objects and then to associate sets of users together who may then be granted *en masse* such pre-defined sets of privileges. For instance, in a large enterprise, employees can be divided into certain categories, with each category having a pre-defined set of database privileges.

9.4.3 Database performance

The DBA is responsible for maximizing the overall performance of a database system. Most multi-user systems allow the DBA to set parameters that assist in the 'tuning' of the system. These include the configuring of items such as how much of the database can be buffered in main memory at a time, how much before image and after image data should be buffered, how many processes a user can instigate at a time, how many locks a transaction can acquire and so on. Database locking is an area that the DBA must closely monitor owing to the potential for what is known as 'deadlock'.

One of the problems with two phase locking is that it increases the possibility for deadlock. Suppose we had two transactions, TA and TB, and two database objects, O1 and O2. We could have the situation arise where TA requires exclusive locks on O1 and O2, whereas TB requires exclusive locks on O2 and O1. We could get the following sequence of events:

1. TA places X lock on O1.
2. TB places X lock on O2.
3. TA requests X lock on O2. It is required to wait.
4. TB requests X lock on O1. It is required to wait.

In a system that does not release locks until a transaction is ready to commit, these two transactions will wait for ever. We say that they are deadlocked. Neither transaction can proceed until it releases a lock. They are both indirectly forcing themselves to wait. In such a situation, the DBA must intervene and terminate one or both of the transactions. The deadlock situation can occur quite subtly, being set off by a chain of lock requests running across a series of transactions that lead back to a transaction that is waiting for a lock.

The DBA must constantly monitor database performance in order that decisions can be made about the amount of resources that should be dedicated to individual users and their applications and to the database as a whole. Monitoring can also assist in the detection of deadlock. Many systems provide monitoring tools to help the DBA in the collection of information about database performance.

An important aspect of database performance is database availability. The DBA should ensure that standard 'housekeeping' routines such as archiving the database and performing upgrades interfere as little as possible with the use of the database. The DBA should monitor the size of the database. If it looks as if it is about to exceed the available disk space, then the DBA must intervene to add more disk space or to stop users from creating new data, otherwise the database will fail. As described above, the DBA must also have catastrophe management in place in order to make the database available as soon as possible after a disaster.

9.4.4 Data administration

Large enterprises frequently require the DBA to perform the function of 'data administration'. This covers topics such as data naming conventions, data definition conventions, processing restrictions and the establishment of an enterprise-wide data policy with accompanying standards of practice.

Summary

- A database transaction is a logical unit of work which may consist of a series of operations which cannot be left in a partial state of completion.
- ROLLBACK and COMMIT protocols exist to enforce the integrity of transactions.
- ROLLBACK and COMMIT protocols require the maintenance of before and after image logs.
- When transactions are executed in an interleaved manner, they can corrupt each other's results unless locking protocols are introduced.
- The two-phase locking protocol ensures that interleaving transactions will leave the database in the state that it would be in if the transactions were executed in a purely serial manner.
- Query optimization techniques can be used to improve the performance of a database.
- Database Administrators are responsible for the recovery and security of databases, enhancing their performance and for the implementation of standards in the use of data.

Exercises

Here is the flights/reservation database originally shown in Chapter 3:

CUSTOMERS

```
----------------------
| CUSTNO  |CUSTNAME    |
----------------------
| 1       | P Jones    |
| 2       | H Chan     |
| 4       | S Abdul    |
| 6       | K Smith    |
| 7       | N Le Mer   |
| -------------------|
```

FLIGHTS

```
-------------------------------------------------------------
| FLIGHTNO | DESTINATION  | DAY       | TIME  | COST  |
-------------------------------------------------------------
| FL2X     | Paris        | Tuesday | 1400  |  78.95|
| HK101    | Hong Kong    | Sunday  | 0900  | 525.00|
| JX74     | Bahrain      | Monday  | 1300  | 275.75|
| ---------------------------------------------------|
```

RESERVATIONS

```
----------------------
| CUSTNO  |FLIGHTNO   |
----------------------
| 1       | FL2X      |
| 1       | HK101     |
| 2       | HK101     |
| 6       | JX74      |
| 7       | JX74      |
| 1       | JX74      |
| -------------------|
```

1 (a) Consider the following two transactions executed in parallel:

Transaction 1
Select sum(cost)
from reservations, flights
where flightno = 'JX74' and
reservations.flightno = flights.flightno;

Transaction 2
Update flights
Set cost = 285.75
where flightno = 'JX74';

List the database operations involved in servicing these transactions. What problem might arise if these transactions were to be executed in an uncontrolled interleaved manner? Explain how this may be overcome by locking.

(b) Likewise, identify the potential problem involved with the following two transactions and how it may be overcome:

Transaction 1
Update Flights
set cost = cost * 1.1;

Transaction 2
Update Flights
set cost = cost + 10.75
where FlightNo = 'FL2X';

(c) Suppose we had foreign key declarations that cascaded the effects of deletions from CUSTOMERS to RESERVATIONS and from FLIGHTS to RESERVATIONS (i.e. deleting a customer results in all of his or her reservations being deleted, and, likewise, deleting a flight will result in all reservations for that flight being deleted). What problem could arise if the following two transactions were to be executed in parallel?

Delete from Flights where Flightno = 'FL2X';
Delete from Customers where Custname = 'P Jones';

What intervention would be required in such a situation?

2 Examine the following database query:

Select CustName, Destination
From Flights F, Reservations R, Customers C
Where F.Flightno = R.FlightNo
and R.Custno = C.Custno
and R.Cost > 100.00
and C.CustName = 'P Jones';

(a) List the sequence of algebraic operations necessary to service this query.
(b) Show how many rows would have to be read, including rows read from temporary tables, in order to service this query.
(c) Derive an equivalent set of algebraic operations using transformation rules. Calculate the number of rows read by this equivalent set and compare your answer to your answer to (b).

Further reading

Date (1995) Chapters 13, 14, 15 and 18
Elmasri and Navathe (1994) Chapters 17, 18, 19 and 20
Gardarin and Valduriez (1989) Chapters 7, 8 and 9
Hughes (1991) Chapter 7
Kroenke (1995) Chapter 15
Korth and Silberschatz (1991) Chapters 9, 10, 11 and 12
Ozkarahan (1990) Chapters 7 and 8
Ryan and Smith (1995) Chapters 10, 11 and 12

CHAPTER 10

Distributed database systems

Up to this point, we have been describing multi-user database systems that have been implicitly 'standalone'. By this we mean database systems that operate independently of other database systems. In the modern world, there is an increasing requirement for database systems to be able to co-operate with other database systems. It has always been possible to perform this in an *ad hoc* manner. However, just as a database system provides an integrated and controlled environment for accessing a set of data, it is also preferable to have an integrated and controlled environment for accessing a set of databases. A distributed database system provides such an environment. When we associate databases together in a distributed system, a set of complexities are introduced which we shall examine in this chapter. There are other means by which data may be shared amongst databases, which we shall also examine in outline in the latter part of the chapter.

By the end of this chapter, the reader should be able to:

1. Define the main characteristics of a distributed database system.
2. Explain the main problems associated with successfully implementing a distributed database system.
3. Describe alternative means of sharing data between databases.

10.1 Aims of a distributed database system

A distributed database system is a collection of logically related databases that co-operate in a transparent manner.

By 'transparent', we mean that each user within the system may access all of the data within all of the databases as if they were a single database. Distributed database systems invariably consist of a number of databases mounted on a number of machines that are connected together over a computer network. Ideally, users and applications should be able to access data without having to know precisely where it is located within the network. Data may thus be moved around the network without applications having to be rewritten. We call this 'location independence'.

Data transparency and location independence are two mutually supportive technical aims of a distributed database system. They exist to support the operational aims of a distributed system. We summarize these in the following paragraphs.

In a large enterprise that operates across a number of sites, there will be many geographically dispersed database users. In a traditional environment, there will exist a single central database with remote terminals at each site accessing that database. This has a number of disadvantages:

1. High communications overhead. A large amount of data transference is involved, which is costly and slow.
2. An overworked central machine exacerbating performance problems.
3. Overreliance on a central site. If the central machine fails, then the entire corporate database becomes unavailable.

The answer to these is to take the corporate database and physically partition it in order that it can be dispersed across a number of sites. Ideally, each site should have stored locally that part of the database which is most relevant to it. For instance, in our banking database, we could have a separate database system at each branch which stored and controlled the Customer, Account and Employee records that are relevant to that branch. The database management system at each branch would have to have an extra component (a 'distributed' component) that would enable applications and users to access data that is held elsewhere as if it was stored locally. Such an environment brings the following benefits:

1. Reduced communications overhead. Most of the data access is local, saving expense and improving performance.
2. Improved processing power. Instead of one machine handling the database, we now have a collection of machines servicing the same database.
3. Removal of reliance on a central site. If a machine fails, then the only part of the system that is affected is the relevant local site. The rest of the system remains functioning and available.
4. The database is brought nearer to its users. When we have data dispersed and stored locally, this can effect a cultural change in an organization whereby the users of the system no longer have to deal with a remote, central bureaucracy in order to access and use the operational data that they require. Local database systems can lead to a much greater user involvement in the management and operation of the database. (Of course, some organizations would not regard this as an advantage.)

Thus, to summarize, the aims of a distributed database are as follows:

1. Data transparency.
2. Location Independence.
3. Reduction of communications overhead.
4. Increased processing power.

5. Removal of reliance on central site.
6. Local autonomy: each database in the system has control over the data stored within it.

The last aim highlights the main feature that differentiates a distributed database system from other forms of database sharing. In a true distributed system, each part is a database management system in its own right which co-operates in a partnership with other database systems.

The implementation of a distributed database system brings with it problems which can, to a greater or lesser extent, compromise some of these aims.

10.2 Implementation of a distributed database system

10.2.1 Fragmentation

In a true distributed database system, the sum of all of the co-operating databases is in itself a database which is effectively fragmented across a number of sites. This fragmentation may be at the inter file level where different files are stored at different sites. This is not what is usually understood by the term 'fragmentation'. This term is generally taken to mean the process by which files (or equivalent logical database objects such as relations) are themselves subdivided and dispersed across a number of sites.

In a distributed system composed of co-operating relational databases, there is the possibility of two types of fragmentation:

1. Horizontal fragmentation. This is the process by which a relation is subdivided into subsets of tuples with each site storing a particular subset, for example in a banking system, a relation of accounts being subdivided into subsets according to the handling branches, with each branch storing and managing its own set of accounts.
2. Vertical fragmentation. This is the process by which a relation is subdivided according to its attributes. We could take a relation of employees and subdivide its attributes so that some of the attribute values pertinent to employees are held at one site, whereas another site holds a different set of attribute values for employees.

In a fragmented system, protocols must exist that enable fragmented relations to be logically reconstructed. In a completely fragmented system, no data is stored at more than one site. This is not possible in the case of vertical fragmentation where the rows themselves are subdivided according to their attributes. In order that the constituent parts of a row can be rejoined, those attributes that uniquely identify a row must be replicated at every site.

10.2.2 Replication

Data replication is the storage of the same data at more than one site, Ideally, this should not occur. However, it frequently exists for reasons of performance, availability and security.

There will almost inevitably exist parts of the system dataset that are of operational use to more than one site. As explained above, one of the aims of a distributed database system is to reduce communications overhead. If there are parts of the corporate database that are being constantly accessed by many sites, then the communications overhead may in fact increase. This is especially the case if widely used parts are dispersed over a number of sites. Each individual site may find itself involved in the process of constantly rebuilding sets of data for application users from data held at a number of sites. Performance will inevitably deteriorate if individual sites are constantly having to access data that is held remotely from them.

The removal of reliance on a central site is another aim of a distributed system. Amongst other things, this increases the general availability of the database, with individual sites being able to function when one of them fails. However, if there exists frequent access to remote data and one of the sites holding a 'popular' section of the dataset fails, then availability becomes compromised, with parts of the operational data required by individual sites being rendered unavailable.

There may be parts of the dataset that are highly crucial to the enterprise. Each site will have its own security facilities for ensuring the recovery of lost data. This is enhanced if the data is held and secured at more than one site.

In practice, most distributed database systems support a certain level of data replication which in itself leads to complexities.

10.2.3 Update propagation

In a non-replicated system, update propagation is not a consideration as only one copy exists of each item of data. However, it is a major consideration in systems that support replication. When an application at one site updates data that is held at another site, some form of protocol must exist to ensure that all of the available copies of that data are consistent.

In a standalone database system, when data is being updated by an application, it is 'locked', meaning that no other application may access it whilst it is being altered. Sometimes an update may affect more than one piece of data, for instance transferring a balance from one account to another. Such an update may only be committed to the database when all of the relevant data (in this case, the balances of two accounts) has been altered. If any part of the update process fails, then a rollback to the previous database state is invoked.

In a distributed environment using replication, individual systems must be able to issue network-wide locks when replicated data is being altered. In this way, when one site is updating an item of replicated data, then it becomes locked at all sites. Once an update is committed at the updating site, there must then follow a network-wide commit where all sites attempt to commit the update. The data must remain locked throughout until all commits are successful. If the update fails at any particular site, then a network-wide rollback must be issued to undo it at all sites where it has been committed. Without these safeguards, different sites could be using different versions of the same data.

This compromises two of the aims of a distributed system. Local autonomy is compromised owing to the facility for systems to issue locks on data that is stored and managed by other systems. Availability can be severely compromised. When a system-wide update is being performed, if one of the sites is not able to complete the commit owing to local system failure, then that part of the database remains indefinitely locked to all sites.

One technique that partly mitigates the problem of availability is the 'primary copy' strategy. In this situation, every database object that is replicated is assigned a site that is designated to hold the 'primary copy' of that object. When a system-wide update is performed, the site that holds the primary copy issues the system-wide locks. Once the primary copy site commits, then the update operation is regarded as complete. This means that all other sites that manage to commit may now start using the database object as if it had been altered everywhere. Sites with local problems that are unable to complete the commit are simply locked out locally from using that particular object. They do not affect the functioning of other sites.

The primary copy strategy is further enhanced by use of the 'two-phase commit' protocol. Individual sites may be unable to commit for a variety of reasons. For instance, a commit that may be perfectly valid at one site may leave the database at another site in an inconsistent state. In the two-phase commit protocol, one site takes responsibility for the co-ordination of commits (in a system using primary copy, this would be the primary copy site). The two phases are as follows:

PHASE ONE: The co-ordinating site sends the update information and a 'Ready-to-Commit?' request to all sites holding a copy of the database object to be updated. Each site performs a check as to whether it can do the commit and sends back a 'YES' or 'NO' signal.

PHASE TWO: If any site sends back a 'NO' signal, then the co-ordinating site issues a system-wide 'Abort' signal, meaning that all sites will discard the update information and proceed as if the 'Commit' warning signal had never been sent. If they all signal 'YES' then a system-wide 'Commit' is issued. Once a site has performed the commit, it can now regard it as complete and release all local locks.

The primary copy strategy and two-phase committing do increase data availability in a distributed database at the cost of a loss of local autonomy as they designate one site to be the 'controller' of a piece of data and/or an update.

10.2.4 Catalog management

A database management system maintains a data dictionary (or 'catalog') that describes all data objects stored and managed by the system. In a distributed environment, each participating database system must have a means of accessing data dictionary entries on data objects stored at other sites. There must exist some form of 'global' catalog which represents the sum of all data dictionaries within the system. There are various approaches that can be taken to the storage and management of the catalog:

1. Completely dispersed. In this scenario, each site only has catalog details for those parts of the distributed database that are stored locally at that site. The problem with this approach is that each time access is required to non-local data, a site must examine the catalogs of all other sites until the relevant data is found. This can lead to severe performance problems when non-local data access is required.

2. Completely replicated. In this scenario, every site has a complete copy of the entire system catalog. This greatly speeds up non-local data access. However, it means that every time a new data object (e.g. a relation, an attribute, etc.) is created at one site, or conversely a data object is deleted, then this update to the catalog must be propagated to all other catalogs within the system.

3. Centralized. In this scenario, as well as local data dictionaries, there also exists at one site a catalog of all data available within the system. Access to non-local data is performed by firstly looking it up at this site. Changes to a local data dictionary must also be propagated to the central catalog. This is essentially a compromise between the two previous approaches and does have advantages over both of them. However, it undermines the principle of no reliance on a central site. If the machine maintaining the central catalog were to fail, then all access to non-local data would be rendered impossible.

4. Persistent identifiers. This is a scheme that is used in principle by a number of systems, though the details will vary. In this scenario, when a data object is created at a particular site, it is given a 'logical' identifier that is exported to the data dictionaries of all other sites. This logical identifier identifies the site where it was created (its 'birthsite'). The birthsite catalog entry of an object keeps track of where it is actually stored. Thus if an object, say a relation, is moved from its birthsite to another site, the catalog entry at its birthsite is altered to

record its new location. It is also added to the local data dictionary of the site where it is now stored. Any other site requiring that object will first examine the catalog entry at its birthsite and use the information stored there to find the object itself. If the object were to move again, then it would simply get deleted from the data dictionary at the site it is leaving, added to the data dictionary of its new site and have the catalog entry at its birthsite altered to record its new location. Again, any other site requiring this object will still only need to access the catalogs of two sites: the birthsite where it was created and the site where it is now stored. This means that objects only become unlocatable if their birthsite has failed.

10.2.5 Distributed query processing

In a distributed database system, the processing of queries that require the examination of data stored across different sites can pose problems. Take the following scenario:

The COD Delivery Company has a distributed database system with two files: Emp and Depts. The Emp file keeps details of employees and is horizontally partitioned across three sites. The Depts file keeps details of departments and is kept entirely at one site. The amounts of data kept at each site are as follows:

SITE1

Depts: 10 records, each 500 bytes long: 5,000 bytes
Attributes include DeptRef (2 bytes), DeptName (20 bytes)

Emp: 100 records, each 100 bytes long: 10,000 bytes
Attributes include EmpNo (10 bytes), EmpName (30 bytes), DeptNo (2 bytes)
All Emp records have value 'Region = 1'

SITE2

Emp: 2000 records each 100 bytes long: 200,000 bytes
All Emp records have value 'Region = 2'

SITE3

Emp: 1000 records each 100 bytes long: 100,000 bytes
All Emp records have value 'Region = 3'

Suppose we had the following query issued at SITE 2:

Select EmpNo, EmpName, DeptName
from Emp E, Dept D
where E.Deptno = D.DeptRef
and Region = 3;

Assuming that all Emp records can join with a Depts record, this query will yield a result consisting of 1000 rows consisting of EmpNo (10 bytes), EmpName (30 bytes) and DeptName (20), making 60,000 bytes altogether (1000 × 60). The ways this result can be put together are as follows:

1. (a) Take the Depts file at SITE1 and transmit its contents to SITE2 (5000 bytes).
   (b) Take the Emp data at SITE3 and transmit it to SITE2 (100,000 bytes).
   (c) Complete the Join at SITE2.
   Total amount of data transference: 105,000 bytes.
2. (a) Take the Depts file at SITE1 and transmit it to SITE3 (5000 bytes).
   (b) Do the Join at SITE3. Transmit the result to SITE2 (60,000 bytes).
   Total amount of data transference: 65,000 bytes.
3. (a) Take the Emp file at SITE3 and transfer it to SITE1 (100,000 bytes).
   (b) Do the Join at SITE1. Transmit the result to SITE2 (60,000 bytes).
   Total amount of data transference: 160,000 bytes.

In a distributed system, the highest performance overhead is the transmission of data. The strategies above vary in their data transference costs from 65,000 to 160,000 units. The differences would be even more dramatic if only a small set of records satisfied the Join condition. Suppose only 10% of employees at SITE3 belonged to a department. This means the result would only be 6000 bytes in size, making the cost of strategies 2 and 3 11,000 and 106,000 bytes respectively.

Ideally, a distributed system should maintain statistical records of the size of datasets held at each site in order that the best strategy for servicing a query may be deduced. Query servicing should also take advantage of fragmentation. The above strategies assume that the query processor at SITE2 'knows' that all Emp records with the Region value of '3' are stored at SITE3. If this information is not available to the query processor, then it has no alternative but to examine the Emp records at all sites in order to find the relevant data. Strategies 2 and 3 can only be executed if a level of co-operation exists between different systems whereby the query processor at one site is able to perform a Join required by a query initiated at another site.

When joining data held at more than one site, one strategy for reducing data transference costs is that of the 'semi-join'. With this strategy, we just send the joining attribute from one site to another, perform the Join with the relevant rows and send back those attributes required by the query to the first site where the Join can now be completed. For instance, with the above query, we could:

1. Send DeptRef values from SITE1 to SITE3 (2 × 10 = 20 bytes).

2. Join these with the Emp rows where Emp.Deptno = DeptRef. Send back to SITE1 the joining column (Deptno) along with the columns required by the result (EmpNo, EmpName), resulting in 42×1000 (42,000 bytes) of data transference.
3. Complete the Join at SITE1 and send the result to SITE2 (60,000 bytes).

Total data transference: 102,020 bytes.

This does not show much improvement. However, if we were to:

1. Send the set of distinct DeptNo values from SITE3 to SITE1 ($10 \times 2 = 20$ bytes).
2. Return the DeptRef, DeptName values that match these numbers ($10 \times 22 = 220$ bytes).
3. Complete the Join at SITE3 and send the result to SITE2 (60,000 bytes).

We get a total data transference cost of 60,240 bytes, the cheapest so far.

Again, the deduction of the best order of events to service a semi-join relies on the query processors having access to detailed statistical information regarding the sets of data held at each site.

10.2.6 Types of distributed database system

Distributed database systems may be broadly classified into those that are 'homogeneous' and those that are 'heterogeneous'.

A homogeneous distributed database system (Figure 10.1) is one where every site has the same type of database management system. When this is the case, each site will require a distributed 'layer' to be added to the local software

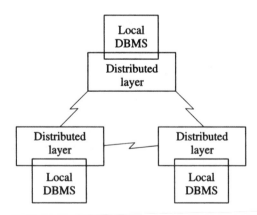

Figure 10.1 Homogeneous distributed database system.

to handle network communication and provide distributed database management facilities.

A heterogeneous distributed database system is one that associates together more than one type of database. The form of implementation will vary according to the degree of heterogeneity, that is how different the various sites are.

Suppose we had two sites that both had relational databases, but these were supplied by different vendors (e.g. ORACLE and INFORMIX). If the ORACLE site wished to access and use the database at the INFORMIX site as if it was part of an ORACLE distributed database it would have to supply a 'gateway' to the INFORMIX site.

A 'gateway' is a layer of software that enables one product to 'look like' another. An INFORMIX/ORACLE gateway enables an INFORMIX database to 'look like' an ORACLE database. Amongst other things, it would supply mappings between INFORMIX data types and ORACLE data types, mappings between the SQL dialects used by the two products, protocols for synchronizing locking and committing routines and so on. The gateway would sit on top of the INFORMIX software, making it 'look like' an ORACLE site. In this way, a similar, but not identical, DBMS can participate in an otherwise homogeneous system (Figure 10.2).

The above solution enables applications at the ORACLE site to use the INFORMIX database as if it were part of a distributed ORACLE system. In order that applications at the INFORMIX site can use the ORACLE database as if it were part of a distributed INFORMIX system, an ORACLE/INFORMIX gateway would have to be supplied to the ORACLE site to sit between the local system and a layer of INFORMIX distributed database software.

When a heterogeneous system is implemented using relational products built around SQL, it is usually feasible to develop gateways that provide a

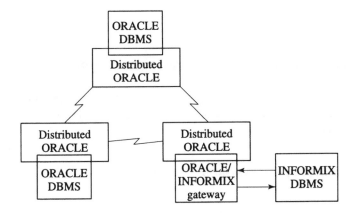

Figure 10.2 Heterogeneous distributed system with a gateway.

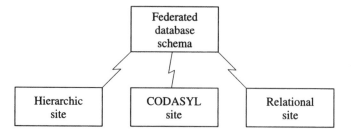

Figure 10.3 A federated heterogeneous distributed database system.

'seamless' interface between the various systems. These enable every site to participate fully as a member of the network, with all of its data objects available to all other sites. It is seldom feasible to overcome completely the inherent incompatibility between systems that are built on completely different principles, such as relational and hierarchic systems. When this is the case, a level of co-operation can be achieved by use of a federated database system.

A federated database system is a collection of independent, locally controlled databases that allow partial and controlled sharing of data. This is achieved by the provision of a 'federated database schema' which provides a high level description of data objects accessible to all sites in the system. In a highly heterogeneous environment, this will probably only represent a very small subset of the entire data content of all the participating databases. Each local site will require an interface that maps objects from its local schema to the federated schema and vice versa. This provides the facility for a distributed system to be implemented that only handles data objects from the federated schema and which communicates via the federated schema interface local to each site (Figure 10.3).

10.3 Non-distributed multi-database systems

A true distributed database system provides a 'seamless' integration between a collection of database systems held at a number of sites. There are other forms of multi-database co-operation.

10.3.1 Client/server systems

Client/server systems are very popular in environments using desktop micro-computers connected by a high speed local area network. In such an environment, machines can be classified as 'clients' or 'servers'.

A client is a machine that provides a 'front end' to a database. By 'front end', we mean anything that provides a user interface to a database, be it an SQL interpreter, a report generator or other database tool, or any application program that has within it embedded calls to a database. When a client application requires a database service, it must send a request to a server. A server is a machine where a database management system is mounted and data is stored. This constitutes a database 'back end'.

The client machines will require an interface that enables network data transfer to take place between their local applications and the network. The server requires an interface that enables data transfer to take place between the network and the database management system (Figure 10.4). In this way, a server can 'service' the database requirements of applications running across a wide range of client machines.

The advantage of this arrangement is that the workload of running applications is taken off the server machine and is exported to the various clients. The server machine becomes a 'dedicated' database machine. Considerations of managing the user interface, handling graphics, processing the application logic and so on are exported to the client. A summary of the different sets of functions is given in Figure 10.5.

There may be more than one server on a given network, meaning that a client may be able to access more than one database. In such a situation, the client application will usually need to provide the network address of the relevant server when sending out a database request. If a database request does not

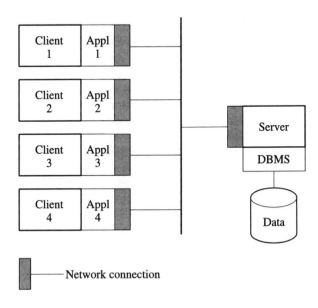

Figure 10.4 A client/server architecture.

Client	Server
Manages user interface	Accepts database requests
Accepts user data	Processes database requests:
	• performs integrity checks
Processes application logic	• handles concurrent access
	• optimizes queries
Generates database requests	• performs security checks
	• enacts recovery routines
Transmits database requests to server	Transmits results of database requests to clients
Receives results from server	
Formats results according to the Application logic	

Figure 10.5 Client/server functions.

require a network address and instead all of the server databases are treated as if they were all part of a unified database, we effectively have a distributed database system.

10.3.2 Shared resource systems

This is an evolution of the client/server environment. In a shared resource system, each client not only runs front end applications, it also has its own database management system. All that resides on the server is the raw data on disk. In this way, the same data can support a set of databases. The individual databases do not inter-co-operate in the manner of a distributed database system. Once data is retrieved from the central repository, its consistency across different platforms cannot be maintained. This type of architecture is suitable for the periodic downloading of data from a central repository to local databases for local processing only.

Summary

- A distributed database system is a collection of co-operating autonomous database systems that can be used as if they were a single database.
- Distributed database systems are required to have strategies for the handling of data fragmentation, data replication, update propagation, catalog management and distributed query processing.

- Distributed databases may be implemented across systems using a homogeneous architecture. In the case of heterogeneous systems, gateways must be provided between the various systems. This gateway may be to a federated database schema that provides a common description of all distributed database objects.
- Client/server and shared resource systems also provide multi-database environments.

Exercises

Here is a restatement of the EverCare County General Hospital scenario:

At the EverCare County General Hospital, patients are admitted and given a unique Patient Id. We record their name, home address and date of admission. They are assigned to a ward and to a consultant. They may then be diagnosed a set of conditions. Whilst in our care, they will receive a set of treatments. Each treatment will have a date and details of the nurse administering the treatment, the drug being administered and the dosage. Drugs have a unique Drug Id, a name and a recommended dosage (which may not be the same as the dosage given in individual treatments). Nurses have a Nurse Id and a name and are assigned to a ward. Each ward has a Sister (who is a nurse). Consultants have a Doctor Id and a name.

Suppose that, amongst other database objects, we have implemented a Patients table and a Consultants table. The Consultants table is held at a central site whereas the Patients table has been horizontally fragmented and stored at three different sites (Central, SiteA, SiteB) with no replication.

Certain distributed physical characteristics of the tables are as follows:

Consultants (Central Site) 100 rows, average row size 256 bytes
Patients (Central Site) 250 rows, average row size 512 bytes
Patients (SiteA) 1000 rows, average row size 512 bytes
Patients (SiteB) 2500 rows, average row size 512 bytes
All Consultant rows contain a Doctor_Id (6 bytes) and a Doctor_Name (30 bytes)
All Patient rows contain a Patient_Id (12 bytes), a Doctor_Id (6 bytes) and a Patient_Name (30 bytes).

Consider the following query:

```
SELECT PATIENT_ID, PATIENT_NAME
FROM PATIENTS P , CONSULTANTS C
WHERE P.DOCTOR_ID = C.DOCTOR_ID
    AND DOCTOR_NAME = 'Dr. Zurelski';
```

Suppose there was one doctor with this name, and this doctor was responsible for 50 patients, distributed across all three sites.

1 What strategies could be adopted for servicing this query if it was executed:
   (a) At Central Site?
   (b) At Site B?
2 For each of the strategies that you have identified, calculate the amount of data transference involved. Use a semi-join where appropriate.

Further reading

Date (1995) Chapter 21
Elmasri and SB Navathe (1994) Chapter 23
Gardarin and Valduriez (1989) Chapter 12
Korth and Silberschatz (1991) Chapter 15
Kroenke (1995) Chapters 16 and 17
Ryan and Smith (1995) Chapter 17

Bibliography

Annevelink, J., Ahad, R., Carlson, A., Fishman, D., Heytens, M. and Kent, W. (1995) 'Object SQL – A Language for the Design and Implementation of Databases', in W. Kim (ed.) *Modern Database Systems*, Addison-Wesley

ANSI/SPARC (1978) 'DBMS Framework: Report on the Study of Data Base Management Systems', *Information Systems*, Vol. 3

Bell, D. and Grimson, J. (1992) *Distributed Database Systems*, Addison-Wesley

Blakely, J.A. (1995) 'OQL(C++): Extending C++ with an Object Query Capability' in W. Kim (ed.) *Modern Database Systems*, Addison-Wesley

Brown, A. (1991) *Object-Oriented Databases: Applications in Software Engineering*, McGraw-Hill

Cattell, R. (ed.) (1993) *The Object Database Standard: ODMG-93*, Morgan Kaufmann

Ceri, S. and Pelagatti, G. (1984) *Distributed Databases: Principles and Systems*, McGraw-Hill

Chen, P. (1976) 'The Entity-Relationship Model: Toward a unified view of data', *ACM Transactions on Database Systems*, 1, March 1976

CODASYL (1975) 'Data Base Task Group Report 1971', Association for Computing Machinery

Codd, E.F. (1969) 'Derivability, Redundancy and Consistency of Relations stored in Large Data Banks', IBM Research Report RJ599, August

Codd, E.F. (1970) 'A Relational Model of Data for Large Shared Databanks', *Communications of the ACM*, 13, June

Codd, E.F. (1979) 'Extending the Relational Model to Capture More Meaning', *ACM Transactions on Database Systems*, 4, December

Cox, B.J. (1986) *Object-Oriented Programming: An Evolutionary Approach*, Addison-Wesley

Darwen, H. and Date, C.J. (1992) *Relational Database Writings 1989–1991*, Addison-Wesley

Date, C.J. (1990) *Relational Database Writings 1985–1989*, Addison-Wesley

Date, C.J. (1995) *An Introduction to Database Systems*, 6th edn, Addison-Wesley

Date, C.J. and Darwen, H. (1993) *A Guide to the SQL Standard*, 3rd edn, Addison-Wesley

Delobel, C., Lecluse, C. and Richard, P. (1995) *Databases: From Relational to Object-Oriented Systems*, International Thomson Computer Publishing

Elmasri, R. and Navathe, S.B. (1994) *Fundamentals of Database Systems*, 2nd edn, Addison-Wesley

Gardarin, G. and Valduriez, P. (1989) *Relational Databases and Knowledge Bases*, Addison-Wesley

Hammer, M. and Macleod, D. (1981) 'Database Description with SDM: A Semantic Database Model', *ACM Transactions on Database Systems*, 6, September

Hawryszkiewycz, I.T. (1991) *Database Anaylsis and Design*, Macmillan

Hughes, J.G. (1991) *Object Oriented Databases* Prentice Hall International

Kent, W. (1978) *Data and Reality*, Elsevier Science

Kim, W. (ed.) (1995) *Modern Database Systems*, Addison-Wesley

Kim, W., Reiner, D.S. and Batory, D.S. (eds) (1985) *Query Processing in Database Systems*, Springer-Verlag

Korth, H.F. and Silberschatz, A. (1991) *Database System Concepts*, McGraw-Hill

Kroenke, D.M. (1988) *Database Processing*, 3rd edn, Prentice Hall International

Kroenke, D.M. (1995) *Database Processing*, 5th edn, Prentice Hall International

Ozkarahan, E. (1990) *Database Management: Concepts, Design and Practice*, Prentice Hall International

Paton, N., Cooper, R., Williams, H. and Trinder, P. (1996) *Database Programming Languages*, Prentice Hall International

Pratt, P.J. and Adamski, J.J. (1987) *Database Systems Management and Design*, Boyd & Fraser

Rolland, F.D. (1992) *Relational Database Management with ORACLE*, 2nd edn, Addison-Wesley

Rolland, F.D. (1996) *SQL Step by Step*, International Thomson Computer Press

Ryan, N. and Smith, D. (1995) *Database Systems Engineering* International Thomson Computer Press

Shipman, D.W. (1981) 'The Functional Data Model and the language DAPLEX', *ACM Transactions on Database Systems*, 6, March

Smith, P. and Barnes, M. (1987) *Files and Databases: An Introduction*, Addison-Wesley

Tamer Oszu, M. and Valduriez, P. (1991) *Principles of Distributed Database Systems*, Prentice Hall International

Teorey, T.J. and Fry, J.P. (1982) *Design of Database Structures*, Prentice Hall International

Ter Bekke, J.H. (1992) *Semantic Data Modelling*, Prentice Hall International

Van der Lans, R.F. (1993) *Introduction to SQL*, 2nd edn, Addison-Wesley

Index